TABLE OF CONTENTS

Top 20 Test Taking Tips

1. Carefully follow all the test registration procedures
2. Know the test directions, duration, topics, question types, how many questions
3. Setup a flexible study schedule at least 3-4 weeks before test day
4. Study during the time of day you are most alert, relaxed, and stress free
5. Maximize your learning style; visual learner use visual study aids, auditory learner use auditory study aids
6. Focus on your weakest knowledge base
7. Find a study partner to review with and help clarify questions
8. Practice, practice, practice
9. Get a good night's sleep; don't try to cram the night before the test
10. Eat a well balanced meal
11. Know the exact physical location of the testing site; drive the route to the site prior to test day
12. Bring a set of ear plugs; the testing center could be noisy
13. Wear comfortable, loose fitting, layered clothing to the testing center; prepare for it to be either cold or hot during the test
14. Bring at least 2 current forms of ID to the testing center
15. Arrive to the test early; be prepared to wait and be patient
16. Eliminate the obviously wrong answer choices, then guess the first remaining choice
17. Pace yourself; don't rush, but keep working and move on if you get stuck
18. Maintain a positive attitude even if the test is going poorly
19. Keep your first answer unless you are positive it is wrong
20. Check your work, don't make a careless mistake

Foundations

Major chest muscles of respiration

Diaphragm
The large dome-shaped muscle that separates the chest cavity from the abdominal cavity

External intercostal muscles
Short muscles located between the ribs

Serratus posterior superior
An upper back muscle originating from the lower neck and attaching to the upper ribs

Levator costarum brevis and longus
Back muscles that attach from the sides of each thoracic vertebra to the tips of the ribs. There are twelve on each side.

Role of chest muscles in inspiration

In the diaphragm, contraction causes the chest to expand drawing air into the lungs.

The external intercostals elevate the rib cage to expand the lungs for inspiration.

The serratus posterior superior elevates the rib cage to expand the lungs for inspiration.

The levator costarum brevis and longus elevate the rib cage to expand the lungs for inspiration

Abdominal muscles of respiration

Latissimus dorsi
Large flat triangular muscle originating from the upper arm extending to the lower back

Rectus abdominus
Thick muscles covering the front part of the abdomen
Internal oblique abdominus
Muscles covering the lateral part of the abdomen

Transverse abdominus
Lateral abdominal muscles lying underneath the internal obliques

Quadratus lumborum
Muscles arising from the upper pelvic bone attaching to the lower vertebral bones of the back

Role of the abdominal muscles in exhalation

The latissimus dorsi keeps the rear part of the abdomen balanced for exhalation.

The rectus abdominus contract the lower back to assist in expelling air out of the lungs.

The internal oblique abdominus contract the abdominal wall to assist in expelling air from the lungs.

The transverse abdominus contract the abdominal wall to assist in expelling air from the lungs.

The quadratus lumborum contracts the lateral portion of the abdominal wall to assist in exhalation.

Phonation

Phonation is the production of sounds of speech. The structure responsible for sound production is the larynx, otherwise known as the voice box. The larynx is in the lower neck and houses the vocal folds. The larynx lies at the top of the trachea (windpipe) and esophagus. The vocal folds are principally involved in the production of sound. Air is exhaled from the lungs and passes through the larynx. As air passes, the vocal folds vibrate to produce sound. These vocal folds are also important to prevent ingested food from entering the lungs. The amount of forced air that passes through the vocal folds controls the volume of speech sounds. The movement of the vocal folds is controlled by the cranial nerve X, otherwise know as the vagus nerve.

Myeloelastic-aerodynamic theory of phonation

Producing sounds requires the rapid cycle of the opening and closing of the vocal folds. As the air leaves the lungs and reaches the vocal folds, air pressure builds and forces the folds apart. This makes the folds vibrate. As air continues to pass through the folds, the increased air speed flowing across the folds forces them to stick together again: this is called the Bernoulli effect. The arytenoid cartilages and associated muscles hold the vocal folds together. The thyroid and cricoid cartilages control tension on the vocal folds and cause changes in voice pitch.

Anatomical structures that are responsible for voice resonance

Resonance is the alteration of sounds produced by the larynx.

The following structures serve to alter sounds:
- Pharynx: located just beyond the throat and nasal cavity. Both air and food pass through this space.
- Nasal cavity: principal in creating /m/ and /n/ sounds
- Velum: soft area in roof of the mouth near the back of the throat that moves back or is lifted in the production of sounds
- Oral cavity: the main resonating source for sounds in English

Mouth structures involved in articulation

Articulation refers to the manner in which the mouth structures move in order to produce speech.

The following mouth structures are important for articulation:

Pharynx
Divided into three parts
1. Laryngopharynx, first portion of pharynx beginning just before the larynx terminating at the base of the tongue
2. Oropharynx, beginning at the base of the tongue and terminating at the soft palate
3. Nasopharynx terminates at the level of the nasal cavity

Soft palate
Located at the back portion of the roof of the mouth. It is also called the velum.

Hard palate
Forms the roof of the mouth

Mandible
The jawbone containing the lower teeth and tongue

Teeth, tongue, lips, and cheeks are the remainder of the mouth structures that are important in speech production.

Role of the mouth structures in articulation

Pharynx
The laryngopharynx and oropharynx give resonance to speech sounds. The nasopharynx gives resonance to the /m/ and /n/ speech sounds.

Soft palate
Elevation of the soft palate during speech causes separation of the mouth from the

nasal cavity. If this function is defective, the voice will sound produce a nasal sound.

Hard palate
The contact of the tongue against the hard palate is essential in producing many speech sounds.

Mandible
This bone is responsible for the opening and closing of the mouth.

Teeth
Aside from chewing, the teeth assist in the production of several sounds. For example, the /th/ sound is produced by the tongue against the upper teeth.

Tongue
Aside from eating, the action of the tongue is important in the production of many sounds.

Lips and cheeks
Their movement is important in the production of all sounds.

Role of the cranial nerves involved in speech production

Cranial nerve 5 (V), trigeminal nerve
Controls the muscles of the mandible causing movement in every direction and innervates part of the soft palate to open the breathing tube.

Cranial nerve 7 (VII), facial nerve
Controls the muscles that lower the mandible and controls the muscles of the lips.

Cranial nerve 10 (X), vagus nerve
Controls the movement of the soft palate (velum) and pharynx.

Cranial nerve 11 (XI), spinal accessory nerve
Controls the movement of the soft palate (velum) and pharynx.

Cranial nerve 12 (XII), hypoglossal nerve
Assists in lowering the mandible and controls all movements of the tongue.

Brain stem

The brain stem is made up of the midbrain (mesencephalon), pons (metencephalon), and medulla (myelencephalon). Cranial nerves V (trigeminal) and VII (facial) arise from the pons thus controlling soft palate, mandible, and lip movements. Cranial nerves X (vagus), XI (accessory), and XII (hypoglossal) arise from the medulla thus controlling soft palate, pharynx, mandible, and tongue movements. The brain stem also integrates with other brain structures to control respiration and alertness. The ability to produce coordinated respiration and levels of consciousness can effect speech production.

Role of the reticular activating system, basal ganglion, and cerebellum in speech production

Reticular activating system
Sits at the core of the brain stem and assists in translating sensory input into motor output. It is also vital in maintaining alertness and consciousness.

Basal ganglion
Lies deep within the brain and serves as a connection between the frontal lobe of the brain with more complex centers of the brain. This structure is responsible for adapting and directing the mechanical movements of speech that have been initiated in the brain cortex.

Cerebellum
Located behind the brain stem and is responsible for the rate of speech.

Role of the cerebrum in speech production

Frontal lobe is the front portion of the cerebrum.

The major areas of speech are located here. The primary motor cortex controls the voluntary movements of the muscles of speech. The supplemental motor cortex controls speech planning. Broca's area is found only on the left side of the cerebrum and is important in the production of the fine-motor muscle activities involved in speech.

Parietal lobe is the upper side portions of the cerebrum.

There are two areas of the parietal lobe important in speech. The supramarginal gyrus integrates sensory inputs allowing oral reading and writing comprehension. The angular gyrus integrates sensory inputs providing reading, writing, and object naming comprehension.

Temporal lobe is the lower sides of the cerebrum.

There are two major areas of speech in the temporal lobe. The primary auditory cortex (left side for most) takes verbal communication and processes the sounds into recognized words. Wernicke's area is responsible for verbal and written language comprehension.

International Phonetic Alphabet

The International Phonetic Alphabet (IPA) was developed by linguists to provide a way to standardize the representation of the sounds of spoken language. Through a system of symbols, speech sounds are standardized according to the manner in which they are pronounced. This allows a uniform method for speech and language professionals around the world to assess and describe spoken words with the use of phonetic transcriptions. Phonetic transcriptions are represented by placing phonemes (the smallest units of sound) between slash marks / /. Allophones (spoken variations of phonemes) are placed between brackets [ ]. Diacritical markers are symbols or marks used over a letter to distinguish its sound in different words.

Recognizing and pronouncing the symbols of the phonetic alphabet

The letters of the phonetic alphabet are listed along with examples of their pronunciation.

/ɔ/ w**a**ll, /b/ **b**ack, /d/ **d**og, /e/ c**a**ke, /f/ **f**at, /g/ **g**ood, /h/ **h**at, /i/ f**ee**t, /j/ **y**ear, /k/ **k**iss, /l/ **l**ate /m/ **m**ug, /n/ **n**ut, /o/ **o**pen, /p/ **p**ull, /r/ **r**an, /s/ **s**ap, /t/ **t**one, /u/ l**oo**p, /v/ **v**est, /w/ **w**ind, /z/ **z**ip, / æ/ c**a**p, /ɔ / c**ou**gh, / ə / **a**bout, / ŋ/ fa**ng**, /ʌ/ c**u**t, /ɪ/ b**i**t, / ʃ / wi**sh,**

/ ʒ / mea**s**ure, / θ / **th**ink, / ð / ra**th**er, /e/ m**e**n, /ʊ / f**oo**t, / ɜ / h**ur**t, / ɚ / lat**er,** /eɪ / l**a**ne, /aɪ/ b**i**ke, /oʊ / c**oa**t, /aʊ / c**ow**, /ɔ ɪ/ b**oi**l, /IU/ m**u**te, / tʃ / **ch**eap, / dʒ / **j**ump

Distinctive feature approach and the place-voice-manner approach to the classification of phonemes

Distinctive feature approach
A vowel or consonant is characterized according to the presence (+) or absence (−) of a particular feature

Place-voice-manner approach
Applies to the classification of consonants based on three phonetic features:
1. Place of articulation: the anatomical location, velum, lips, or tongue, where sounds are initiated. For example, placing the

tongue against the back of the upper teeth produces /l/.

2. Voicing: refers to the presence or absences of sounds that are produced via the vibration of the vocal folds. Linguists refer to voiced vs. voiceless sounds; for example, /b/ is a voiced sound while /p/ is voiceless.

3. Manner of articulation: the method of which the vocal cord moves in the production of sounds. For example, the /n/ is produced by air passing from the vocal folds through the nasal cavity.

Four dimensions of mouth movement in the production of vowel sounds

Lip position makes sounds either rounded or unrounded. Vowel sounds produced with the lips in a circular position are said to be rounded. Those that are produced with the lips in a relaxed position are said to be unrounded.

Tense vowels are produced with more muscular tension and lax vowels are produced with less.

Tongue height produces vowel sounds that are said to be high, middle, or low with regard to where they are produced in the mouth.

Tongue position forward or retracted produces vowel sound that are said to be front, central, or back with regard to where they are produced in the mouth.

Ways that sounds can change one another when used together in speech

Phonetic adaptation
Refers to the alteration in the movement of the physiologic vocal structures in the pronunciation of a phoneme due to the preceding phoneme.

Assimilation
Refers to the alteration of a speech sound because of an adjacent sound. For example, in the phrase *paint zone* the /z/ is now voiceless because of the preceding voiceless /t/.

Coarticulation
Refers to both the process of adaptation and assimilation whereby speech sounds vary due to the influence of adjacent sounds. Two different articulators move at the same time to produced two different sounds. For example, examine the variations between the /k/ sounds in the words *keep* and *cool*.

Suprasegmental

Suprasegmentals (properties of prosody) are features of speech that give speech added meaning and context. Suprasegmentals can be influenced by gender, emotion, or culture. However, there are several suprasegmentals that are most important in the impact of speech production:

- Length of vowels and consonants
- Syllable stress
- Rate of speech
- Pitch or tonal change of words or sounds
- Volume or loudness of speech
- Juncture, pauses between words; sometimes called vocal punctuation

Frequency and pitch

Sound is a result of vibrations of molecules through air, liquid, gas, or solids. Frequency is one of two important features of vibrations of sound. This is the measurement of the number of cycles of vibratory motion per second (Hz). The properties of the vibrating object affects the frequency; however, the medium (air, liquid, gas, or solid) through which sounds are transmitted does not affect its frequency. However, solids with a higher

- 9 -

density, such as metal, will transmit sounds faster than more elastic materials.

Pitch is the change in perceived sound. High frequency sounds are perceived as higher pitch. The human ear can perceive frequencies of 20 Hz to 20,000 Hz but is more responsive to frequencies below 1,000 Hz.

Amplitude and loudness

Along with frequency, amplitude is one of two important features of the vibratory motion of sound. Amplitude refers to the strength of the sound. Another way to characterize amplitude is sound pressure. Higher amplitudes produce more intense sounds. Loudness refers to the perception of sound amplitude. Higher amplitudes are perceived as louder sounds. The units of sound loudness are called decibels (dB). The loudness of normal conversation speech typically is between 50 and 70 dB. Sounds that exceed 100 dB may be damaging to the ear.

Five important components of language

Phonology
The physical production of voiced sounds

Morphology
The study of the structure of words

Syntax
The manner in which words are brought together to form a meaningful sentence

Semantics
The meaning that is expressed in a word, phrase, or sentence

Pragmatics
The use of words, phrases, or sentences in the correct social context

Morpheme

A morpheme is the smallest grammatical unit of language. It may be a word, prefix, or suffix. It is distinctive from phonemes in that it always has meaning. There are two major categories of morphemes: free and bound. A free morpheme is one that forms a word or can stand alone, like the words cat or pray.

A bound morpheme is a grammatical unit that attaches to words to create other words but cannot form a word alone. An example of a bound morpheme is the prefix dys– that forms the word dysfunction.

Several important varieties of morphemes are the inflectional type that mark plurality or tense, such as the endings –s, –ing, and –ed.

Derivational morphemes are those that produce additional word meanings when placed in front or at the end of words, such as our previous example dys– as in dysfunction and –ness in the word laziness.

Mean length of utterance in morphemes

The mean length of utterances (MLU) in morphemes is an important tool in describing children's speech development. The MLU is calculated by dividing the number of morphemes by the number of utterances.

To calculate MLU, choose 100 consecutive utterances and count all morphemes, even if used incorrectly. Do not count repeating words like no, no. Do not count extraneous words like um.

- At ages 1 to 2, children should have an MLU of 1.0 to 2.0
- At ages 2 to 3, expected MLU 2.0 to 4.0

- At ages 3 to 4, expected MLU 3.0 to 5.0
- At ages 4 to 5, expected MLU 4.5 to 7.0
- At ages 5 to 6, expected MLU 6.0 to 8.0
- At ages 6 to 7, expected MLU 6.5 to 8.5
- At ages 7 to 8, expected MLU 7.0 to 9.0

Semantics in language development

Vocabulary development

Important aspects of vocabulary development include the number of words used and understood. Also important is the familiarity with opposites, synonyms, homonyms, humor, and symbolic language. This development depends upon the extent of the child's exposures.

The idea of fast mapping refers to the ability of a child to gain knowledge of new words and concepts with a small number of exposures to them.

Word relationships

Children in the early stages of speaking (1 to 2 years) may use overextensions (e.g., uses mama to refer to all women) or underextensions (e.g., only the child's favorite train can be a toy). The ability to categorize words is important in language development.

Pragmatics in language development

Language function

Children should be able to expand the ability to label and describe objects. They must develop conversational skills such as taking turns while speaking, maintaining topical conversation, and being logical. Language context should be coherent and intelligible as they grow older.

Pragmatic skills

There are several important pragmatic skills in language development. These include the ability understand and use indirect speech and the ability to maintain effective discussion (discourse.)

Both language function and pragmatic skills may be influenced by culture.

Semantic relations that young children (12 to 18 months) in the single-word phase (holophrastic stage) should be able to express verbally

Action: Example: Car *go*
Attribute: Example: Yummy cookie
Denial: refers to a refutation in response to a statement or question. Example: No doggy
Disappearance: Example: Wagon gone
Existence: Example: That car
Locative action: Example: Truck here
Possession: Example: Dolly mine
Recurrence: Example: More juice
Rejection: Example: No milk

Semantic relations that children 18 to 24 months in the two-word phase should be able to express verbally

Action-object: Example: *Drive car*
Agent-action: Example: *Boy sing*
Agent-object: Example: *Mommy hat* (Mommy's hat)
Action-locative: Example: Go park (Let's go to the park.)
Demonstrative-entity: Example: *That toy* (not this toy, but *that* toy)
Entity-attributive: Example: *Big horse*
Entity-locative: Example: *Dolly chair* (The dolly is on the chair.)
Instrumental (verb and noun): Example: Sweep broom (sweep with the broom)
Notice: Example: *Bye kitty*
Nomination: Example: *That horse* (That is a horse.)
Recurrence: Example: *More cookie*

Developmental milestones of speech and language during the first year of life

Birth to 3 months:
- Vocalizes with cooing sounds
- Tracks voices or faces with eyes
- Reacts to loud noises or pain by turning head or crying
- Smiles in response to stimuli

3 to 6 months:
- Uses various vocalization sounds, which mature into multisyllables
- Recognizes and responds to familiar faces

6 to 12 months:
- Understands a few words or simple commands
- Recognizes own name
- Communicates needs by gesturing to objects
- Attempts to imitate speech

Developmental milestones of speech and language during years 1 and 2

12 to 18 months
- Follows simple requests
- Requests objects
- Names 5 to 10 objects
- Language mostly consists of nouns
- Begins to express own emotions and experiences
- Begins to initiate conversation
- Uses single words (holophrases) to express objects, needs, and actions
- 18 to 24 months
- Uses multiword responses (2 to 3 words)
- Uses verbs and adjectives in combination with nouns
- Can express up to 50 words and understand nearly 200 words by age 24 months
- Can use the personal pronoun, usually *me*

Developmental milestones of speech and language during years 2 through 4

2 to 3 years
- Starts to use plurals, personal pronouns, and regular past tense verbs; misuses irregular past tense verbs
- Can express about 500 words and understands about 3,500 words
- Can use 3 to 4 word responses and can now ask simple questions
- Can follow two-step requests
- Can state age, name, and some body parts
- Demonstrate some intent in most aspects of communication
- 3 to 4 years
- Uses plurals, past tense, prepositions, pronouns, some irregular words, possessives, and conjunctions
- Starts to use and understand complex expressions and questions
- Able to use about 1,000 words and can understand about 4,000 words
- Understands comparative words and opposites
- Most speech comprehensible to others

Developmental milestones of speech and language during years 4 through 8

4 to 5 years
- Uses complete sentences, future tense, possessive pronouns, and irregular plurals
- Able to use about 6,000 words and can understand about 9,000 words
- Understands simple time concepts
- Begins to define and inquire about words and concepts
- Able to tell stories and jokes
- All speech comprehensible to others
- 5 to 6 years

- Uses concepts learned from ages 4 to 5 with fewer grammatical errors
- Understands spatial relationships• Uses superlatives, adverbs, and conjunctions to join complex sentences; understands explicative language
- 6 to 7 years
- Has mastered most tense and plural forms and is using –*ing* ending words (gerunds)
- Able to perform simple reading and writing
- 7 to 8 years
- Able to converse at nearly adult level
- Able to retell a complex story with appropriate spatial content, social meaning, and figurative expressions

Nativist, behaviorist, and social interactionism theories

Nativist theory holds that children have an innate or genetic ability to learn and organize language but need the presence of other people in order to learn language to its full potential.

Behaviorist theory holds that the acquisition of language is similar to any learned behavior. Children are conditioned by positive or negative reinforcement to learn language. Furthermore, a particular language is learned as a product of a particular environment.

The social interactionism theory of language acquisition holds that language is acquired through interaction with the environment. This theory holds that language is learned by the drive to be social.

Jean Piaget's stages of cognitive development

Jean Piaget was a Swiss developmental physiologist who was well known for his work in developing his theory of cognitive development. He observed thousands of children and theorized that there were four stages of cognitive development.

1. Sensorimotor stage (birth to 2 years): This stage begins with the development of reflexes, habits, and coordination. Children develop coordination, object permanence, and begin creativity.
2. Preoperational stage (2 to 7 years): Child begins to use mental symbols to represent objects (symbolic functioning). Child can attend only one aspect of a situation (centration) and is egocentric in his thinking.
3. Concrete operations stage (7 to 11 years): Child is able to use logic appropriately.
4. Formal operations stage (after age 11): Child begins to develop the ability to think abstractly.

Information processing theory of cognitive development

The information processing theory is that children learn to think the same way that a computer processes information. Just like a computer, a human takes information, organizes it, stores it, and relates it in order to present it in a logical way by actions, speech, or writing. The theory holds that information gained from previous experience is translated or programmed, and this ability to encode and generalize information is central in problem solving. Once encoded, input is stored in the brain in the form of memory. The important components of memory are sensory units (the part of the brain that receives all the information from the environment), short-term memory (the part of the brain where information is

- 13 -

stored temporarily), and long-term memory (the part of the brain where information is held indefinitely). Furthermore, the information processing theory says that humans have a finite capacity for amount and type of information it can handle. The theory further purports that humans, especially children, can learn to improve the efficiency with which they process information and improve their ability to learn. This can be achieved by creating a more receptive learning environment that facilitates increased attention, organization, illustration, and repetition.

Distinctive features concept of classification of word sounds

In the distinctive features concept, phonemes have unique characteristics that distinguish them. These unique sounds are characterized using a binary system to indicate the presence (+) or absence (-) of the particular sound feature. The important features that represent the major classes of sounds are

- Consonantal: sounds made by the constriction of the vocal tract. Example: consonantal (+) /g/ in the word *gate* and the nonconsonantal (-) /h/ in the word *hat*.
- Sonorant: sounds made without turbulent airflow in the mouth and can be produced continuously at the same pitch. Example: sonorant (+) /m/ in the word *make* and nonsonorant (-) /d/ in the word *dog*.

Manner of articulation concepts

Manner of articulation features
- Nasal: sounds produced with the production of air through the nasal tract, as in the sounds /n/ and /m/.
- Voiced: sounds made by vibrating the vocal tract. Example: voiced

(+) /d/ in the word dog and the unvoiced (-) /p/ in the word pet.
- Strident: nonsonorant sounds made with turbulent airflow and are produced using high mouth friction. Example: strident (+) /f/ in the word face and nonstrident (-) /s/ in the word sat.
- Continuant: sounds produced with a continuous stream of air through the vocal tract. Example: continuant (+) /w/ in the word wind and noncontinuant (-) /t/ in the word time.
- Lateral: sounds produced by the elevation of the center of the tongue to the roof of the mouth. Example: lateral (+) /l/ in the word lake and nonlateral (-) /r/ in the word rat.

Place of articulation concepts of distinctive features approach to word sounds

Place of articulation features
- Coronal: sounds produced by using the tip of the tongue in the mouth anteriorly, as in the sound /l/, extended as in /th/, or more posterior as in the sound /d/. An example of a noncoronal sound is /j/ in the word *jump*.
- Dorsal: sounds produced with the midportion of the tongue in the mouth in the high position, as in the sound /g/, in the low position as in the sound /h/ in the word *hang*, or back position as in the /k/ as in the word *kite*. An example of a nondorsal sound is /w/ in the word wind.
- Labial: sounds produced using the lips. Example: labial (+) /b/ in the word *ball* and nonlabial /h/ in the word *hat*.

- 14 -

Manner of articulation concepts of the place-manner approach to word sounds

Stops (plosives)
Produced by stopping the airflow through the oral and nasal cavities. Stop phonemes: /b/, /d/, /g/, /k/, /p/, /t/

Nasals
Produced by passing air from the vocal tract through the nose. Nasal phonemes: /m/, /n/, /h/

Fricatives
Produced by creating friction and forceful air through the vocal tract. Fricative phonemes: /f/, /h/, /s/, /v/, /z/, /t/, /d/, /ʃ/,   / ʒ/

Affricatives
Phonemes that begin their sound like a stop and releases like a fricative. Affricative phonemes: /tʃ/, /dʒ /

Glides
Produced without creating major friction or major obstruction of the vocal tract. They are pronounced by changing the movement of the vocal tract during pronunciation. Also called semivowels or semiconsonants, they always precede vowels. Glide phonemes: /w/, /j/

Liquids
Produced with the least amount of friction or obstruction of the vocal tract. Liquid phonemes: /l/, also called a lateral due to release of air on the sides of the tongue; /r/, also called a rhotic because sound is made by placing back of tongue against the alveolar ridge

Place of articulation concepts in the place-manner approach to word sounds and list the phonemes in each category

Bilabials
Produced by placing the lips together. Bilabial phonemes: /b/, /m/, /p/

Labiodentals
Produced by placing the bottom lip against the upper teeth. Labiodental phonemes: /f/, /v/

Linguadentals
Produced by the tongue contacting the upper teeth. Linguadental phonemes: /t/, /d/

Lingua-alveolars
Produced by the tip of the tongue contacting the alveolar ridge. Lingua-alveolar phonemes: /d/, /l/, /n/, /t/, /s/, /z/

Linguapalatals
Produced by the tongue contacting the roof of the mouth. Linguapalatal phonemes: /j/, /r/, / tʃ /, /dʒ /, /ʃ /

Linguavelars
Produced by the back of the tongue contacting the velum. Linguavelar phonemes: /k/, /g/, /h/

Glottal
Sound is produced by passing air through the larynx (vocal folds). Glottal phoneme: /h/

African American English

African American English (AAE) is thought to have its origins in West African tribal languages. During the slave trade, many Africans developed a language of communication among each other and with Americans already living here. This language was further refined in the southern United States. The prevalence of

AAE used among African Americans is highly dependent on socialization. Most users can switch between Standard American English and AAE. The ability to speak AAE has no bearing on intellectual ability. The factors that influence the use of AAE are

- Age: Younger persons use AAE more frequently than older persons do.
- Location: There is more AAE spoken in rural locations than in urban ones. AAE is more prevalent in southern states than in the west.
- Socioeconomic status: AAE is spoken more frequently in those of lower income areas compared to higher income areas.
- Social and peer group: Those persons who have more associations with Standard American English speakers are less likely to use AAE.

Phonemic patterns of African American English

- Diphthongs are reduced to monophthongs. For example, *fly* /flaI/ is pronounced *fla*.
- Consonant clusters at the end of words are reduced. For example, the word *past* is pronounced *pas*.
- •The /th/ sound /ð/ in the beginning of some words is rep laced with /d/, and the / θ / sound at the end of some words is replaced with /f/, /d/, /t/, or /v/. For example, the word *this* becomes *dis*; the word *booth* becomes *boof*.
- When /r/ sounds are at the end of words, they are dropped unless followed by a vowel. For example, the word *pour* becomes *po*.
- The terminal /l/ sound is often deleted. For example, the word *fool* becomes *foo*.

- When a nasal /n/ or /m/ sound follows a vowel, the nasal consonant is sometimes deleted and the vowel is nasalized. For example, the word *man* becomes *mã*.
- When the vowels *i* and *e* come before a nasal sound, they are both pronounced /I/. For example, the words *thin* and *then* are pronounced the same.

Grammatical patterns of African American English

- The verb *to be* is either omitted in sentences or used differently to mark aspect in verb phrases (deletion of copulas). For example, *She cookin'* = She *is cooking*. *She be cookin'* = She *is always cooking*.
- The reversal in order of phonemes containing s-clusters. For example, the word *ask* becomes *aks*, and the word *grasp* becomes *graps*.
- The words *ain't* and *can't* are use to produce negative sentences. For cxample, *She ain't had no books* = She *had no books. Can't nobody tell him nothin'* = No one *can tell him anything*.
- Contractions are dropped and the simple pronoun is used. For example, *Where your hat?* = *Where's your hat?*
- There is a lack of subject verb agreement. For example, *Mary walk to the store*. = *Mary walks to the store*.

Phonemic patterns of Spanish-influenced English

- The substitution of /ch/ for /sh/; for example, the word *ship* is pronounced *chip*.

- The substitution of /b/ for /v/; for example, the word *vote* is pronounced *bote*.
- The sound /th/ becames /d/, /t/, or /z/; for example. the word *thing* becomes *ting*.
- The sound /j/ becomes /y/; for example, the word *jump* becomes *yump*.
- The sound/l/ is pronounced /i/; for example, the word *fit* becomes *feet*.
- The omission of /h/ at the beginning of words; for example, *huge* becomes *uge*.
- The substitution of /θ / for /s/; for example, *estranged* becomes *ethranged*. This is exclusively found in speakers from Spain.
- The terminal /s/ is deleted in many words in the Caribbean Spanish accent.

Accent modification in speech pathology

An accent is the particular pronunciation of English words based on the country of origin or particular region of the United States. Some persons may want to reduce their accent to improve other's comprehension or to obtain a particular job requiring a high level of Standard English pronunciation. Those persons wishing to reduce their accent will call on a speech pathologist. Although an accent is not considered a speech disorder, there are important aspects of training Standard English. There is typically no reimbursement on state or private health plans for this service. Accent modification is not a part of any school service. Therefore, it is usually a private pay therapy. Accent modification begins with a full assessment of pronunciation patterns. Training is directed toward mouth position, intonation, and speech rhythm training.

Basic interpersonal communication skills (BICS) and cognitive-academic language proficiency (CALP)

Children who acquire two languages simultaneously from infancy (simultaneous bilingual acquisition) tend to learn both languages with minimal difficulty. However, when a second language is introduced before the complete proficiency of the first language is gained, there is typically a decrease in deficiency of both languages for a time. Those children who immigrate into the United States speaking a different language may take an average of 2 years to develop a proficiency in spoken English if there is normal exposure to the language. However, these children may take 5 years to develop a level of academic proficiency in English. This gap between basic interpersonal communication skills and cognitive-academic language proficiency is an important realization when educating English-as-second-language students. These children are at risk of being labeled as having communication or speech disorders.

Individuals with Disabilities Education Act (IDEA)

The Individuals with Disabilities Education Act mandates educational services and provides rights to children with a range of physical, cognitive, and emotional disabilities. Among those protected are children with speech, communication, or learning disabilities. Individual states may also allow for certain circumstances in which children need special education. Certain children who are culturally and linguistically diverse and in need of speech therapy come under the protection of the IDEA. The IDEA mandates the following:
- Materials used in evaluations must be selected and delivered in a way that is not racially

Copyright © Mometrix Media. You have been licensed one copy of this document for personal use only. Any other reproduction or redistribution is strictly prohibited. All rights reserved.

discriminatory or culturally biased.

- Evaluations must be made available in the language most efficiently used by the client.
- English deficiency is not a sole determining factor of a child's qualification for the term *disabled*. Therefore, testing must be directed at evaluating the specific disability rather than for English proficiency.
- Multicultural education should be available as needed for those clients with speech disorders.

Innateness, motherese, functional core, semantic features, and critical age hypotheses of language acquisition in children

Innateness hypothesis
Humans are born with an innate universal grammar.

Motherese hypothesis
The acquisition of language is dependent upon the language of the caretaker.

Functional core hypothesis
Children develop language by defining objects by their functional quality and then by applying conceptual features later.

Semantic features hypothesis
Children acquire a body of basic universal features that define objects. These features expand and become more sophisticated over time.

Critical age theory
The critical period of language acquisition begins at age 2 and ends at age 12. This theory has been largely refuted.

Sequential memory

Sequential memory is the ability to remember details in a particular order. Many children have poor sequential memory, especially those with dyslexia.

Visual sequential memory is required to recall letters, words, and numbers. Poor visual sequential memory causes reading, writing, spelling, and enumeration difficulties. Young children have difficulty learning the alphabet, shapes, and numbers. Many have difficulty with recall of subjects presented to them visually. They often misspell, miscopy, and rearrange letters, words, and numbers. They have difficulty with relating a story in a logical order.

Auditory sequential memory deficits may also be present, which cause sequence errors when verbalizing long words and sentences.

Audiometer equipment check

An audiologist should always perform an equipment check. Put on the earphones and listen to the tones while switching across the frequencies. This is done to ensure that the machine is generating all frequencies that will be used in the hearing test and also to make sure they are not audibly distorted. Second, listen closely while using the interrupter switch to start and stop each tone. This is done to make sure no switching transients are audible. Switching transients are "pops" or "clicks" heard when a pure tone is turned on or off suddenly. Audiometers have a circuit to start and stop tones smoothly and gradually, which eliminates switching transients. If switching transients are audible, the patient may respond to these rather than to the pure tones, making the test invalid. Third, turn on the masking noise to make sure it works and that its output levels match the dB levels on the dial.

Biological check of audiometer

First, allow the audiometer to warm up for 10 minutes. This check should only be done if you have normal hearing. If you do not, have a colleague with normal hearing listen for you. Set the audiometer's frequency to 1000 Hz and the hearing level dial to 40 dB. Put on the earphones and listen, switching the tone from one ear to the other. When the strength of the tone is equal on both sides, gradually lower the level toward 0 dB. You should be able to hear the tone at or near 0 dB with normal hearing if the machine and earphones are working properly and the sound levels in the earphones are the same as or very close to the values indicated on the hearing level dial. This procedure is known as a "biological check" of an audiometer's calibration.

Audiometer's masking level dial

With respect to the masking level dial on an audiometer, linearity of attenuation means that the masking level dial increases or decreases the noise output by the numerical increment shown on the dial. In other words, if you turn the dial up 10 dB, the noise output level should go up by 10 dB. Conversely, if you turn the dial down 10 dB, the noise output level should go down by 10 dB. One way to check this is to use a sound level meter or vacuum tube volt meter (VTVM). Take readings with the masking level dial set at regular intervals, working from the highest level to the lowest level.

Air-conduction calibration check

First, you should test and determine hearing thresholds in both ears for 10 young adults who have normal hearing. Add up the left ear results for all ten subjects and divide the sum by 10. Then, add up the right ear results for all ten subjects and divide that sum by 10. This will yield a mean (average) right ear and left ear threshold for the audiometer and earphones you are using. The mean thresholds you obtain should be the same as or very similar to the 0 dB setting on the audiometer's attenuator dial. If they are not, the test results obtained with that audiometer should be adjusted to eliminate the difference to the nearest 5 dB.

Checking audiometer calibration with bone conduction

Audiometer calibration is harder to check with bone conduction than with air conduction if you do not have calibration equipment. This is because any ambient or random noise coming into the ears via air conduction will mask bone conduction of sound at levels near threshold in subjects with normal hearing. In reality, there is more noise in most clinical test rooms than there should be ideally, which poses a problem. An alternative solution (Carhart, 1950) exists to test subjects with pure sensorineural hearing loss. Air conduction and bone conduction testing should be done on 10 to 12 ears. If all test subjects have pure sensorineural hearing loss, the thresholds for air conduction and bone conduction should be equal. With accurate calibration of air conduction receivers, the mean (average) of air conduction thresholds can be used as a standard, and the mean (average) of bone conduction thresholds can be matched to that standard.

Components required for sound production

Four basic components required for sound production are vibration, force, medium, and hearing mechanism. Vibration is simple harmonic motion (i.e. pure tones) or complex harmonic motion (i.e. human voices). Vibratory motion is oscillation, or up and down movement, that occurs in cycles. The number of cycles in a given time period is known as frequency. A frequency of one cycle per second equals one Hertz (Hz). Each cycle generates one sound wave. Sound waves are sinus, or sine, waves with peaks and valleys. The distance between two consecutive peaks of a wave is the wavelength (λ). Force is the degree to which a sound wave displaces a medium's molecules. The medium through which a sound wave travels has a different impedance, or resistance, against the force than the medium of the hearing mechanism. The force of a sound wave is determined by pressure gradients, or differences, between adjoining zones in a wave. The velocity (speed) of molecules in a medium is related to the physical properties of the medium and to its pressure. Force determines sound intensity.

Anatomical structures required for speech sound production

Anatomical structures required for speech sound production include:

- (1) sternum (breast bone) – supports the ribs, protects the heart and lungs; (2) lungs – supply air to vibrate vocal folds; (3) larynx – contains the vocal folds, functions as a valve to admit/stop airflow; (4) vocal folds or cords (contained in larynx); (5) trachea (windpipe, airway); (6) thyroid cartilage – largest laryngeal cartilage; (7) cricoid cartilage – laryngeal cartilage; (8) esophagus (throat, alimentary canal); (9) epiglottis – flap covering the trachea when food is being swallowed to stop it from moving from the esophagus into the lungs via the trachea; (10) soft palate (velum) at the back of the oral cavity – opens/closes to admit/stop air; (11) hard palate – thin bony plate of the skull in the roof of the mouth; (12) nasal cavities – influence the degree of vocal resonance; (13) hyoid bone – anchors the tongue, attaches to laryngeal cartilages; (14) tongue, (15) lips, and (16) teeth – all shape speech sounds; and (17) lower jaw (mandible) – shapes speech sounds.

Phonetic representation of speech sounds

Speech sounds are usually represented phonetically by the International Phonetic Alphabet (IPA), which resembles the alphabets of English and Romance languages, but differs in that many of its symbols are not alphabet letters. For example, the vowel sound in the words hat, cat, sat, mat, that, etc. is represented by the symbol /æ/, named "ash," which is not an alphabet letter. The vowel sounds in unstressed syllables, such as the ones in "about," "sorted," and "comma," are represented by the symbol /ə/, called "schwa," which is not an alphabet letter. The consonant sounds in "she" and "show" are represented by the symbol /ʃ/, which is not an alphabet letter. The consonant sounds in "beige" and "pleasure" are represented by the symbol /ʒ/, which is not an alphabet letter. The initial consonant sound in "thin" and the final consonant sound in "oath" are represented in the IPA by /θ/, or theta, which is an alphabet letter in Greek but not in English or Romance languages.

Auditory system

The parts of the auditory system are: the outer ear, the middle ear, the inner ear, and parts of the nervous system involved in auditory sensation and its integration with other sensory or motor systems. The outer ear is an acoustic device. It is protective, and collects acoustic energy. The middle ear is an acoustic device and a mechanical device. It collects acoustic energy. Its ossicles (tiny bones) are set in motion by that energy, and their movements mechanically transmit energy to the inner ear. The inner ear is a mechanical, hydraulic, and biological device. Transmission of energy via the hair cells is mechanical. The inner ear is filled with fluid that reacts to changes introduced by energy, meaning it is also a hydraulic device. The inner ear analyzes energy it receives in terms of frequency, intensity, complexity, and temporal features. It transmits this information to the central nervous system via the auditory nerve. Therefore, it is also a biological device.

Auricle and the external auditory meatus

The auricle, or pinna, is skin-covered cartilage and ligaments. Its ridges and depressions combine to form a complex resonator for high-frequency sounds and their localization. It is most efficient at collecting sound frequencies above roughly 500 Hz. Lower frequencies have wavelengths larger than the pinna, and can therefore move around it. The pinna's resonance affords selective tuning of the peripheral auditory mechanism. The outer two-thirds of the meatus is cartilaginous, and the inner third is comprised of skull bone. Skin over the meatus has hair follicles and cerumen glands. The hairs and the waxy cerumen produced are protective. The meatus is heavily innervated for tactile sensitivity and pain by the trigeminal (V) and vagus (X) cranial nerves. The meatus also functions as a resonator. It reinforces sound energy with wavelengths four times its own length. Normally, these wavelengths are between 3500 and 4000 Hz. The meatus's resonance amplifies sound frequencies between 3000 and 4000 Hz by 10 to 15 dB.

Ossicles of the middle ear

The ossicles, or tiny bones, are the malleus (the hammer), the incus (the anvil), and the stapes (the stirrup). When the acoustic energy of sound waves reaches the middle ear via the outer ear, the tympanic membrane (eardrum), which is a soft tissue structure, vibrates and causes the malleus to move. The malleus strikes the incus and causes it to vibrate. The incus's vibration moves the stapes to press against the oval window, which is a soft tissue structure into which the stapes's foot plate fits. The oval window bulges from the pressure and transmits the sound energy to the cochlea of the inner ear. From the inner ear, the energy is transmitted via the auditory nerve to the central nervous system. It is then interpreted by the auditory areas of the brain.

Middle ear response to acoustic energy in terms of acoustic impedance

Acoustic impedance is determined by mass, stiffness, and friction (or resistance). The inner ear has much greater impedance than air does. The middle ear mechanism adjusts for this difference by augmenting the effective pressure of acoustic energy hitting the eardrum. This is possible because the eardrum is about 17 times larger than the stapes's foot plate, and because the malleus and incus work together as a lever. If there were no middle ear and sound reached the inner ear, an estimated 99.9% of it would not be absorbed by the inner ear, but rather reflected back into the air. This would be due to a difference in impedance. The middle ear increases the pressure of sound energy by 17 times from where the eardrum vibrates to where the much smaller stapes's foot plate moves. Pressure equals force per unit area, so the much smaller area of the stapes's foot plate is subjected to greater pressure than the eardrum.

Embryology of the outer ear in a developing human embryo

The external auditory meatus or ear canal is derived from the ectoderm, the outer layer of the embryo which forms first. The ectoderm eventually differentiates during development into the epidermis (outer skin), nervous system tissues, and teeth. The external auditory meatus is formed from the first pharyngeal cleft. The pinna or auricle is formed from the fusing of six separate auricular hillocks, or ruminates. Three are anterior to (in front of) the external auditory meatus, and three are posterior to (in back of) the external auditory meatus.

Embryology of the middle ear in a developing human embryo

The first pharyngeal pouch differentiates during development into the middle ear cavities and the eustachian tubes (one of each for each ear). The lining of the first pharyngeal pouch, and hence the lining of the cavities and tubes, is epithelium. The epithelium develops out of the endoderm, the inner layer of the embryo. The endoderm also eventually develops into the linings of the respiratory system and the digestive system. The first two ossicles, the malleus and the incus, form out of the first pharyngeal arch. The third ossicle, the stapes, forms out of the second pharyngeal arch. The pharyngeal arches are considered a mesenchyme, which is a collection of loosely packed, unspecialized cells that eventually develop into the connective tissues, cartilage, bones, blood, heart, renal tissues, smooth muscles, and lymphatic vessel tissues. Mesenchyme derives from (is part of) the mesoderm, the middle embryonic layer between the ectoderm and the endoderm.

Embryology of the inner ear in a developing human embryo

An embryo has two ectodermal (outer) depressions (one on each side of the head) called otic placodes. During development, the ectoderm thickens to form the otic placodes. These then invaginate, creating a single, pear-shaped, cystic, closed otic vesicle lined with epithelium. When this first forms, it is called an otocyst. The otocyst then differentiates into two compartments. The larger portion forms the vestibular pouch, which will hold the vestibular system. This system includes the semicircular canals, utricle, and saccule, which all contain sensory receptors. The vestibular system governs the sense of balance and spatial orientation. The smaller portion of the otocyst forms the cochlear pouch. This will hold the cochlea, the organ of the inner ear that transmits sound energy along the auditory nerve to the brain.

Presbycusis

Presbycusis is the sensorineural hearing loss associated with aging. It may be mild, moderate, severe, or profound. In general, however, most adults experience some hearing acuity loss as they grow older. One type of damage that may contribute to presbycusis is a loss of hair cells, which means there are fewer functioning cells overall. Another contributing factor is the deterioration of the stria vascularis in the scala media or cochlear partition, the membranous labyrinth between the scala vestibuli and the scala tympani. The three scala are the cochlear ducts. The stria vascularis, a strip of specialized cells, secretes endolymph (fluid) to supply the scala media. Degradation of the stria vascularis contributes to hearing loss. Another contributing factor is a loss of nerve fibers in the auditory nerve, which reduces its ability to transmit signals to the brain. Finally, mechanical impairment of normal cochlear function can contribute to presbycusis.

Etiologies you would suspect for sudden-onset hearing loss or fluctuating hearing

Teen or young adult who recently had mumps or an upper respiratory infection; and an older adult with high blood pressure

In a teen or young adult who recently had mumps or an upper respiratory infection, one suspected etiology would be viral labyrinthitis. This infection can result from an infection of the sinuses and/or other parts of the upper respiratory system, such as influenzas or common cold viruses. It is even more likely to develop as a result of the mumps virus. The mumps virus is relatively rare today due to vaccines, but it is still seen occasionally. In an older adult with hypertension (high blood pressure) and related cardiovascular (heart and circulatory) disease, one suspected etiology related to sudden-onset hearing loss would be a vascular accident in the inner ear. In the same way that strokes, or cerebral hemorrhages, can damage the brain, blood vessels in the inner ear can hemorrhage and cause damage in the inner ear. This can result in sudden hearing loss.

Fluctuating hearing acuity occurs along with sudden or gradual hearing loss

Overall hearing acuity tends to deteriorate progressively, but it can also fluctuate over the shorter term as a result of any or all of the three following etiologies. First, Ménière's disease, which affects the vestibular system and causes vertigo and tinnitus, can cause hearing loss. It is also associated with fluctuations in hearing acuity. Second, congenital syphilis, even if the infection was treated at some time in the past, can cause

hearing loss and fluctuations in hearing acuity. Even though this disease is treatable, it can at times go undetected and/or untreated. In these cases, it can be passed from mother to child, and can affect the child's hearing. A final etiology that would be suspected is Cogan's syndrome, which is an interstitial keratitis that is not syphilitic in origin. It is associated with audio-vestibular types of symptoms. Conducting a series of repeated audiograms can establish, confirm, and document fluctuations in hearing acuity in these types of cases.

Hearing loss in a patient's right ear if you knew the patient had a stapedectomy or a stapes mobilization in the left ear that improved hearing in that ear

If a patient had hearing loss in the left ear and had a stapedectomy (removal of the stapes and replacement with an artificial stapes) or a stapes mobilization, wherein a fixed stapes is freed to move normally so sound can be transmitted to the inner ear, a likely cause for the fixation is otosclerosis. This condition, which seems to have a genetic component, causes abnormal bony growth in the middle ear. The excess bone can "freeze" the stapes so it cannot move, causing conductive hearing loss. Removing the interfering bone will free the stapes and allow it to move in some cases. In other cases, the stapes is too compromised to save, so it is removed and replaced. If a patient's hearing in their left ear improved after one of these surgeries, the hearing loss was likely due to otosclerosis. Therefore, otosclerosis would also be suspected in the right ear.

Why someone with conductive hearing loss finds it easier to hear conversation in a car with the windows open than someone with normal hearing

The individual's conductive hearing loss will mask some of the ambient noise entering through the car windows. People with normal hearing can hear all of the ambient noise, and it interferes with their ability to hear conversation. Because of this, they will speak louder. The person with conductive hearing loss hears less interfering noise. They can also hear the others' voices better when they talk louder over the ambient noise they can hear fully. For similar reasons, people with conductive hearing loss are likely to speak more quietly, while those with sensorineural loss tend to speak more loudly. In conductive hearing loss, bone conduction is greater than air conduction, so affected individuals can hear their own voices in their heads. With sensorineural hearing loss, both bone conduction and air conduction are equally reduced. There is no change in the difference between the two.

Hearing of low, middle, and high frequencies

Hearing acuity for high frequencies is most often affected in presbycusis, or hearing loss as a result of aging. It is uncommon for the ability to hear low or middle frequencies to be compromised to the same extent. Some noise-induced hearing loss can affect the ability to hear middle or low frequencies, but this is not caused by aging. One effect of high-frequency hearing loss is that a person can often hear adequately in a quiet setting, but has trouble understanding conversations when there is background noise. For instance, they may have trouble hearing at a party, public event, or large meeting. Another effect is that a person can often hear conversation, but has trouble discriminating high-frequency sounds in words, such as /s/, /ʃ/, /t/, or /θ/. This can make it hard to distinguish "fish" from "fist," or "fit" from "fifth." Many people compensate by determining the correct word through the context of the conversation or the sentence.

However, context may not always provide sufficient information.

Tinnitus

Tinnitus is a noise that a person hears in the ear(s) that is not caused by any external sound source, but is instead caused internally. It may be constant or intermittent. It can vary in intensity. Those who experience it describe it variously as ringing, humming, rushing, roaring, buzzing, hissing, chirping, etc. When there is fluid in the middle ear, the noise may pulse in time with the person's heartbeat. In these cases, the patient may describe it as a swishing or thumping sound. Tinnitus can be caused by any type of hearing loss, regardless of its degree of severity. Chronic or acute suppurative otitis media and secretory otitis media (middle ear infections producing pus or fluid) can both cause tinnitus. Ménière's disease can also cause tinnitus. Hearing loss caused by any etiology can result in tinnitus. If the hearing loss is unilateral, the tinnitus will occur in the impaired ear only.

Vertigo

Many people define vertigo as dizziness, though a more accurate definition is false perception of movement, or a spinning/whirling sensation, of either oneself or one's surroundings. Auditory system etiologies that can cause vertigo include Ménière's disease; labyrinthitis (inner ear inflammation), which is often caused by viral or bacterial infections; or acoustic neuroma, a benign tumor on the acoustic (auditory) nerve that causes unilateral tinnitus and hearing loss. Benign positional vertigo, which is not usually serious, can be caused by nerve inflammation; inner ear surgery; an overdose of aspirin, Dilantin, or alcohol; head injuries; and labyrinthitis. Non-auditory etiologies include multiple sclerosis (MS), cerebellar hemorrhage

- 24 -

(bleeding into the base of the brain), restricted blood flow to the back of the brain, migraines, and head and/or neck trauma. One difficulty for the examiner is that patients may use "dizziness" to describe a variety of symptoms. They may mean they are experiencing vertigo, but they may also use the term to describe faintness, lightheadedness, weakness, or clumsiness. They may also mean they are feeling off balance, weak, tired, confused, etc.

Otorrhea

Otorrhea refers to aural discharge or some kind of fluid coming out of the ear. This may be pus and/or mucus, blood, or cerebrospinal fluid. Otorrhea may accompany conductive, sensorineural, or mixed hearing loss (all types of hearing loss). If the discharge persists or comes and goes over years, an infection is the most likely cause. A clear discharge that occurs immediately after severe head trauma can be caused by a ruptured eardrum and/or a fracture to the base of the skull. A transverse fracture across the petrous bone will likely cause total sensorineural hearing loss. A longitudinal fracture can dislocate the ossicular chain, causing conductive hearing loss. Infections and trauma can both cause bloody aural discharge. In chronic suppurative otitis media, the presence of hemorrhagic granulation tissue in the middle ear can cause bleeding. In acute suppurative otitis media, the tympanic membrane can rupture and cause bleeding. In both cases, bloody otorrhea results.

Conditions where severe earache accompanies hearing loss

Acute suppurative otitis media is one condition that can cause severe earache with hearing loss. One-sided, severe, persistent aural pain with hearing loss is often a symptom of a malignant growth in the external auditory meatus or the middle ear. If the aural pain is severe and deep with hearing loss, and facial pain and double vision (diplopia) are also present, there could be suppurative otitis media involving the apex of the petrous bone, which is close to the gasserian ganglion and the abducens nerve (hence the diplopia). The combined symptoms of earache, discharge from the ear, and double vision are called Gradenigo's syndrome. A very severe earache with sensorineural hearing loss can be symptomatic of Ramsey Hunt syndrome, also known as herpes zoster oticus. This viral infection can be diagnosed by the presence of vesicles that form on the pinna and in the external auditory meatus.

Aural sensation of fullness or pressure along with hearing loss

Patients with primary endolymphatic hydrops (also known as Ménière's disease) or secondary endolymphatic hydrops often have a sensation of fullness or pressure along with hearing loss. (The cause of Ménière's disease is unknown. Secondary endolymphatic hydrops can be caused by head trauma, ear surgery, other inner ear disorders, allergies, or systemic disorders like diabetes or autoimmune diseases.) Secretory otitis media may also cause this sensation. Any infection creating fluid in the middle ear that causes conductive hearing loss can also result in a feeling of fullness or pressure. The sensation may be constant or intermittent. It may accompany vertigo and decreased hearing, or may occur on its own. Patients may say they feel there is water in their ear(s). They may also say it sounds (to them) like their head is in a bucket when they talk. In a smaller number of cases, they may also complain that the affected ear(s) feel(s) numb or dead.

Recruitment

Recruitment refers to a substantial decrease in the difference between an individual's hearing threshold, most comfortable loudness levels, and uncomfortable loudness levels. Normally, there is a broad range of dB levels between these points. A person can hear everything perfectly at one dB level, but can also hear at many levels louder before loudness is great enough to cause discomfort. A person with hearing loss who is experiencing recruitment has a higher hearing threshold and a lower uncomfortable loudness level than normal. Thus, the range within which they can hear everything without discomfort is very small. An example is an older person with presbycusis who says "What? What?" when a speaker uses normal loudness, but snaps "You don't have to shout; I'm not deaf!" when the speaker raises his/her voice (usually a lot instead of a little). This person is not simply being difficult. The speaker's normal loudness is insufficient, but the raised voice exceeds the hearer's comfort range.

Hyperacusis

Hyperacusis is defined as a higher than normal sensitivity to noise or loud sounds. This can be caused by Ménière's disease when the patient has sensorineural hearing loss due to the disease. This increased sensitivity can be substantiated by finding evidence of recruitment during audiometric testing. Hyperacusis can also occur in patients who have lesions on the seventh (facial) cranial nerve that cause paralysis of the stapedius muscle. Such patients may report hypersensitivity to louder sounds in the ear in which the stapedius muscle is paralyzed. Hyperacusis is most often associated with normal hearing. When the clinical impression is a paralyzed stapedius muscle, this impression may be

substantiated by testing the patient using a modified acoustic impedance bridge (Brooks, 1973) as well as a pure tone screening.

Diplacusis

Diplacusis is defined as a distortion of heard pitch accompanying hearing loss. Sound is heard at a different pitch in the affected ear than in the normal ear. The kind of hearing impairment that is accompanied by diplacusis is usually caused by endolymphatic hydrops. This is either Ménière's disease [primary idiopathic endolymphatic hydrops (idiopathic means its etiology is unknown)] or secondary primary endolymphatic hydrops caused by head trauma, ear surgery, other inner ear disorders, allergies, or systemic disorders such as diabetes or autoimmune diseases. Diplacusis is not found to occur as frequently as either aural fullness/pressure or hyperacusis. This may mean it occurs less often, or it may simply mean it is reported less often, as many people do not notice if they do not have a good sense of pitch. Patients more likely to notice the difference are mainly musicians or those with musical ability.

Including ocular disorders in a hearing impairment history

Because of the arrangement of the cranial nerves, ocular disorders often accompany hearing loss. The presence of an ocular disorder can help diagnose the cause of hearing loss. One example is if there is conductive hearing loss and double vision (diplopia). These could be due to a nasopharyngeal tumor. These same symptoms could be due to suppuration in the apex of the temporal bone's petrous pyramid. Another example is that a patient presenting with sensorineural hearing loss and diplopia could have multiple sclerosis (MS). Another example is that a patient with sensorineural hearing loss and uveitis could have sarcoidosis. Symptoms of Vogt-Koyanagi-Harada syndrome include hearing loss, uveitis, poliosis, vitiligo, alopecia, and meningeal irritation, so this is another example. One more example is that sensorineural hearing loss and interstitial keratitis can be caused by Cogan's syndrome or congenital syphilis. As these examples are serious conditions, early diagnosis is important.

Anatomical parts in addition to the ears that should be examined in a patient presenting with aural symptoms

In addition to the ears, there should be a complete examination of the head and neck. This should include the nose, mouth, pharynx, larynx; the vasculature of the head and the neck (assessed via palpation); and an evaluation of the functioning of the cranial nerves and the cerebellum. Most examinations and their interpretation should be made by an otologist. The audiologist should also be fully informed of the exams conducted and the interpretations. In cases where a speech-language pathologist is responsible for the audiological examination instead of an audiologist (as is the case in, for instance, many school systems and some nursing homes), this professional should also be informed of test results and interpretations. The patient's presenting complaints and the preliminary findings of examinations will determine which other specialists (e.g. ophthalmologist, neurologist, neurosurgeon, internist, etc.) should examine the patient and which additional laboratory tests should be ordered.

Auscultation

Auscultation is listening to the patient's ear by using a stethoscope or, less often, an ear-to-ear tube. One end is placed in the patient's ear and the other end in the examiner's ear. When a patient complains of hearing a pulsating noise or click in his/her ear, auscultation can aid diagnosis. For example, if the examiner hears a bruit in or near the patient's ear, there could be a fistula in a blood vessel (an arteriovenous fistula). This noise can help with the diagnosis. In cases of atherosclerosis, there could be a plaque in the carotid artery or somewhere in the carotid arterial system. This would also cause a bruit near the ear that the examiner could hear, helping to diagnose this condition. A third condition is palatal myoclonus from a lesion on the brain stem, which can cause a repeated clicking in the patient's ear that the examiner can hear.

Inspection of the pinnae and EAMs in cases of congenital atresia

If the examiner finds the patient has a microtic pinna (microtia is a condition wherein the pinna is abnormally small) and congenital atresia of the external auditory meatus, this means the condition originated during the first trimester of the mother's pregnancy. Because of the early onset, both the outer ear and the canal are abnormal, and will require more surgical reconstruction. If the examiner finds the patient has a normal pinna but congenital atresia of the external auditory meatus, this means the condition originated later in the fetus's development. It also means there is a very good chance that the ossicular chain is intact. There is roughly a 50% probability that the tympanic membrane is intact. Findings such as these can help to predict the extent of surgery that will be needed and how difficult reconstruction that will enable auditory functioning will be.

Symptoms that can be found via aural inspection and palpation

Inspection and palpation of the pinna can allow for the identification of

- 27 -

cartilaginous defects. These can be caused by trauma, infection, or chronic relapsing polychondritis. They may also be related to disorders of the middle or inner ear. Inspection and palpation of the mastoid process can allow for the identification of swelling, tenderness, fluctuation, and discoloration caused by suppurative mastoiditis. If pressing on the tragus causes pain or discomfort, this can allow for the identification of external otitis. If cholesteatoma causes a fistula into the horizontal semicircular canal, pressing on the tragus can cause nystagmus (involuntary eye movement) and vertigo. When a patient has pulsating tinnitus, palpation over the carotid artery may yield a palpable thrill, which could be caused by a fistula. If a patient has symptoms of visual impairment, hearing impairment, and headaches, and palpation of the superficial temporal artery causes tenderness, beading, and induration, this can help to diagnose arteritis (arterial inflammation, in this case of the temporal artery).

Abnormalities that can be seen and some things that should be done during otoscopic examination

Using an otoscope, Siegle's otoscope, binocular dissecting microscope, or ear speculum and head mirror, the examiner can see canal abnormalities such as wax buildup, abrasions, infections, and tumors. Any obstructions should be removed from the canal to make a full examination. However, if pus is present, the examiner should take a specimen for culturing and analysis first. The tympanic membrane can be visualized as normal, or as flaccid, thickened, scarred, bulging, retracted, discolored, or perforated. If a patient has secretory otitis media, middle ear fluid may be visible behind an intact eardrum. Air bubbles in the fluid may be visible. If the examiner suspects fluid but cannot be sure whether it is present, a diagnostic myringotomy (incision in the eardrum) may be done. With active, chronic suppurative otitis media, if the eardrum is ruptured, hemorrhagic granulation tissue growing through the rupture may be visible. If there is an attic defect, a cholesteatoma may be seen.

Siegle's otoscope and a binocular dissecting microscope during an otoscopic examination

The Siegle's otoscope can create positive and negative pressures on the tympanic membrane. This is useful for testing the mobility of the tympanic membrane. If the membrane has been perforated and there are secretions (as there are in secretory otitis media), the Siegle's otoscope can also suction those secretions through the perforation. The Siegle's otoscope can also be used in the examination to test for the presence of a fistula in the horizontal semicircular canal. Using a binocular dissecting microscope will allow the examiner to inspect and palpate the tympanic membrane and/or tympanic cavity with a probe. This can frequently give the examiner information about middle ear pathology and its degree of involvement that could not otherwise be determined during the otoscopic exam.

Eustachian tube function

One reason normal eustachian tube function is important is because it is a prerequisite to a successful myringoplasty if one is needed. The Valsalva or Politzer maneuver can be used to test eustachian tube function. The Valsalva maneuver is holding one's nose shut, closing one's mouth, and blowing. This pushes air into the eustachian tube. The Politzer maneuver is swallowing water while a Politzer bag, Senturia apparatus, or similar equipment forces air into one nostril while the other is clamped shut. With normal functioning, inflation of the eustachian tube results from either maneuver. The implication if

- 28 -

these fail is defective eustachian tube functioning. One alternative is catheterization. The eustachian tube can be inflated with air sent via a cannula introduced through the nose. Another alternative is to conduct impedance audiometry, which can also give the examiner information that is useful with respect to the functioning of the eustachian tubes.

Examining the nasopharynx

The nasopharynx should always be examined thoroughly during any aural examination. A good time to do this is when testing for normal eustachian tube function, as these areas are related. The examiner can make a thorough, systematic visual examination of the nasopharynx using a nasopharyngeal mirror. If any abnormality at all is noted, even if it is very tiny or seems insignificant, the examiner should take a biopsy of it. If a patient has secretory otitis media on one side and the clinician suspects that a nasopharyngeal tumor is the cause of this inflammation, but a growth cannot be seen upon visual inspection, imaging tests should be done to try to locate such a neoplasm. If imaging does not clearly reveal any mass, it could be due to the size, placement, or positioning of the mass. In this case, multiple blind biopsies can also be taken of the nasopharynx to aid in diagnosis.

Principles of psychoacoustics

Hearing is not just a mechanical process of receiving sound waves. It also involves sensation and perception. A mechanical sound wave in the air is transformed within the auditory system into neural action potentials. These are carried by nerves to the brain, which perceives and interprets them. In converting mechanical stimuli to neural stimuli, the inner ear performs considerable signal processing. As a result, some differences in sound

wave forms may not be perceptible to the hearer. Techniques of electronic audio compression, such as those used in MP3s, find this limitation an advantage they can use. Also, the human ear's response to various loudness levels is nonlinear. Telecommunications networks and audio noise reduction systems both take advantage of this by nonlinearly compressing sound data for transmission, and then expanding the data for playback. Because of the ear's nonlinear reaction, sounds close in frequency can produce intermodulation distortion products called phantom beat notes.

Limits of human hearing perception with respect to frequency or pitch

A normal human ear can potentially hear sounds between 20 Hz to 20 kHz (20,000 Hz). Hearing acuity for higher frequencies decreases with age. Most adults with normal hearing cannot hear above 16 kHz. The frequency of the human voice tends to range between 2 kHz and 4 kHz (2,000-4,000 Hz). In a clinical setting, changes in pitch that are larger than 3.6 Hz within the octave of 1,000 to 2,000 Hz can be perceived by the human ear. In some cases, smaller differences can be perceived. For example, two competing pitches can cause phase variance, called beating, so that the interference of the two is heard as a frequency difference pitch.

Limits of human hearing perception with respect to intensity

The human ear can hear a tremendous range of sound intensity. Human eardrums sense changes in pressure as small as 2×10^{-10} atm (atmospheres) and as great as or greater than 1 atm. One atmosphere equals 191 dB. This is the largest pressure variation an undistorted sound wave can have in the Earth's atmosphere. Larger sound waves exist on Earth as shock waves. When sound pressure is measured logarithmically, the reference point for all pressures is 1.97385×10^{-10} atm. This defines the lower limit of audible sound for human ears as 0 dB. The upper limit is not as clearly defined, but for practical purposes can correspond to a level causing physical harm and/or hearing loss. Time of exposure to loud sounds also determines damage. For example, a person may hear sounds up to 120 dB for a short duration and experience pain or discomfort but not hearing loss, but long durations of exposure to sounds above 80 dB can cause permanent hearing loss.

Acoustic cues related to speech perception

Acoustic cues are various properties of speech sounds' waveforms. They help listeners differentiate speech sounds corresponding to different phonemes (abstract representations of individual speech sound units). Voice onset time (VOT) is one of the most studied acoustic cues. It signals the difference between devocalized and vocalized stops. For example, the consonants /t/ and /d/ are articulated the same, but /t/ is unvoiced and /d/ is voiced. VOT helps listeners tell the difference. There are cues indicating differences in the placement of articulation. These include the tongue's position (protruding, or in the front, middle, or back of the mouth) and whether it is touching the hard palate, the alveolar ridge, or the teeth. Additionally, there are cues signaling differences in the manner of articulation. These include whether the air stream is stopped and released (in stops or plosives) or emitted with friction (in fricatives and affricates) with consonants, whether vowels are nasalized or denasalized, etc. Such cues are combined in speech to help listeners recognize specific phonemes, and hence specific words.

One problem is that a single cue can signal more than one dimension of linguistic relevance. For example, in English, vowel duration can cue whether that vowel is stressed or not; whether the consonant following that vowel is voiced or unvoiced; what the vowel is in cases where there are two that sound similar, such as /æ/ and /ɛ/ in American English; and even, according to some experts, whether the vowel is "long" or "short." Another difficulty is that several different acoustic cues can signal one linguistic unit. For example, a classic experiment by Alvin Liberman in 1957 showed that the formant transitions in the onset of the consonant sound /d/ will vary according to the vowel that follows it (/di/, /da/, or /du/, for example). Regardless of the different shapes of the formants and their transitions, however, listeners will still perceive it as /d/.

Acoustic standards in ANSI

Most ANSI acoustic standards are developed by an Accredited Standards Committee (ASC). ASC, or "S," committees are S1 – Acoustics; S2 – Mechanical Vibration and Shock; S3 – Bioacoustics; and S12 – Noise. S1, S3, and S12 are most relevant to audiology. Administration of ASCs is by Secretariats or organizations. The Secretariat for S committees is the Acoustical Society of America (ASA). To develop a standard, someone must submit a proposal. The Secretariat manager evaluates it and confers with the ASC chair. If the chair approves it, committee members vote on the proposal. If they approve, a working group whose members represent groups relevant to the standard is formed. This group writes a draft standard. Individual experts designated annually by each S committee evaluate the draft and all members vote. With a majority consensus, it becomes a standard. Standards are voted on for reaffirmation, revision, or withdrawal every five years. Developing standards can take years.

Speech cannot easily be segmented into single perceptual units

As listeners, we perceive speech in a linear fashion as a series of separate units, such as phonemes, syllables, words, phrases, sentences, etc. However, speech is not produced in the same linear way. The individual sounds actually overlap, resulting in coarticulation. A spectrogram of a spoken phrase made up of several separate words may show no discernible divisions between the speech sounds. Produced sounds run together acoustically, even though we perceive them as separate due to our ability and need to differentiate among them. Speech sounds are influenced by their contexts (the other sounds coming before and after them). This influence crosses the boundaries of syllables and even words. An example is the differential influence of the following vowel on the formation of /d/, as demonstrated by Liberman. Thus, it is not easy to try to segment sequences of speech into individual perceptual units.

Lack of invariance

One source of variation is context-induced variation. Acoustic properties of speech sounds are influenced by their phonetic surroundings. For example, with VOT, the differentiation between vocalization and devocalization values varies among velar, alveolar, and labial stops; among stressed and unstressed syllables; and according to the position within the syllable. A second source of variation is different speech conditions. One speech condition is the tempi or speeds at which people speak. Second, many phonemic differences are temporal in nature. For instance, vowels and consonants are short or long, voiced or unvoiced, stops or glides, fricatives or affricates. Another speech condition is

enunciation. In connected speech, the typical speaker has sloppy articulation. Articulation can vary according to whether the speaker is more careful or sloppier when speaking than the typical person. A third source of variation is the speaker. Pitch and resonance vary among individual speakers according to age, sex, size of vocal tract, and psychological characteristics. Regional dialects and foreign accents also produce individual variations in the acoustic structure of speech sounds.

Perceptual constancy

Perceptual constancy is a characteristic found in many areas of human perception, including vision (shape, color, size, distance, location, and lightness), music (the ability to identify an instrument despite variations in pitch, loudness, environments, and players), and speech. It means we adjust for, or filter out, variations to identify a common category. One example of perceptual constancy is vocal tract normalization. This means that people recognize common speech sounds despite differing pitches and resonance among speakers by adjusting their perceptual systems for the acoustic properties of each individual speaker. Another example is speech rate normalization, meaning that people adjust their perception of sound duration for the tempo or rate at which an individual person speaks. Without perceptual constancy, we would not be able to recognize the same words in the same language when they are spoken by different speakers. Obviously, this would severely limit communication. Perceptual constancy lets people understand spoken language despite speech differences among speakers.

Categorical perception

Categorical perception has to do with how people differentiate their perception of speech sounds. People perceive speech sounds categorically. Phonemes are categories of speech sounds. People are more apt to observe differences between phonemes or categories than differences within one phoneme or category. Thus, perceptual space between phonemes is subjective. For example, in 1970, Lisker and Abramson used an artificial continuum between a vocalized and devocalized labial stop (/b/ and /p/). Each point on the continuum has a different amount of VOT. A pre-voiced /b/ had a VOT of -10. An unaspirated /p/ had a VOT of 0. By increasing the VOT by increments of 10, the researchers found that the end of the continuum was a strongly aspirated /p^h/. With seven sounds on this continuum, listeners perceived the first three as /b/, the last three as /p/, and the middle point as the boundary between voiced and unvoiced phonemes. Their perception of the continuum was discontinuous, separating the vocalized and devocalized categories.

Test to identify either of two phonemes on a VOT continuum, and a test to discriminate between two phonemes with different VOT values but an equal VOT distance from each other

A test to identify whether a speech sound is in the voiced or unvoiced category on a VOT continuum (an identification or categorization test) would yield the result that a listener's categorizing function is discontinuous rather than continuous. Even when sounds are presented on a continuum, they are perceived as discrete by listeners, enabling them to categorize sounds as separate phonemes. A test to discriminate between two sounds with different VOT values but an equal VOT distance from each other (20 milliseconds, for example) would yield the result that listener responses would be equal to chance (around 20%) when the two different sounds are within the

same category, but would be close to 100% when the two sounds are in separate categories. The conclusion that could be drawn from both tests is that listener sensitivity to the same increment of VOT varies according to whether the sounds are within or across phonemic boundaries.

Bottom-up and top-down processing

With respect to speech perception, bottom-up processing means that the smallest distinguishable unit of speech sound, such as an individual phoneme, will be recognized first. The next largest unit, such as a syllable, will be recognized next, followed by a word, etc. Conversely, top-down processing means that a larger unit, such as a whole sentence (or in some cases even a whole conversation) would be recognized first. Then, increasingly smaller units such as words, syllables, and phonemes would be identified. While both processes occur in speech perception, the larger context often gives listeners information that helps them to identify the smaller pieces within that larger context. For example, in experiments, when the same words are presented to listeners in isolation and in the context of a sentence or phrase, the accuracy of the listeners' perception is greater when words are presented in context than when they are presented in isolation.

Phonemic restoration effect

The phonemic restoration effect means that listeners can compensate for the absence, distortion, or noise masking of a phoneme by using the surrounding phonemic context (if it is more clearly audible) in conjunction with their knowledge of the spoken language. In 1970, Richard M. Warren demonstrated this by presenting listeners with a word in which he substituted a sound like a cough for one of the phonemes. The listeners had no trouble restoring the actual phoneme in their perception of the word. In fact, they were not even able to pinpoint which of the phonemes in the word had been changed. This showed that our perception can automatically correct words with phonemic errors or distortions so that we hear what we expect to hear and (usually) what we would normally hear if the error or distortion was not present. This relates to perceptual constancy with other sources of variation in addition to individual speakers.

Garnes and Bond's 1976 experiment with "carrier" words

In 1976, Garnes and Bond studied how semantic knowledge affects speech perception. They used word series wherein only the initial phoneme differed (for example, may, bay, day, gay, etc.). These differences occurred gradually on a continuum. They inserted these words into various sentences. Each sentence only made sense with one of the words. When the initial sound of a target word was close to a division between two distinct phonemes on the continuum so its sound was ambiguous, listeners were likely to compensate using the context of the sentence's meaning to determine what the word was, and hence what phoneme its initial sound was. This demonstrates top-down processing, as the subjects used higher-level processing (semantics) to understand a whole sentence, and then used that understanding to discern a single ambiguous word (morphology) by its context. They ultimately selected which phoneme the ambiguous sound represented (phonemics) based on the word. Therefore, processing proceeded from high to low.

Language development in infants with respect to categorical perception

Infants can hear even the smallest differences in speech sounds quite early, and are able to discriminate among all phonemes that can be produced. The more they hear their native language spoken, the more selective their discrimination becomes. They begin to disregard non-pertinent differences such as variations that occur within the same phoneme, and start to attend to phonemically distinctive differences. Thus, their perception becomes language-specific and categorical in nature. Research conducted with infants has found that they learn to discriminate among different phonemes for the vowels in their native language by the time they are around six months of age. Research has also found that infants learn to discriminate among different phonemes for the consonants in their native language by the time they are around 11 to 12 months of age.

Studying speech perception in babies

Researchers have used the head-turn method and the sucking-rate method to study speech perception in babies. When they present one-day-old newborns with their mother's normal speaking voice, their mother's voice speaking in a monotone, and a stranger's voice, babies only turn their heads to the sound of their mother's normal speech. When they present a human sound and a non-human one, babies only turn their heads to the human sound. Some researchers believe babies' auditory learning begins in the womb, as they can hear voices and other sounds in utero. To study effects of sound on sucking rate, the baby's normal rate is established as the baseline first. Sucking rate increases when a sound stimulus is introduced, and then levels off as the baby becomes habituated to the sound. When a new stimulus is introduced while the first sound is still present in the background, the baby's sucking rate will increase again in response if the baby perceives the new sound as different.

Difficulties posed by language differences for learners of a foreign language

A foreign language will often contain some phonemes not used in the learner's native language. If a learner tries to assimilate the foreign language's elements into his/her native language's system because other components in both languages are the same instead of accommodating by adding unfamiliar features to his/her repertoire, s/he will have trouble with the unfamiliar features. A phonemic example is the difficulty Japanese learners of English have discriminating between /r/ and /l/. There is no /l/ in Japanese, and learners often experience difficulty producing /l/ because they tend to assimilate this unfamiliar phoneme into their familiar /r/ category. A morphological example is that Chinese learners of English tend to omit articles in English such as "the" or "a" and "-s" endings for plural words because these do not exist in their language. A syntactic example is that German learners of English may place the verb at the end of a sentence ("I was happily down the street walking," for example). This reflects the grammatical structure of German.

Models of language learning proposed by Best and Flege in 1995

In 1995, Best proposed a Perceptual Assimilation Model related to different languages and learning across languages. This model describes the possible patterns in which learners of foreign languages are likely to assimilate structural categories (such as phonemes) of foreign languages into the categorical system of their native language. It also predicts the outcomes of such assimilation. Also in 1995, Flege proposed a Speech Learning Model related to the learning of a second language. This model posits that a sound in the second language is more easily acquired by the learner when it is more markedly different from any sound in the learner's first language. On the other hand, a sound in the second language that is more similar to a sound in the learner's first language will be harder to acquire. This is because the more unfamiliar sound is perceived by the learner as more distinctive, while sounds that are similar in both languages can confound the learner.

Prevention and Identification

Vestibular injury

After a vestibular injury, sensations of imbalance or vertigo can continue. This can be caused by inadequate compensation of the central nervous system. It can also be caused in some cases by the patient's developed strategies for controlling their posture. These strategies compensate for the disequilibrium, but can also cause the patient's balance to be unsteady under some circumstances. Vestibular and balance rehabilitation programs can be helpful to patients with such residual symptoms. A comprehensive program of vestibular rehabilitation is usually delivered by a physical therapist or an occupational therapist who has received training pertinent to vestibular rehabilitation. According to ASHA policy, it is within the scope of practice for an audiologist to provide consultations to these therapists, to serve as a member of an interdisciplinary team formed for management of patients with balance disorders and/or dizziness, and to perform canalith repositioning procedures included in vestibular rehabilitation.

Testing cranial nerves and the auditory nerve during a routine otolaryngology examination

In addition to the auditory (-vestibular) (eighth) cranial nerve, an otologist should test the trigeminal (fifth), abducens (sixth), facial (seventh), glossopharyngeal (ninth), vagus (tenth), accessory (eleventh), and hypoglossal (twelfth) cranial nerves. Paralysis of the hypoglossal (twelfth) nerve on one side is indicated by deviation of the tongue to indicated by deviation of the tongue to the opposite side when protruded. Long-term paralysis is indicated by muscular atrophy. Soft palate deviation to one side and vocal fold fixation on the opposite side indicate paralysis of the vagus (tenth) nerve on the side of the vocal fold fixation. Lesions can cause all of these signs. A chemodectoma of the jugular foramen can affect the ninth, tenth, eleventh, and twelfth cranial nerves. Symptoms include paralysis of the tongue, palate, and vocal cords; decreased tactile sensation in the pharynx (glossopharyngeal nerve); and weakness in the sternocleidomastoid and trapezius muscles (accessory nerve) on the side where the lesion is located.

Observing eye movements and testing corneal reflexes in connection with audio-vestibular problems

When patients present with audio-vestibular complaints, the examiner should always look for spontaneous nystagmus. If observation shows that one eye stops moving laterally at the midline, this indicates lateral rectus paralysis. The abducens (sixth) cranial nerve is affected. There could be a nasopharyngeal tumor or an infection in the petrous apex. Corneal reflexes should then be tested. If the reflex is reduced or absent on one side, this means the trigeminal (fifth) cranial nerve is affected. It may indicate a larger acoustic neuroma. In this case, the examiner should also test sensations of touch, pain, and temperature in the parts of the scalp and face innervated by the ophthalmic, maxillary, and mandibular portions of the trigeminal (fifth) cranial nerve. One-sided paresis of the trigeminal nerve's motor division can be identified by palpating both temporal and masseter muscles while the patient is clenching his or her teeth.

Approaches that can aid differential diagnosis of either inner ear pathology or a cerebellar disorder

Since the cerebellum coordinates motor functions and the inner ear's vestibular system manages balance and spatial orientation, it can sometimes be hard to differentiate between the two. Observing a patient's gait can help. With a vestibular problem, the patient's gait may be ataxic (drunken, reeling). With a cerebellar problem, the patient's gait may show a loose appearance in the extremities. If the patient exhibits tremors during voluntary movements, cerebellar disease is more likely. Testing the patient's coordination can also assist in diagnosis. The finger-nose-finger test, wherein the patient alternates touching the examiner's finger and his or her own nose, can reveal various degrees of terminal incoordination. The degree of incoordination can help narrow the diagnosis. Rapid alternating movements (diadochokinesia) should also be tested by having the patient rapidly turn his or her hand to face up and down. This can help with differential diagnosis of an inner ear problem.

Divisions of the auditory (eighth cranial) nerve

The two main divisions of the auditory nerve are the cochlear and vestibular nerves. Audiometric testing can usually distinguish between a lesion on the cochlea and a lesion on the auditory nerve. Audiometric testing can also sometimes localize a central auditory lesion. Unlike audiometric testing, vestibular testing cannot differentiate between cochlear and auditory nerve lesions. However, vestibular testing can often help determine the difference between a peripheral vestibular lesion and a lesion in the cerebellum or brain stem. Stimulation of the vestibular system, specifically of the semicircular canals, can elicit nystagmus (involuntary eye movements). Measurement of the characteristics and duration of the nystagmus, which can be both grossly observed and objectively measured, can help an examiner assess the functioning of the semicircular canals.

Cold caloric, bithermal caloric, rotation, and positional nystagmus tests

Cold caloric testing assesses each labyrinth. When the head is tilted back 60 degrees to make the horizontal semicircular canal vertical, introducing cold water or air to the inside of one ear changes inner-ear temperature and produces a current in the fluid. A patient with normal vestibular function experiences vertigo. Results can be: both labyrinths are normal; one labyrinth is less active; both labyrinths are hypoactive; or one or both labyrinths do not respond. Bithermal caloric testing stimulates each ear with alternating cold and warm water/air. This can help deduce labyrinthine activity and directionality. Rotation tests turn the patient in a swivel chair 10 times in 20 seconds while the head is tilted forward 30 degrees. Subsequent nystagmus is then observed. Unlike caloric tests, this stimulates both labyrinths, yielding less information. However, rotary testing can help in drug toxicity if caloric stimulation evoked no response by discovering residual vestibular function. Positional testing rapidly places the head in different positions. Elicited positional nystagmus objectively identifies vestibular dysfunction. Continuous positional nystagmus can indicate central nervous system dysfunctions; patients may have mild or no vertigo.

Radiologic imaging exams

X-rays can show sclerosis and inadequate aeration of the mastoid process. They can show rarefied areas of the mastoid process resulting from cholesteatoma. X-rays can also show enlargement of the external auditory meatus or erosion of the petrous pyramid, both of which can indicate the presence of an acoustic neuroma. Tomography of the petrous bone can help in identifying and describing a fracture, in diagnosing labyrinthine otosclerosis, and in visualizing the ossicles. Pantopaque myelography of the posterior fossa can help in the diagnosis of smaller acoustic neuromas. If a patient has a glomus jugulare or glomus tympanicum tumor (also known as temporal bone paragangliomas) or a tumor on either the jugular foramen or the bottom of the middle ear, delimiting the area of the tumor is aided by selective external and internal carotid arteriography. These and other imaging tests should always be used in conjunction with histories, physical examinations, and laboratory tests.

Collapsible external auditory meatus

Sometimes, tissues in an individual's EAM are flaccid, and collapse from the pressure of audiometer earphones. This is known as a collapsible meatus. An example of how such a patient might present is as follows: A child's audiogram shows 20-30 dB of conductive hearing loss in one ear. The otoscope, however, shows a normal eardrum and a slightly narrowed but essentially normal meatus. Recent ear infections should be ruled out, as should a family history of congenital hearing impairment or otosclerosis. Once these are ruled out, a simple way to confirm collapsible meatus is to insert a small plastic tube into the meatus to hold it open. If repeating the audiogram with this tube in place yields a more normal hearing level reading in that ear, the presence of collapsible meatus is confirmed and no treatment is needed. While this procedure is simple, an examiner unfamiliar with collapsible meatus will not know to perform it, and will be confounded by unexplained conductive hearing loss as a result.

Foreign bodies

A foreign body in the external meatus is one source of conductive hearing loss. While one might expect this to be the first factor that would be looked for and ruled out, foreign bodies in the external meatus are sometimes not considered or found. While young children are notorious for inserting small beads, beans, or other objects into their ears, they are not the only ones who may have foreign bodies in their ears. Adults can have cerumen (wax buildup) that can become dry and impacted (pushed against the eardrum), or they may even have insects or other objects in their ears. If an otoscopic examination is not done closely and carefully enough, these objects can be missed in some cases. This issue can be complicated by the presence of some sensorineural hearing loss, as the patient will be diagnosed with a mixed hearing impairment. With the etiology of the conductive component unknown, some patients have unnecessarily been prescribed hearing aids.

External otitis

Symptoms of external otitis include reddened, swollen outer ear skin and pus in the external auditory meatus. The etiology is most often an infection. Bacterial infections are much more common than fungal infections as etiological organisms for external otitis. Taking a culture of the pus found in the ear canal can determine which type of infection is responsible. External otitis is treated with repeated, thorough cleansings of the external auditory meatus. Water is kept out of the affected ear and a local antibiotic is applied. The specific type of medication should be chosen based on the specific type of bacterium or other organism that is causing the infection, as certain drugs are more effective against certain organisms than others. If external otitis has been present for a long time, it may require lengthy and persistent treatment to be successfully resolved.

Osteomas vs. malignant neoplasms of the EAM

Osteomas, or bony growths, of the bony portion of the external auditory meatus are not unusual. They are most often small in size and do not affect hearing. In the somewhat rare event that an osteoma grows big enough to block the canal, removing some of the occlusive bone can reopen the canal and restore the patient's hearing. On the other hand, malignant neoplasms of the external auditory meatus, such as epitheliomas or carcinomas, are life-threatening. These kinds of tumors dictate more aggressive treatments intended to keep the patient alive. In these cases, the patient's hearing acuity is considered of low importance unless or until the cancer has been brought under control, is in remission, or has been eradicated.

Congenital atresia of the EAM

Congenital atresia of the EAM can involve one or both ears. It may be partial or complete. It may be membranous or bony. The pinna may be normal, tiny, deformed, or missing. The tympanic membrane may be normal, defective, or missing. The ossicular chain may be normal or defective. If the atresia is on one side, surgical reconstruction of that meatus is not considered an emergency since the child can communicate normally with one normal ear. If a child has complete bony atresia, reconstruction should be delayed until s/he is older. It should not be done if chances are slim to none that the procedure will restore hearing to within 20-30 dB of the normal ear. A child with bilateral bony atresia cannot hear or communicate normally, and treatment should be done as soon as possible. Bone-conduction hearing aids can help, and surgical reconstruction should be done on at least one side to allow for the use of an air-conduction hearing aid.

Etiologies of chronic secretory or serous otitis media in children and adults.

Blocked eustachian tubes make the middle ear absorb air, causing negative pressure and affecting mucosal vessels. Mucus enters the tympanic cavity, causing conductive hearing loss. This is one etiology of chronic serous otitis media. If the eustachian tube can inflate, lymphatic drainage is another source of middle ear fluid. Some children have repeated attacks of acute suppurative otitis media. Antibiotics control this, but the middle ear may still be full of fluid between episodes. This is often due to enlarged adenoids. Tubal inflations and oral decongestants often resolve this. If they don't, antibiotics are also given. If these fail, adenoidectomy and fluid removal via myringotomy are indicated. Removing the adenoids can resolve obstruction, but poorly performed surgery can cause scar tissue. This can block the tube just as the adenoids did, causing permanent secretory otitis media. In adults, nasopharyngeal neoplasms are the most common etiology. If the origin of persistent otitis media is unknown, inserting tubes can be very beneficial.

Otosclerosis

Otosclerosis is an abnormal growth of bone in the middle ear cavity. Histological studies of large samples have found that this condition is found in more than eight times as many members of the white population as members of the black population, supporting a considerable genetic component. Studies have found that a minority of those (approximately one eighth) diagnosed with otosclerosis had ankylosis of the stapes foot plate, which is known as clinical otosclerosis. Labyrinthine otosclerosis can cause sensorineural hearing loss, but the condition occurs more often in the middle ear than the inner ear, and therefore more often results in conductive hearing loss. Hearing impairment usually begins around the age of 30 and progresses as time goes on. The impairment may be observed in only one ear, but both ears are usually involved. Otoscopic examination will occasionally show Schwartze's sign, a red color from the promontory.

Stapedectomy over the earlier fenestration surgery for otosclerosis

One advantage when the stapes foot plate is fixated by otosclerotic bone growth is that stapedectomy can close the air-bone gap (i.e. bone conduction is worse than air conduction, indicating hearing impairment). Therefore, unlike fenestration, it helps patients whose cochlear function is not normal. Another advantage is that stapedectomy does not leave the patient with a hole from the mastoidectomy as fenestration would. One disadvantage of stapedectomy is that one of its possible complications is sensorineural hearing loss. If a patient has bilateral hearing impairment and is a candidate for stapedectomy, the ear with the most sensorineural loss should be chosen because of the risk of further sensorineural hearing loss. The patient should be informed of the risk of further sensorineural hearing loss. The patient should also be informed of the maximum gains he or she should expect. For example, the surgery may enable the patient to benefit more from a hearing aid rather than restore hearing.

Traumatic injuries that can cause conductive hearing loss

Foreign bodies in the canal can cause skin abrasions, eardrum perforation, and ossicular chain disruptions. Head injuries, especially if the ear is hit, can tear the eardrum and disrupt the ossicles. The most frequent ossicular disruption is incus (anvil) dislocation. The severity of conductive loss corresponds to the severity of injury. With traumatic eardrum perforation, the perforation's margins should be realigned immediately with a dissecting microscope. In these cases, they will usually heal. With persistent, small perforations, the margins can be cauterized and the hole temporarily patched. Such conservative treatments can be done in the office on adults, but general anesthesia is needed when they are done on children. Conservative treatments may need to be repeated multiple times for perforations to heal, or to conclude they will not work. If they do not work, myringoplasty is indicated. If there was both perforation and ossicular disruption, ossicular reconstruction may be done at the same time as myringoplasty. These operations may also be done separately, with the myringoplasty coming first.

Underlying condition that must be ruled in or out with chronic suppurative otitis media

Cholesteatoma must be ruled in or out. If present, surgery is indicated. If the cholesteatoma is not well-defined and easy to entirely remove, modified radical mastoidectomy is indicated. Eardrum perforations can be closed during the same surgery. Ossicular damage can also be reconstructed or, depending on the case, repaired during a separate surgery. Complications of chronic suppurative otitis media include facial nerve paralysis, meningitis, and brain abscess. Without cholesteatoma, infection management begins with daily cleansing and antibiotics appropriate to the organism diagnosed. If these fail, simple or modified radical mastoidectomy and eardrum reconstruction are indicated. If there is ossicular damage, this should be repaired in a later, separate surgery after the ear has dried out and healed. With inactive chronic suppurative otitis media, the ears are dry and/or the infection is controlled. However, middle ear defects remain, indicating reconstruction of the eardrum, ossicles, or both. Surgery prerequisites are sufficient eustachian tube function and cochlear reserve.

Congenital anomalies in the tympanic cavity

Beyond congenital atresia of the meatus and a defective or missing eardrum, congenital anomalies within the tympanic cavity include a missing oval window, congenital ankylosis of the stapes foot plate, a missing long process of the incus, fusion of the incus and malleus, or ankylosis of the malleus. With ankylosis of the stapes foot plate, a stapedectomy can be done. A missing oval window is more technically challenging because the facial nerve usually overlies that area. Fenestration of the horizontal semicircular canal is a way to treat an absent oval window without damaging the facial nerve. Nearly every anomaly of the ossicular chain can be treated with a specific surgical procedure. As long as the correct procedure is chosen, the result is better hearing in a large proportion of patients. Therefore, the prognosis for such surgeries is usually good.

Myringoplasty

During a myringoplasty, the surgeon should also look for any disease in the tympanic cavity and check the ossicular chain for any defects. If it is found that otosclerotic bone growth has fixated the stapes, a stapedectomy should not be done at that time. This is because the risk that creating an opening to the inner ear will cause sensorineural hearing loss is too high. The stapedectomy, if it is indicated, should be performed later, after the tympanic membrane is healed. On the other hand, if any damage or defects are revealed in the incus and/or the malleus, these are usually repaired at the same time that the myringoplasty is being performed.

Kinds of hearing loss otosclerosis can cause

When otosclerosis fixates the stapes foot plate, it causes conductive hearing loss. If the bony growth affects the cochlea as well as the stapes foot plate, it can cause mixed (i.e. conductive and sensorineural) hearing loss. Whether surgery will restore hearing to a usable degree or not depends on the amount of loss that is sensorineural. Otosclerosis can also cause pure sensorineural hearing loss in the case of labyrinthine otosclerosis, also called cochlear otosclerosis. Labyrinthine otosclerosis is diagnosed by tomography visualizing the abnormal bone. Sensorineural hearing loss secondary to labyrinthine otosclerosis occurs quite frequently. In these cases, there is often dizziness along with hearing loss because the vestibular system is compromised, which disrupts the equilibrium. Long-term therapy with sodium fluoride, calcium gluconate, and Vitamin D combined can often stop the progression of otosclerosis and hence the progression of hearing loss. Sometimes, some patients experience considerable improvement in their hearing with this treatment.

Perilymph fistula

A perilymph fistula is an abnormal hole or opening in the oval window or round window that allows perilymph fluid to leak from the inner ear into the middle ear. It can be a later complication of stapedectomy. Another cause is trauma to the head and/or the ear. A third instance is when it occurs spontaneously. Usually, a perilymph fistula results in sensorineural hearing loss. Sometimes, it results in mixed hearing loss when there is a conductive component as well. However, it is very rare for it to cause only conductive hearing loss. A common symptom of perilymph fistula is dizziness. A perilymph fistula can develop in the oval window, in the round window, or in both the oval and round windows at the same time. The treatment indicated is to repair the ruptured window membrane(s) surgically. The prognosis is a reasonably good probability of restoring hearing acuity if the perilymph fistula receives early treatment.

Ototoxic drugs

Ototoxic drugs are medications that have toxic effects on the auditory system in particular. They generally cause sensorineural hearing loss, which is permanent and cannot be reversed or treated. Some of these drugs may be antibiotics. One exception regarding irreversible hearing loss caused by ototoxic medications is aspirin. If it is taken in large doses, aspirin can be the cause of sensorineural hearing loss that may be mild to moderately severe. This loss tends to be fairly uniform across all tones and frequencies, producing a relatively flat audiogram curve. However, in the case of aspirin, unlike other ototoxic medication, if the patient discontinues taking this drug, the patient's hearing will usually be restored within 24 to 48 hours of discontinuing its use.

Cogan's syndrome

Cogan's syndrome is a nonsyphilitic interstitial keratitis associated with audio-vestibular symptoms. It is considered an inflammatory autoimmune disorder. Some clinicians have suggested it is one manifestation of polyarteritis nodosa (also known as periarteritis nodosa or panarteritis nodosa), also called Kussmaul-Meier disease, an autoimmune type of vasculitis. Cogan's syndrome involves both ears (usually simultaneously or nearly so) and causes end-organ type hearing loss with rapidly progressing loss of cochlear and vestibular function. Untreated, it progresses quickly to total deafness, and can also lead to blindness. Symptoms include corneal inflammation, fever, fatigue, weight loss, dizziness, and hearing loss. Many patients have symptoms in other body systems and exhibit signs and symptoms of systemic disease. Early treatment of Cogan's syndrome with a short course of corticosteroids in fairly high doses may stop the progression. If not, immunosuppressants such as cyclosporine, methotrexate, or azathioprine can help. Extensive damage may indicate cochlear implant surgery to restore hearing.

Additional conditions that cause end-organ sensorineural hearing loss

In addition to Cogan's syndrome, other conditions that cause end-organ types of sensorineural hearing loss include: temporal arteritis, an inflammation of the temporal arteries; chronic relapsing polychondritis (also called chronic atrophic polychondritis, Meyenburg-Altherr-Uehlinger syndrome, von Meyenburg's disease, generalized chondromalacia, and systemic chondromalacia), which causes the cartilage to deteriorate in locations such as the ears, nose, throat, heart valves, ribcage, and joints; disseminated lupus erythematosus, a systemic autoimmune disease of the connective tissues; and Wegener's granulomatosis, a type of autoimmune vasculitis causing end-organ damage. Treatment for any of these is the same as it is for Cogan's syndrome. The immune system is suppressed with various medications. Steroids may be tried; if ineffective, other immunosuppressants can be used. In some cases, a combination of several of these medications is used. In addition to these conditions, idiopathic (of unknown etiology) bilateral hearing loss that progresses rapidly has sometimes been helped by steroids.

Auditory symptoms secondary to congenital syphilis or sarcoidosis

In patients with congenital syphilis, even when it has long since been treated, audio-vestibular symptoms may develop. They will involve both ears. Hearing acuity will fluctuate initially, but cochlear and vestibular function will deteriorate rapidly shortly after. Symptoms and audiometry results are consistent with secondary endolymphatic hydrops. This is thought to be due to hypersensitivity. Sarcoidosis, a systematic granulomatous inflammatory disease, can sometimes cause sensorineural hearing loss. Hypersensitivity is also one of many possible causes. Treatment is the same as it is for congenital syphilis. In both cases, steroids may help. However, their constant use will eventually be required, which can cause undesirable side effects. If steroids are going to lead to improvements in hearing, these improvements are usually observed within the first week of treatment. Biologics like Remicade (infliximab) that block tumor necrosis factor-alpha can help, but carry increased cancer risk with long-term use. Enbrel (etanercept), another tumor necrosis factor-alpha inhibitor, has actually been found to cause sarcoidosis when used to treat rheumatoid arthritis.

Thyroid disorders

Three types of thyroid disorders can cause end-organ sensorineural hearing loss. One is endemic cretinism. This congenital condition characterized by hypothyroidism and severely stunted physical and mental development is caused by a maternal dietary iodine deficiency. Due to iodized salt, this condition no longer exists in North America, and has only a very small incidence in South America. However, it is still a public health problem in less developed countries of the world, especially in Asia. While iodine deficiency and hypothyroidism can be treated, the congenital retardation of development cannot. A second thyroid disorder is Pendred's syndrome, a genetic disorder causing goiter, sensorineural hearing loss, and hypothyroidism. The hypothyroidism can be treated, but there is no treatment for the disorder itself. A third thyroid disorder is adult myxedema. This is infiltration of the subcutaneous tissues with mucin caused by thyroid dysfunction. This is the only treatable one of the three. Thyroid medication that restores euthyroid function may improve hearing.

Vascular accident

Vascular accidents occurring in the cerebrum are commonly known as cerebrovascular accidents, cerebral hemorrhages, or strokes. However, vascular hemorrhages or accidents can also occur to blood vessels in the inner ear. If this blocks the internal auditory artery or cochlear artery, it can cause a sudden onset of sensorineural hearing loss that is severe or total. A difficulty in differential diagnosis can arise with sudden hearing loss due to viral labyrinthitis. Both conditions can have the same presentation. If an elderly patient with cardiovascular disease who has not recently had any upper

- 42 -

respiratory infection experiences this kind of hearing loss, it is reasonable to assume that it is secondary to an inner ear vascular accident. Some have suggested that treatment with anticoagulants within a few hours of the accident can restore or improve hearing. Vasodilators are often also recommended for treating this problem.

Ménière's disease

Ménière's disease symptoms are end-organ sensorineural hearing loss, tinnitus, episodes of vertigo, and a feeling of fullness/pressure in the affected ear(s). About 20% of patients eventually have both ears affected. The severity of the hearing loss fluctuates initially, but hearing deteriorates progressively over the long-term. Histologic changes are dilation of the endolymphatic system, especially of the cochlear duct and saccule. Medications are not known to prevent hearing deterioration, but can control vertigo attacks. These include vasodilators, diuretics, anti-motion sickness medications, anti-cholinergic drugs, tranquilizers, sedatives, and the OTC nutrient formula Lipo-Flavonoid. While tack surgery to decompress the labyrinth and endolymphatic subarachnoid shunt surgery can control vertigo without vestibular system damage or additional hearing loss, and may sometimes improve hearing, there is a significant risk that hearing after the operation will get worse. Differential diagnosis from acoustic neuroma is necessary. Neuroma more severely affects vestibular function than early Ménière's, usually before affecting auditory acuity. If the tumor is too small for audiometry to reflect it, diagnosis is done by imaging and vestibular testing along with history.

Early intervention with hearing-impaired children

If hearing loss is discovered before a baby is six months old, habilitation rather than remediation is possible because groundwork for language learning can be laid during the baby's normal developmental time. The younger a child is when he or she is able to hear speech, the fewer auditory deprivation effects will occur and the less he or she will compensate using other senses. Auditory-vocal skills are easier to develop concurrently with locomotive, cognitive, and social development skills. Using hearing aids at earlier ages gives babies a longer time to develop hearing and speech skills. Adults reinforce babies' vocalizations, thereby increasing them. Babies' responses reinforce and increase adults' vocalizations directed towards them. Babies nearing a year of age are learning to crawl and walk, distracting their primary focus from auditory-vocal behavior. An early start gives babies a basic phonetic repertoire on which language is built. It may be smaller than the repertoire of babies with normal hearing, but will still be better compared to intervention with toddlers.

Determining whether a hearing-impaired child will acquire spoken language

Three factors that determine whether a hearing-impaired child will acquire spoken language are: the teacher or clinician's competence and ability to guide the parents, how well the parents can understand and apply the principles of early language development, and how intact (relatively) the child's central nervous system and brain are. The five behaviors that indicate a hearing-impaired child is in the beginning stages of language learning are: the child looks at and/or listens to people when they talk, the child has a varied phonetic repertoire, the child communicates vocally, the child modifies his or her tone of voice to express emotions, and the child shows symbolic behavior such as shaking the head to indicate "no," nodding the head to indicate "yes," and making other communicative gestures. These behaviors mean the child is ready to associate meanings with sound patterns s/he and other people produce.

Checking the language comprehension of a hearing-impaired child

A hearing-impaired child's parent can say as s/he offers the child a drink, "Do you want a drink?" Seeing the bottle or cup helps the child understand the verbal message. Later, the parent can ask the child the same question without the drink. If the child licks his/her lips, makes sucking gestures, or looks in the direction of where the drink comes from, this indicates comprehension. Parents can write down the phrases most commonly used during routine activities, such as eating meals, washing, dressing, and playing. They can record the dates when the child comprehends phrases with nonverbal cues and, later, without them. This procedure helps parents find out which phrases or words usually understood by young children are not being understood by their child. Parents, teachers, and clinicians should also give children enough exposure to words/phrases required for everyday communication, such as the child's name, "Mommy," "Daddy," and names of siblings and pets.

Questions and answers adults can use with a hearing-impaired child to evaluate and facilitate basic language comprehension

Parents, teachers, and clinicians should often ask questions such as "Where's Mommy/Daddy?" and give the answer ("There s/he is") until the child can answer without coaching. They can ask the child to point out favorite toys/objects. They should not just ask these in a test situation while objects are on a table, but should build them into natural situations of everyday life or games. Hide and Seek works well, as young children enjoy running and finding the person, animal, or object they are asked to locate. As the child's vocabulary grows, adults should ask "What's that?", "Who's that?", and "What is ___ doing?" and help the child answer. Helping the child understand and appropriately answer questions will facilitate the child's asking questions him- or herself to get information. Adults should also monitor what parts of speech the child understands (i.e. just people/object nouns or also "no," "more," "all-gone," "up," "on," "off," "out," "hot," etc.).

Evaluating and facilitating a hearing-impaired child's use of expressive language

Asking the child questions can not only check comprehension, but also expression. A young child's phonology can be evaluated through his/her responses Teachers/clinicians can encourage transfer of sounds from the child's phonetic to phonologic repertoire. More accurate pronunciation facilitates others' understanding of the child's speech. It also helps children recall a word from long-term memory to compare with a new, similar word. If the teacher/clinician finds a sound missing from the child's repertoire, s/he can help the child develop it phonetically and transfer it to phonology as soon as possible. Parents should listen carefully to their child. If a child says /o/ for "no" or /a/ for "on," s/he may not have /n/ in his/her repertoire. Adults should not be surprised if the child only uses vowels or monosyllables initially, if approximations change phonetically, or if commonly used words are suddenly not used. This

- 44 -

developmental stage corresponds to one that also occurs in children with normal hearing.

Checking a hearing-impaired child's vocabulary

Once a child's vocabulary is around 50 words, it is useful to check his or her vocabulary against a list of 500 words (such lists have been created by audiological researchers). As the child's vocabulary grows, a list of 2,000 words should be used. Parents should record if the child understands a word, whether the child understands it with or without cues, and if the child imitates it or uses it spontaneously. The teacher/clinician reviews the list with parents and confirms words s/he believes are only understood with cueing. The point of this is not to give a precise vocabulary word count, but to see if it is increasing at a sufficient rate and if there are noticeable gaps needing special attention. It should be determined whether the child uses verbs, adjectives, question words, negatives, function words, and demonstratives as well as nouns; and whether s/he uses abstract verbs such as "want," "need," "like," "get," and "have" as well as concrete ones like "walk," "run," and "jump."

Spoken word combinations used by a hearing-impaired child

A hearing-impaired child must have developed a substantial single-word vocabulary that s/he uses freely in social interactions before s/he can be expected to use word combinations. A child with normal hearing may have a 250-word vocabulary before trying to form phrases. Two-word phrases characteristic of telegraphic speech are common in hearing-impaired children and in those with normal hearing. The child must also be cognitively mature enough to express ideas linguistically. A child in the telegraphic stage might say, "Daddy shirt,"

and may mean "This is Daddy's shirt," "Daddy, help me take my shirt off," etc. The child knows there is a relationship between objects, but cannot express it precisely. In this respect, hearing-impaired children and those with normal hearing are cognitively equal. Physical maturation and practice are required to develop the articulatory skill needed to use possessives (-s as in "Daddy's," for example). Function words such as "more" or "off" must be learned before combining them with content words. For example, a child must learn "more" before saying "more juice."

Facilitating learning and the use of function words by a hearing-impaired child

We naturally tend to stress content words ("Take your shoes off"). If a child is using single words too long, adults can alternatively stress the function word ("Take your shoes off. That's right; off they come."). This directs the child's attention to the preposition. If a child wants help and says "shoe" to his mother, she can say, "Yes, that's your shoe" and wait instead of helping immediately. The child may then say "off." If so, she can say, "Oh, you want Mommy to take your shoe off." This is done to encourage the child to say "shoe off" while helping him remove it. If the child does not say "off," the mother can prompt him to say it, and then possibly elicit "shoe off" while helping. When children are younger, they need more assistance, which provides many opportunities for language learning. When they become more independent, it is more difficult as artificial situations must be used.

Child's progression from using telegraphic phrases to using kernel sentences

A kernel sentence is a phrase with a subject, a verb, and an object. It does not

- 45 -

contain the function words that would make it a grammatically complete and correct sentence. Adults can build on a child's existing two-word utterances by providing feedback and cues to encourage the child to add a third word to create a kernel sentence. For example, if a child says "Go work," the mother may ask, "Who's going to work?" If the child replies "Daddy," the mother can say, "Yes, Daddy's going to work." Then the child might say "Daddy go work." This is a kernel sentence. If the child says "doggie eat," the mother may say "The doggie is eating what?" The child may respond, "eat bone." Then the mother can say, "Tell Daddy: The doggie is eating a bone." With this encouragement and cueing, the child may then say, "Doggie eat bone," which is also a kernel sentence.

Building on a hearing-impaired child's existing words and phrases with asking the child to imitate full sentences

As an example, suppose the hearing-impaired child stands by the door saying, "Go out." If the mother says, "Say: I want to go out," expecting him to imitate this, he may be unable to reproduce a sentence of that length and complexity. Overusing imitation can result in the purpose of spoken language – communication – being lost. However, imitation can help develop motor speech patterns. If Billy really wants to go outside, the mother can exploit this motivation by saying, "Who wants to go out? Do you want Mommy to go out? Do you want Daddy to go out?" Being anxious to go out, Billy may come up with the expanded utterance "Billy go out" or "Me go out." His reward will be getting to go outside, which reinforces this communication. Using this technique is better for guiding the child to consider what he has to say to communicate what he needs or wants in a way that will allow him to get it.

Language training programs using imitation

Children with normal hearing but delayed language development may have intellectual disabilities; other, less global cognitive impairments; autism spectrum disorders; emotional disturbances; environmental deprivation; or no symptoms other than language delay. Some special language programs for these children use reduced models similar to the telegraphic phrases used by young children to express semantic relations ("girl run," "in house," etc.). These are not as appropriate for hearing-impaired children because language-delayed children with normal hearing can hear normal speech patterns outside of training. but hearing-impaired children cannot; this method focuses on production more than comprehension; reduced forms modeled by adults are unlikely to enable children to form complete sentences independently; and hearing-impaired children tend to be rather rigid in their retention of learned material, so teaching them incorrect forms would only necessitate their unlearning these later. Exposure to normal models is more desirable for hearing-impaired children.

Personal hearing protectors

Earplugs and earmuffs are one type of hearing protector. Pre-molded earplugs are more hygienic as they avoid the contamination of hand-shaping, but may not fit as well. Formable earplugs can be shaped by the wearer. Their advantage is that they conform to the shape of the individual's ear canal. A disadvantage is contamination by handling (users should always wash hands first). Custom-molded earplugs are cast from each individual's ear canals. Their advantage is that they offer the most perfect fit. Disadvantages are their expense to employers and the time needed to make them. Semi-insert earplugs are soft and attached to a band that helps keep them in place. Their advantage is quick insertion and removal. Their disadvantage is lack of custom fit. The advantages of earmuffs are that they are not inserted into the meatus, are more hygienic and possibly more comfortable, and create a seal around the ear. Some earmuffs or earphones also use noise-canceling technology. Disadvantages are that these hearing protectors may not fit properly or may cause discomfort when used by those who wear glasses or have hair in the way.

Noise reduction ratings for personal hearing protectors

The United States Environmental Protection Agency (EPA) requires that all personal hearing protection devices be labeled with their noise reduction rating (NRR), which gives an estimate of the device's attenuation. Researchers (Park and Casali, 1991; Berger et al., 1998) have found that manufacturers' labels significantly overestimate their devices' attenuation in the field. Thus, OSHA recommends that employers subtract 7 dB from the manufacturer's NRR. NRRs are usually provided in a C-weighted format, while the OSHA standard for a maximum time-weighted average level of exposure of 85 dB is measured on the A (slow response) scale. To translate the recommended reduction of the C-weighted NRR to the A-rated level, 7 dB must be subtracted. To meet the OSHA standard of a safety factor of 50%, the number remaining after this calculation is done must be divided by two. Therefore, the figure representing OSHA's recommendation for noise reduction is calculated using the formula $(NRR - 7)/2$.

Hearing conservation programs for the workplace

Hearing conservation programs for workplaces are devised to prevent noise-induced hearing loss. The Occupational Safety and Health Administration (OSHA) requires such programs "whenever employee noise exposures equal or exceed an 8-hour time-weighted average sound level (TWA) of 85 decibels measured on the A scale (slow response) or, equivalently, a dose of fifty percent." (Code of Federal Regulations, Department of Labor). The Mine Safety and Health Administration (MSHA) requires hearing conservation programs with the same standards, but does not require them in writing as OSHA does. The OSHA standard has program requirements including administrative and engineering controls, monitoring, testing, use of hearing protectors, training, and record keeping. Sound surveys are usually conducted to identify work areas with potentially high exposure to noise by using sound level meters. Type 0 SLMs are precision meters used in laboratories. Type 1 SLMs are meters used to take precision field measurements. Type 2 SLMs are less precise, and are used to take all-purpose measurements.

Functions of audiometric testing when used in workplace hearing conservation programs

Audiometric testing conducted as a part of workplace hearing conservation programs can identify workers who have lost substantial amounts of their hearing acuity; workers who are in the process of losing hearing acuity; and workers whose hearing loss is permanent, which is known as noise-induced permanent threshold shift (NIPTS). Employee training in hearing conservation programs, which OSHA requires be conducted annually, can have a significant positive effect on worker compliance with protective measures, and hence on prevention and/or reduction of noise exposure and of resulting noise-induced hearing loss. Researchers (Williams, 2004; Joseph et al., 2007) have found that

"...even with a very modest amount of instruction attenuation performance can be significantly improved." In other words, employees who receive annual training in using personal protective equipment and other preventive measures do a significantly better job of preventing overexposure to noise that would cause damage to their hearing.

Information items OSHA requires in record keeping for workplace hearing conservation programs

OSHA requires that all workplace hearing conservation programs keep records of the following: the employee's name and job classification, the date of each audiogram obtained, the name of the audiometric examiner for each test, the date of calibration of the audiometer for each test, the date and results of the employee's most recent noise exposure assessment, and the levels of sound pressure of background noises in the audiometric examination booths used for the testing. Records of noise exposure measurements must be kept on file for at least two years. Audiometric testing records must be kept for as long as the worker is employed at that workplace. Access to these records must be given to the employee, to former employees, to representatives individual employees may designate, and to the Assistant Secretary of the U.S. Department of Labor.

Government involvement in program evaluation of occupational hearing conservation programs

The National Institute for Occupational Safety and Health (NIOSH) provides a checklist to aid evaluation of the effectiveness of hearing conservation programs. NIOSH recommends that less than 5% of employees exposed to noise have a Significant Threshold Shift of 15 dB in the same ear and at the same frequency. A current trend is to focus on prevention rather than conservation. A "buy quiet" policy is an approach that supports prevention. Many manufacturers are redesigning noisy machines and tools to run more quietly, so employers can implement this policy by purchasing quieter equipment. New York City's Department of Environmental Protection produced a guide sheet on vendors and products to help contractors comply with city noise regulations. Using its research results, NIOSH made a database of sound exposure levels for users of hand-held power tools. Contractors can use this database to monitor the limits of their noise exposure and take precautions to prevent hearing loss.

Statistics and observations regarding the incidence and prevalence of hearing loss in babies and children

The most common congenital condition found in newborns is hearing loss. Despite this, not all neonates are given routine hearing testing. Roughly three out of every 1,000 babies are born with significant hearing loss. Many more are born with milder levels of hearing loss. It is possible to test babies for hearing loss, even neonates who are only a few minutes old. Testing the hearing of newborn babies is easy, safe, and painless. Approximately 15% of children between the ages of 6 and 19 have unilateral or bilateral hearing loss. Children who receive early intervention (before the age of six months) have significantly better language development than those who receive intervention after the age of six months, according to National Institute of Health (NIH) studies confirming earlier research. Only 7% of deaf children are born into deaf families, while 93% are born into hearing families.

Educational implications of hearing loss in children

Any amount of hearing loss can interfere with a child's education. Children with even mild to moderate hearing loss may not hear up to half of the information in a classroom discussion. Hearing loss in children, if not addressed, compromises their language and speech development, their academic abilities, their educational progress, their self-images, their emotional development, and their social development. The average age at which hearing loss is diagnosed in children is two and a half to three years old, which is beyond the critical period for language and speech development. This can mean developmental deficits in language and speech that can never be recouped. Research finds that an estimated 90% of learning by young children is incidental. They learn by hearing conversations going on around them, which shows the value of early intervention. Of children with only minimal hearing loss, 37% fail at least one grade in school.

Statistics about children and hearing loss in the United States

More than a million children in the U.S. have hearing loss. At least 5% of children aged 18 years and younger have hearing loss. One of every 22 infants born in the United States has some type of hearing problem. Six of every 1,000 babies in the U.S. are born with hearing loss; one of every 1,000 is born with a severe or profound hearing deficit. Out of every 1,000 children in the United States, 83 have hearing loss deemed educationally significant. Seven of every 1,000 school-aged children in the United States have bilateral, educationally significant hearing loss. Between 16 and 19 of every 1,000 school-aged children in the U.S. have unilateral, educationally significant hearing loss. Around nine of every 1,000 school-aged children in the country have severe to profound hearing loss. Ten of every 1,000 U.S. school-aged children have permanent sensorineural loss. Around 30% of children with hearing loss also have another disability.

How hearing status influences the way children learn to read

Children with normal hearing first learn to discriminate speech sounds; then they learn to understand speech; and then they learn to use speech themselves as their language and articulation skills develop. Children learn to read after they have learned to speak. They normally learn to read by associating the words, phrases, and sentences in written language with their spoken counterparts. Thus, the learning of reading has an auditory basis in children with normal hearing. Reading skills are acquired most efficiently when children have a foundation that includes a sense of hearing and previously acquired spoken and heard language. Children who are born with profound deafness will not develop a language system that includes an auditory basis. As a result, although these children may still be able to learn to read, they typically do not read at their grade level and have a great deal of difficulty attaining grade-level reading skills.

Minimal hearing loss for children attending regular schools

Many children with small threshold changes, unilateral loss, or conductive losses that fluctuate show no problems with face-to-face communication. As a result, their linguistic and academic risks are overlooked. One child's detailed evaluation or an assessment of group performance will reveal deficits in multiple areas that would not otherwise be obvious. While 37% of children with minimal hearing loss fail at least one grade, only 2% of children with normal hearing do. Hearing only 10 dB below normal thresholds decreases an individual's subjective sense of loudness by half for speech sound signals. This emphasizes the impact of even "minimal" hearing loss on a student. Students in regular schools must hear to learn. A 20 dB loss means hearing only one quarter of what the teacher says. The student may comprehend most of it, but will suffer greater fatigue, will have a poorer understanding of grammatical elements expressed by less-audible phonological cues, and may "tune out" and/or act out in school.

Hearing Loss Association of America (HLAA)

The HLAA recommends that the U.S. Department of Education implement guidelines for a nationwide hearing screening program. Their minimum requirements for guidelines are: all children in lower grades and some upper grades should have hearing screenings; tympanometry should be routine for lower grades; the program should be conducted only by specially-trained staff supervised by certified audiologists; and parents should be informed if their children do not pass the whole screening, physician referrals made, and follow-ups done with parents for compliance and with schools for academic management. Other guidelines are that children with permanent hearing loss or conductive losses who are unresponsive to treatment should have comprehensive audiological, speech, language, educational, and psychosocial evaluations. Private and parochial schools should be included, as should public schools. In addition to mitigating the impact of hearing loss on students' educational and psychosocial progress, HLAA believes the existence of the program itself would communicate the importance of hearing for learning to society.

Ambient noise problem with audiometry in public schools

A typical problem in public schools is that the rooms used for audiometric testing are adjacent to cafeterias, cafeteria lines, auditoriums, gymnasiums, playgrounds, and even power plants. This means ambient noise levels are much higher than they should be for good testing conditions. Too much background noise will result in many false failures on audiometric tests. Most public schools cannot afford to soundproof testing rooms, and many do not have the space to relocate testing rooms to other, quieter areas. Some public health departments have had good success with the use of mobile testing units. The American Speech and Hearing Association (ASHA) has guidelines and the American National Standards Institute (ANSI) has established standards for the maximum allowable ambient noise levels for pure tone audiometers. This is expressed as sound pressure level (SPL) at a hearing level (HL) of zero, the threshold for normal hearing. ASHA's guidelines are related to ANSI standards.

Drugs and substances that can be ototoxic

Aminoglycoside antibiotics like gentamicin and tobramycin can be toxic to the cochlea, though the toxicity mechanism is inadequately understood. N-acetylcysteine given with aminoglycosides may prevent damage. Gentamicin's toxicity is sometimes utilized to treat Ménière's disease. Erythromycin and other macrolides can induce reversible ototoxicity, especially in patients with liver or kidney disease or recent organ transplants. Loop diuretics like furosemide and ethacrynic acid can be ototoxic. Chemotherapy drugs containing platinum, such as cisplatin and carboplatin, can cause dose-dependent ototoxicity with tinnitus and high-frequency hearing loss. Vincristine and other vinca alkaloids can also cause reversible ototoxicity. High doses of aspirin and other salicylates can be ototoxic, causing bilateral hearing loss and high-frequency tinnitus. This can be reversed by discontinuing the medication. Other ototoxic substances include heavy metals such as lead and mercury, and quinine. Symptoms of ototoxicity are tinnitus (ringing or noise in the ears), vertigo (disequilibrium), and hearing loss, which can be mild, moderate, or profound.

Infection control procedures

The simplest but most important infection control measure, according to the Centers for Disease Control (CDC) (2009), is hand-washing to prevent infection spread. OSHA standards require employers to make facilities available and employees to wash their hands after exposure to blood or other potentially infectious matter. Disinfection and sterilization of surfaces and instruments are procedures especially important in healthcare facilities, as is personal protective equipment such as gloves, face shields, gowns, bonnets, goggles, shoe covers, surgical masks, CPR masks, etc. Healthcare workers should be vaccinated against infections to which they are exposed. When no vaccine exists, post-exposure prophylaxis is possible. For example, antibody injection within four hours of exposure to the HIV/AIDS virus can precipitate viral particles out of the bloodstream. Surveillance by an infection control practitioner that is facilitated by computer software can investigate for possible infections of the blood, urinary tract, surgical sites, and pneumonia. In some cases, isolation is used to prevent infection spread.

Intervention for Communication Difficulties

For the client who is experiencing problems with communicating as a result of having a hearing impairment, the audiologist is responsible for: (A) developing and providing a program of intervention for the client that is designed with the goals of improving the client's receptive and expressive communication abilities and making it easier for the client to engage in these processes in mind; (B) providing programming to the client with the intended goal of conserving hearing and speech; and (C) functioning as an intermediary between the client, the client's family, and other agencies or organizations involved in managing communication disorders that are caused by or related to the client's hearing loss. Note: Under the services and procedures included, the final two services and procedures listed are (IV) Re-evaluation of the Client's Status and (V) Evaluation and Modification of the Intervention Program.

Specific language impairment (SLI)

Specific Language impairment (SLI) is a developmental communication disorder that is a pure language impairment. Children with this disorder have normal physical and intellectual development. Their language delay cannot be attributed to any physical cause of developmental abnormality, such as brain injury or autism. These children have impaired expressive and receptive language skills.

Specific features include:
- Failure to use or correctly apply plurality, possessive words, articles, past tense, comparative words, and irregular words
- Inability to form or understand long/complex sentences
- Inability to initiate or maintain age-appropriate conversation

- 51 -

Intellectual disabilities and autism

Intellectual disabilities refers to an impairment of intellectual functioning (IQ <70) due to genetic defects or injuries during gestation or at birth. Intellectually disabled children have significant delays in all of the components of language. Although grammatical development occurs in a normal sequence, the language of children with intellectual disabilities usually lacks variety and complexity. It is typical for children to have language that is concrete and repetitive.

Autism spectrum disorder refers to an impairment of social and communication skills. Autistic children may have low, average, or superior intelligence. They often engage in repetitive behavior activities. The language problems with autism run the gamut from severely delay in words, content, structure, and grammar to the inability to make meaningful sentences, despite a large vocabulary. They are unable to interact with others and often do not respond to their names. When they do speak, they may not make good eye contact. Repeating words or phrases (echolalia) is very common.

Asperger's syndrome

Asperger's syndrome refers to a subset of children on the autism spectrum scale. This disorder affects mostly males. These children have deficits in social interactions.

Their repetitive behaviors are similar to other children with autism; however, their language and intellectual abilities are at the higher end of the spectrum scale. Given social interaction problems, language issues are primarily due to poor pragmatics. Therefore, improving the social context of language is the training goal when working with these children. Given the propensity to engage in repetitive behaviors, these children must learn to reduce or eliminate perseverant language.

Brain injuries that affect speech and language in children

Traumatic brain injury results from a blow or a penetrating trauma to the head. Physical trauma may cause transient or long-term deficits in speech comprehension, speech fluency, speech pragmatics, and memory. The most common forms of traumatic brain injury are caused by motor vehicle accidents, falls, sports injuries, firearms, and physical abuse.

Cerebral palsy is a group of early childhood, nonprogressive disorders that cause neurological and motor abnormalities. This disorder is caused by brain injury during pregnancy (e.g., infection, trauma), during delivery (e.g., low oxygen, premature delivery), or just after delivery (e.g., infection, trauma). Children with cerebral palsy typically have movement disorders, such as paralysis, spasticity, seizures, or ataxia (imbalance), or hearing deficits. Language development may range from normal to severe speech articulation abnormalities (dysarthria).

Poverty

Although poverty does not directly cause learning disorders, it can be a contributing factor in many ways. Some low-income families have limited access to health care. Children who have poor health may have difficulty learning. Mothers without prenatal care may have low birth weight children that can go on to learning difficulties. Furthermore, some children born into poverty have a low level of academic and social stimuli at home, which hampers their ability to learn language. Many of these children have delayed speech, poor development of vocabulary, and reading difficulties.

Parental drug and alcohol abuse

Many children from households where parents abuse alcohol or drugs may suffer from neglect or emotional or physical abuse. These children are most likely to develop expressive language delays.

Fetal alcohol syndrome refers to physical and cognitive disorders that occur in children whose mothers used excessive amounts of alcohol during pregnancy. Children with this disorder may have low birth weight, facial abnormalities, and small head circumference. They may have profound cognitive, neurological, and motor developmental delay. They also may have organ development abnormalities.

Speech and language problems seen in drug and alcohol exposure are gross and fine motor delay; poor eye contact; emotional lability or depression; poor social interactions; lack of attention; poor memory and poor articulation, vocabulary, and communication in general.

Attention deficit hyperactivity disorder (ADHD)

Children with attention deficit hyperactivity disorder (ADHD) have problems with inattention, hyperactivity, or impulsivity, or all three. It is typically diagnosed during the preschool or early elementary school period, given that typical children may not have mastered attention skills before this period. Language problems that may be associated with ADHD are:
- Difficulty processing auditory stimulation
- Difficulty following instructions
- Reading and writing difficulties
- Poor expressive language

- Difficulty in engaging in normal conversational discourse
- Poor social interactions

Phonological processes

The term phonologic processes refer to the manner in which children pronounce speech sounds. Phonological processes can also be referred to as speech errors made by children.

The three major categories are:
- Substitution: The child substitutes one class of speech sounds for another. For example, the child may pronounce the word rat as *wat.
- Assimilation: The child pronounces phonemes similarly to a nearby phoneme. For example, the word cat is pronounced tat.
- Syllable structure processes: The child alters an entire syllable by deletion or alteration of its sound. For example, the word potato is pronounced tato.

Substitution phonological processes

Affrication: An affricative is substituted for a fricative or a stop. For example, the word cheek becomes teek.

Backing: A posterior pronounced phoneme is replaced by an anterior one. For example, peach is pronounced peat.

Deaffrication: A fricative is substituted for an affricative. For example, the word catch is pronounced cash.

Depalatization: An alveolar fricative or affricative is substituted for a palatal fricative or affricative. For example, the word fish becomes fis.

Gliding: The phonemes /l/ and /r/ are replaced with /j/ and /w/. For example,

- 53 -

the word below becomes beyow and the word run becomes wun.

Stopping: A fricative or an affricative is substituted by a stop. For example, the word zipper becomes dipper.

Velar fronting: An alveolar or dental placed consonant is substituted by a velar consonant. For example, the word coat becomes toat.

Vocalization: A vowel is substituted for a consonant. This most commonly occurs in words containing an /l/ or /r/ such that these consonants are replaced with the sounds /o/ or /u/. For example, father is pronounced fatho, and bottle is pronounced bato.

Assimilation phonological processes

Progressive assimilation: a change in the pronunciation of a phoneme because of the effects of a proceeding phoneme. For example, the word zip becomes dip.

Reduplication: duplication of a syllable. For example, the word water becomes wawa.

Regressive assimilation: a change in the pronunciation of a phoneme because of the effects of a preceding phoneme. For example, the word pass becomes pat.

Voicing assimilation: a phoneme is either voiced or devoiced incorrectly. For example, the word card becomes cart, and the word pig becomes big.

Syllable structure processes

Consonant-cluster reduction: A consonant is deleted from a syllable containing adjacent consonants. For example, the word play becomes pay.

Metathesis: Sounds in a word are reversed. For example, spaghetti becomes pisgetti.

Epenthesis: An /a/ or schwa sound is added to a word. For example, black becomes balack.

Diminutization: An /i/ sound is added to the end of a word. For example, the word doll becomes dolly.

Weak (unstressed) syllable deletion: The unstressed syllable of a word is deleted. For example, the word wagon becomes wag.

Final consonant deletion: The final consonant in a word is omitted. For example, the word hat becomes ha.

Articulation errors

Articulation errors occur in children due to some physical inability to produce the correct sound. Thus the child has neurological or motor deficiencies that cause articulation errors. The major physical disorders that may lead to articulation problems are:

- Structural abnormalities of the facial and oral anatomy
- Poor oral-motor coordination
- Hearing loss
- Orofacial myofunctional disorders: abnormality in tongue position at rest and/or when swallowing. The tongue protrudes forward on or past the teeth.
- Dysarthria: a speech-motor disorder due to a neurological injury such as trauma, cerebral palsy, or tumors
- Apraxia: difficulty initiating speech due to deficits in motor planning

Types of articulation errors

Devoicing: the limit or absence of vocal cord vibration to produce sounds. For example, the word pad becomes pat.

Labialization: production of phonemes using excessive lip rounding. For example, the word grow becomes gwow.

Lisp: the production of /s/ or /z/ sounds with tongue touching or protruding through the front teeth (frontal lisp) or with air escaping over sides of the tongue (lateral lisp)

Nasalization: sounds produced by allowing air to escape through the nose

Omissions: deletion of phonemes of words. Ex. hat becomes ha.

Pharyngeal fricative: production of fricatives by using the pharynx
Position error: mispronunciation of phonemes in the initial, middle, or final position of a word

Substitution: the exchange of one class of speech sounds for another. For example, the child may pronounce the word rat as wat.

Stridency deletion: the substitution or deletion of one sound for another. For example, hair becomes air, or chew becomes tew.

Unaspirated: sounds that are normally produced with aspiration (e.g. /p/, /k/, /t/) are pronounced without a strong release of air though the mouth

Vocalic error: mispronunciation of consonants in initial (prevocalic), middle (intervocalic), and terminal syllables (postvocalic)

Abnormalities of the facial and oral anatomy

Ankyloglossia (also known as tongue tie) is a congenital anomaly causing limited mobility of the tip of the tongue. This is due to a short and thick frenulum, which attaches the bottom of the tongue to the floor of the mouth. In infants, this condition may effect feeding due to difficulty swallowing and sucking. Later, speech may be affected. However, not all children with ankyloglossia will have articulation deficits. A v-shaped notch at the tip of the tongue, decreased tongue mobility, and tongue protrusion can identify children with this anomaly. Some children will have difficulty producing the lingual phonemes, such as /t/, /d/, /z/, /s/, /θ/, /ð/, /n/, /l/. There is controversy whether surgical repair of this condition is necessary.

Oral malocclusions may cause articulation errors. Malocclusions are the misalignment of the upper dental arch (maxilla) and the lower dental arch (mandible). It may also refer to the misalignment of individual teeth. Malocclusions may be inherited, as those seen in tooth overcrowding or large spaces between teeth. Accidents and thumb sucking may also be a cause of malocclusions.

Irwin and Weston's paired-stimuli approach

Irwin and Weston's paired-stimuli approach utilizes words already in the child's vocabulary. An articulation error sound is targeted. Four key words are created, two with the target sound in the initial position and two with the targeted sound in the final position. Ten pictures that suggest words with the targeted sound are selected corresponding to each key word. The key words are arranged around the target word, and the child says the key word, the target word, and the key word again (training string).

The child must master the pronunciation 9 out of 10 times without reinforcement before moving to the next sound.

Cognitive-linguistic approach to articulation-phonological therapy

Cognitive-linguistic approach: This procedure focuses on the pattern of sounds rather than on the treatment of individual sounds.

Distinctive-features approach: Through language sampling, an omitted distinctive feature is identified and that feature is trained with the expectation that it will be generalized among like phonemes.

Minimal-pair-contrast approach: A minimal pair is a set of words that differs by a single phoneme, and that single phoneme conveys a totally different meaning. This approach uses contrasts of features in phonemes (e.g., bilabial consonants, alveolar lingual consonants) of paired words to teach the distinctions in the sounds. The sound used in error is paired with a corresponding substitute. The child will presumably generalize the correct sound to other words containing phonemes of the same feature.

Treatment of phonologic disorders that use the cognitive-linguistic approach

The phonological-knowledge approach is used to treat phonological deficits in children. In this form of therapy, the child's phonological inventory of sounds is assessed. Treatment is directed toward those sounds that are most mispronounced and then progresses to those that are mastered. The child's knowledge of phonological rules is thus expanded.

The phonological-process approach (Hodson and Paden's cycles approach) is used for children with many misarticulated sounds and whose language is very difficult to understand. The child's various phonological processes (errors) are assessed and targeted for treatment. Therapy runs in a cycle of 5 to 16 weekly sessions. A phonological error pattern is treated in one therapy session, and all are addressed within one treatment cycle. In each session, target words are reviewed, and new ones are practiced.

Metaphon therapy

Metaphon therapy is based on children's phonological awareness and capacity to control the structure of language. This therapy is best used with preschoolers with moderate to severe phonological disorders. The approach relies on the assumption that phonological errors are due to incorrect acquisition of the rules of phonology as opposed to difficulty in the motor production of sounds. Furthermore, real-life materials are used as analogies for speech sounds.

Neurological causes of phonation disorders

Paralysis of the vocal folds can be caused by trauma, tumors, strokes, and nerve injury. This may lead to changes in voice volume and pitch. Therapy is aimed at increasing volume and pitch, improving breath control, and optimizing neck and head positioning.

Sposmodic dysphonia are involuntary movements of the muscles of the larynx causing voice breaking and difficulty saying words. Brain stem dysfunction is thought to be the cause of this voice disorder. Botox injections, vocal cord relaxation techniques, medications, surgical widening of the glottis, and recurrent laryngeal nerve resections are among the possible treatments.

Neurological diseases, such as multiple sclerosis, myasthenia gravis, ALS, and Parkinson's disease, may cause vocal cord dysfunction.

Paradoxical vocal fold motion (vocal cord dysfunction) is an episodic abnormal closure of the vocal folds while talking or breathing. Persons with this disorder may wheeze and have hoarseness or difficulty breathing and behave like that of an asthmatic. Local irritants, exercise, acid reflux, coughing, shouting, and stress can trigger spasms. Therapies are aimed at instruction in relaxation of the vocal mechanism.

Scaffolding

Scaffolding refers to the modification or simplification of language to match the student or client. This type of technique is very useful when teaching students a second language. The instructor simplifies language to the level of the student by shortening sentences, using present tense, and avoiding abstract language. The use of visual aids and sentence and paragraph completion prompts are useful in scaffolding language instruction. Exercises that require some hands-on activities are very effective to facilitate learning. When the student becomes more efficient in the language, the scaffold techniques are gradually decreased and then stopped. It is important to involve caregivers and other members of the student's speech and language team before starting this technique.

Assessment

Assessment of communication skills and intervention for hearing-impaired individuals

Regarding the assessment of communication skills and intervention for hearing-impaired individuals, audiologists must be able to conduct all evaluative measures in the client's preferred communication mode, or arrange for this. They must be able to conduct and analyze applicable standardized and non-standardized measures of speech and voice production. They must be able to conduct and analyze applicable standardized and non-standardized measures of language comprehension and production skills, and/or alternative communication skills such as signing. They must be able to conduct and analyze applicable standardized and non-standardized measures of auditory, visual, and auditory-visual communicative skills. They must be able to describe clients' communication skills derived from comprehensive communication abilities assessments, and to ascertain and express the communication needs of people with hearing loss. They must be able to make and carry out rehabilitation plans according to clients' communication skills and needs, and must be able to develop and implement systems to monitor and measure the applicability of plans.

An individual who wants to know whether hearing aids will help his or her hearing

First, the individual should see an ASHA-certified audiologist to have an audiological assessment and to determine if medical referral is needed. Next, the person should get a professional hearing aid candidacy evaluation from the certified audiologist. The client should buy the hearing aid the audiologist recommends. The buyer should make note of the trial period, the sales contract, warranty information, and the hearing aid's features. Then, the client should attend hearing aid orientation and rehabilitation with the audiologist. The client should ask the audiologist what other devices can be used in conjunction with the hearing aid(s) for large areas or difficult listening environments. The client should report any communication problems s/he experiences, as the hearing aid might just need a simple adjustment. If not, the audiologist can identify and usually resolve the source of the problem(s). The client should have regular follow-up care to facilitate adjustment and to monitor any hearing changes.

Validity and reliability as they relate to assessment instruments

Assessment instruments must be both valid and reliable for their results to be accurate and meaningful. Validity means that an instrument tests/measures what it purports to test/measure. Reliability means that an instrument's administration can be repeated and can obtain consistent results across repetitions. A test may be reliable but not valid. For example, it may yield the same results when replicated, but may not measure what it is meant to measure. However, the converse is not true. A test that is valid will not be unreliable (assuming the variable measured is not changed). Normally, instruments that are valid are also reliable. Because they measure what they are intended to measure, they can be replicated with the same results. Validity is situation-specific in that an instrument may be valid for some purposes but not others. Reliability is not situation-specific in that a reliable instrument should yield consistent results upon replication, regardless of purpose.

Construction and selection of assessment and intervention instruments

The purpose of an instrument must be made clear and its target population must be defined. Its rationale should come from relevant empirical research, clinical experience establishing its need, and/or theoretical foundations from areas such as psycholinguistics, linguistics, neurophysiology, perception, psychophysics, developmental psychology, social psychology, cognitive science, etc. Content must relate to the instrument's purpose, come from satisfactory knowledge bases, be culturally/linguistically sensitive relative to designated populations, and specify suitable bases for item selections. Subject samples should be representative of the target population, which should be described. Samples should also reflect assumptions that are the instrument's foundation. Scoring procedures for instruments should be clearly specified. For standardized tests, applicable origins of measurement error and the degree of error (if determined) should be reported. When citing test-related research, research designs, sampling procedures, sample sizes, and test conditions should be included. Findings reported should include standard errors of measurement, inter-rater reliability, test-retest reliability, alternate-form reliability, and internal consistency.

Guidelines regarding assessment and treatment of multicultural clients

Speech pathologists must be mindful of cultural differences that may affect the delivery of treatment in certain populations. Many aspects of speech that are found in a particular culture may affect the evaluation and treatment process. Care must be taken not to misinterpret these culturally different communication styles as speech or intellectual deficits. Furthermore, some standardized tests may not be appropriate in the assessment of some clients due to cultural differences. Therefore, it is important that speech pathologists be aware of differences in communication styles that are culturally based. Any multicultural or multilingual information that affects communication should be incorporated in the assessment and treatment plan. Treatment should not be directed toward changing culturally specific speech, but to treat any specific speech or reading disorders that exist. Culturally sensitive testing materials should be used when appropriate.

Assessment of culturally and linguistically diverse clients

- Speech pathologists should exercise caution when using standardized tests for evaluations. Care must be taken to ensure that the tests do not hold bias for particular clients, which may inhibit an adequate assessment. Standardized tests translated into alternative languages are not recommended. Tests developed particularly for certain populations are more relevant.
- Dynamic assessment using the classroom and natural environment is an alternative to standardized tests.
- The use of an interpreter is acceptable; however, this method should be administered wisely. Choose a qualified interpreter with the caregiver's permission when a minor or legally conserved person is involved. Make sure that the interpreter has a clear understanding of all objectives and is aware of the client's background and needs.
- Speech therapy in the client's native language is an acceptable practice when appropriate.

Therapy should be directed at the speech therapeutic objectives rather than correcting grammatical errors.

Assessment of child hearing loss

The child should have a pediatric medical examination. If there are no congenital deformities and there is no possibility of intellectual disabilities, a family history, prenatal history, natal history, and neonatal history should be obtained. Maternal rubella, especially in the first trimester, can cause severe bilateral sensorineural hearing loss in the child. A history of threatened abortion(s) or other conditions causing anoxia (oxygen loss) can also cause hearing loss. Infections such as syphilis can cause hearing loss; both parents and the child should be tested if this is suspected. Multiple abortions before the successful pregnancy can be one cause of infections. Erythroblastosis fetalis due to Rh incompatibility of the parents can cause hearing loss. Natal as well as prenatal anoxia can cause hearing loss. Some antibiotics can cause hearing loss when given to newborns. Serious illnesses such as meningitis in neonates can also cause hearing loss.

Initial observations that an audiologist or otologist should make when he or she sees a patient for the first time

When an audiologist or otologist sees a patient for the first time, he or she should try to observe things such as: whether the patient responds to normal speech; whether the patient appears to be alert; whether the patient appears to be normally developed or underdeveloped; whether the patient exhibits stigmata of any syndrome(s) such as Down syndrome or Vogt-Koyanagi-Harada syndrome, wherein hair loss and loss of skin pigmentation may be evident; whether the patient demonstrates an abnormal gait or other gross motor deficits; whether the patient's affect seems normal or suggests depression, paranoia, or apathy; and whether the patient's voice sounds normal or monotonous, which can be due to long-term, severe sensorineural hearing loss. Simple initial observations such as these can be very important to the overall evaluation of the patient, and can direct the clinician's selection of later, more detailed assessments.

Purpose of electronystagmography (ENG) in otologic assessment

The purpose of ENG in otologic assessment is to test vestibular function. It can measure spontaneous nystagmus, position-induced nystagmus, nystagmus induced by caloric (temperature) stimulation of the ears, and nystagmus induced by rotating the patient. An electronystagmogram is often taken clinically before, during, and after bithermal caloric ear stimulation. Duration of nystagmus and maximum intensity are the data usually obtained. Sometimes, data regarding duration is not obtained. Maximum intensity is a measure of eye speed during a ten second interval at the response peak. One major advantage of ENG is that the patient's eyes can be closed or open. Closed eyes prevent the decrease in intensity of vestibular nystagmus caused by eye fixation. Open eyes can reveal cerebellar nystagmus that vanishes with closed eyes. Another advantage of ENG is that it allows greater accuracy by making correcting for spontaneous nystagmus during bithermal caloric testing relatively straightforward. A third advantage is that ENG creates a permanent nystagmus record for future use.

Purpose of speech audiometry

The purpose of speech audiometry is to try to measure a person's ability to understand everyday conversational speech. Speech audiometry can be used to get a measurement of the person's speech threshold (as opposed to pure-tone hearing threshold). Speech audiometry can be used to cross-check the results of pure tone audiometric testing. Speech audiometry can be used to measure a person's ability to recognize speech heard at dB levels that are above his or her hearing threshold ("supra-threshold speech"). Speech audiometry can be used to assist a clinician in making a differential diagnosis when the etiology of a hearing loss is in question, especially when two different conditions can cause similar symptoms. Speech audiometry can be used to get a measure of a person's capability for auditory processing. Speech audiometry can also be used to help the examiner arrive at an estimate of a person's communication functionality.

Audiological assessment in terms of the three aspects of hearing loss

The purpose of audiological assessment is to get quantitative and qualitative information on hearing loss in terms of the amount, the type, and the configuration. The amount of hearing loss is a quantitative measurement expressed in dB. It is tested using pure tones at frequencies between 500 and 4000 Hz. The severity of hearing loss can be classified as Mild (from 20-40 db), Moderate (from 40-60 dB), Severe (from 60-80 dB), and Profound (80 dB or above). The type of loss is related to the location of damage in the auditory system. It is classified as conductive, related to the outer and/or middle ear; sensorineural, related to the cochlea, inner ear, and/or auditory nerve; mixed, a combination of conductive and sensorineural; or a central auditory processing disorder, related to the brain. Loss configuration is qualitative. Determining the configuration of hearing loss involves distinguishing between bilateral or unilateral loss; symmetrical or asymmetrical loss; high-frequency or low-frequency loss; flat, sloping, or precipitous loss; progressive or sudden loss; and stable or fluctuating loss.

Audiological assessment in terms of previously diagnosed hearing loss

In addition to being used to help diagnose hearing loss, audiological testing is also used to monitor diagnosed hearing loss. After diagnosis, a plan to treat and manage the hearing loss is developed. This can include a prescription for hearing aids and/or assistive devices, medical and/or surgical interventions, aural habilitation or rehabilitation, and periodic assessments. After the plan has been implemented, the relative stability of the hearing loss should be monitored regularly for improvement in hearing due to intervention, any progression of the loss, any fluctuations in acuity, and any new conditions affecting the original loss. The patient's hearing acuity when hearing aids and/or assistive devices are used should be monitored and documented. This can involve real ear measurement, functional gain assessment, listening checks, electroacoustic analysis, and informal functional assessment conducted in the patient's usual listening environment (e.g. in school, at work, or at home).

Taking a case history during audiological assessment

The audiologist will ask the reason for the visit; if the patient has noticed hearing difficulty (and if so, what type of difficulty is being experienced and how long it has been going on); when the patient thinks the hearing difficulty started; if one or both ears seem affected; whether the trouble was sudden or gradual; if the patient is experiencing tinnitus; if the patient has a history of ear infections; if the patient noticed ear pain and/or discharge; if the patient ever feels dizzy;

whether there is a family history of hearing loss; whether men's, women's, or children's voices are harder to hear; whether people say the patient talks too loudly; whether people say the patient's TV volume is too loud; if the patient often has to ask others to repeat what was said; whether the patient can hear but not understand speech; if the patient has a history of exposure to noise at work, in military service, or during recreational activities; and if there are certain situations wherein it is harder to hear, such as in a car, in large groups of people, at a theater, in noisy restaurants, etc.

Depending on the child's age, cognitive level, ability to hear and understand, and ability to respond using speech or other methods of communication, an audiologist will ask the child's parent(s), caregiver(s), teacher(s), therapist(s), or other responsible adult(s) present all of the same questions asked of an adult patient. In addition, the audiologist will ask for the following information regarding a child: the status of the child's speech and language development; the health and medical history of the child; whether or not the child recognizes familiar sounds, and how the child responds to these; whether or not the child exhibits a startle response to sudden, loud sounds; whether or not the child has been diagnosed or identified as having any other disabilities (and if so, what they are); and whether or not the child has previously had hearing screenings and/or hearing tests (and if so, when they were conducted and what the results were)..

Performing a physical examination of the ear and canal

An audiologist will visually examine the pinna for any malformations. The audiologist will use an otoscope, which has a magnifying lens and a light, to examine the external auditory meatus (canal) and tympanic membrane (eardrum). The audiologist looks for cerumen (earwax) and/or foreign objects that may be obstructing the canal. The audiologist otoscopically examines the tympanic membrane for rupture, perforation, flaccidity, signs of fluid, redness, discoloration, retraction or bulging, swelling, scarring, thickening, or other signs of infection. The audiologist will make a physician referral if his or her observations indicate any of the above. Following physical examination, an audiologist will conduct a pure-tone audiometric test, plotting hearing dB levels for each frequency tested on an audiogram. The audiologist will also ascertain the patient's speech reception threshold, which is the lowest dB level at which the patient can hear speech half the time. The audiologist will then evaluate word recognition, which is the patient's ability to identify words at a comfortable level of loudness.

Audiological measures of middle ear function

Measurements that give the examiner information regarding outer and middle ear status are known as acoustic immittance measures. One component of immittance measurement is tympanometry. Tympanometry assesses eardrum function, and can identify wax buildup in the canal, eardrum perforation, and fluid in the middle ear. Another component of immittance testing is acoustic reflex measurement. This tests the acoustic reflex, or the stapedius reflex, wherein the stapedius muscle reacts to sudden loud sound by pulling the stapes foot plate away from the oval window. This has the effect of damping the inner ear's sound transmission, preventing noise-induced hearing loss. Testing this reflex can give information pertinent to middle ear function, hearing loss, and diagnosis. Following the full audiological evaluation, the audiologist develops a profile of the patient's hearing abilities and needs by reviewing each part of the assessment. If indicated, the audiologist recommends medical and/or educational referrals; sensory assessment; hearing aid and/or assistive listening device assessment; assessments for aural rehabilitation, speech, and language; and/or counseling.

Air conduction test

When testing air conduction hearing, the audiometer's earphones are placed over the patient's ears. The audiometer sends pure tones via the earphones through the air into the ear canal. The patient is instructed to raise a hand or finger, point to the ear hearing the tone, press a button, or speak (say "yes," "left," "right," etc.) to show s/he hears the tone. With infants, audiologists observe behavioral changes, such as sucking activity (starting or stopping, or increased or decreased speed, for example); increase or decrease in other motor activity; looking for the sound; and/or other signs of attention to the tone. Correct responses are rewarded by allowing the child to view an animated toy. This is called visual reinforcement audiometry. Conditioned play audiometry can be used with young children. Instead of raising a hand, pointing, etc., they may be instructed to drop a block in a box, put a ring over a rod, or string a bead as the response.

Bone conduction test

With bone conduction testing, the pure-tone audiometer presents the same tones and frequencies as it would during air conduction testing. However, instead of earphones, a small vibrator is placed on the temporal bone behind the ear or on the forehead to introduce tones. This bypasses any obstructions of the outer and/or middle ear. Tones reach the nerve via skull vibration. Therefore, bone conduction tests inner ear function

separately from outer and middle ear function. The difference between the two is that air conduction testing will show conductive and/or sensorineural hearing loss, whereas bone conduction testing will show only sensorineural hearing loss. By comparing the results of air conduction testing to the results of bone conduction testing, the audiologist can deduce whether any problem(s) in the outer or middle ear are causing hearing loss. Matching air and bone conduction results indicate sensorineural loss. Disparate results mean an air-bone gap, indicating conductive or mixed (both conductive and sensorineural) loss.

Components tested in speech audiometry

In speech audiometry, speech reception threshold (SRT) and speech recognition are tested. SRT is determined using spondees. Spondees are two-syllable words with equal stress on both syllables (baseball, cowboy, or airplane, for example). The audiologist speaks each word, and the patient repeats it or points to a corresponding picture. The audiologist repeats each word, gradually decreasing its loudness. The lowest dB level at which the patient can hear and repeat the word half the time is the SRT. Word recognition is typically tested using monosyllabic words (high, knees, or come, for example). The audiologist or a recording speaks each word at a constant, comfortable loudness level throughout testing. The patient repeats each word or points to a corresponding picture. The examiner documents the percentage of words repeated correctly for each ear. Normally, word recognition is tested in a quiet environment. To test hearing with background noise, word recognition can also be tested using recorded noise sent via the audiometer.

Supra-threshold SRA

Supra-threshold SRA refers to Sound Recognition Ability at hearing levels above the individual's hearing threshold. It is expressed as the percentage of words correctly identified at the intensity level of their presentation. For example, it might be 100% at 60 dB and 90% at 30 dB. In general, the results of supra-threshold sound recognition ability testing can be predicted by referring to the amount, type, and configuration of the hearing loss identified by pure tone audiometric testing. Thus, these two different measures will (or should) show a correlation. Materials used to test supra-threshold SRA include phonemes, syllables, words, phrases, sentences, discourse (i.e. speeches, monologues, etc.), nonsense words, synthetic sentences (syntactically incomplete recorded sentences created for testing that are often used with a competing recording), speech presented amidst background noise, and filtered speech (i.e. some frequencies of the speech sounds are filtered out, which makes speech recognition more difficult).

SDT and SAT

SDT stands for Speech Detection Threshold and SAT stands for Speech Awareness Threshold. These two terms are synonyms. The Speech Detection Threshold is the lowest level of loudness (measured in dB) at which the person tested detects speech sounds. Speech detection threshold can be used to test speech recognition when the person tested cannot respond to the spondaic (two-syllable words with equally stressed syllables) stimuli used to test Speech Recognition Threshold (SRT). SDT can be obtained using materials other than spondees. The test taker does not have to recognize or repeat words, or even identify them as speech, but must indicate detection of the sound. The threshold for SDT has been found to be roughly 10 dB better than it is for SRT. In addition, it should be taken into account that audiometers are normally calibrated according to levels of speech recognition rather than levels of speech detection.

Plotting frequency and intensity on an audiogram

Frequency or wavelength, perceived as pitch, goes from left (lowest) to right (highest) along the X (horizontal) axis of the graph. Frequencies audiologists test include 125, 250, 500, 1000, 2000, 3000, 4000, and 8000 Hz. Intensity, perceived as loudness, goes from top (softest) to bottom (loudest) along the Y (vertical) axis. It is measured in decibels (dB). The audiologist plots a point corresponding to the lowest dB level at which the individual can hear each frequency, using O for the right ear and X for the left ear. The Xs and Os are connected to create a line or curve for each ear. If this line's configuration is flat, the person's acuity is equal for every frequency presented. If it slopes down at the right, low-frequency hearing is better and high-frequency hearing is worse. If it rises to the right, high-frequency hearing is better and low-frequency hearing is worse. Symmetrical configuration shows equal hearing levels in both ears. Asymmetrical configuration means hearing levels are different for each ear.

Pure tone average

The pure tone average is a representation of the amount (extent or degree) of hearing loss in each ear. It is measured in decibels (dB). Unlike some other audiological measures such as word recognition and supra-threshold SRA, it is not expressed as a percentage. An audiologist calculates pure tone average after completing pure-tone audiometric testing and plotting an audiogram. The person's hearing thresholds at 500, 1000, and 2000 Hz (the main speech frequencies) are averaged respectively for each ear. For example, if someone's threshold in the right ear is 20 dB at 500 Hz, 40 dB at 1000 Hz, and 60 dB at 2000 Hz, the average is 40 dB, which indicates moderate hearing loss. If the left ear thresholds are 10 dB at 500 Hz, 20 dB at 1000 Hz, and 30 dB at 2000 Hz, the average is 20 dB, which indicates mild hearing loss.

Auditory evoked potentials

Auditory evoked potentials are electrodiagnostic test procedures that yield information about the condition of the neural pathways, or routes of transmission along the nerves, to the brain and within the brain. One indication for auditory evoked potentials is when patients report perceptions or show signs or symptoms of a disorder or disease of the central nervous system. Another indication for these is when patients cannot be tested with behavioral methods. Babies, for example, cannot follow instructions. Children or adults with cognitive impairments may not understand instructions; those with physical disabilities may be unable to indicate responses; those with behavioral problems or mental illness may be unable to respond, or may respond inconsistently, inaccurately, or inappropriately; and all of these individuals may be incapable of sustained attention. Auditory brainstem response (ABR) is a type of auditory evoked potential often used with infants. Electrodes placed on the head record brainwave activity in response to sound stimuli.

OAE

OAE stands for otoacoustic emissions. Otoacoustic emissions are produced by the cochlea in the inner ear when it is stimulated by an incoming sound signal.

When sound waves stimulate the cochlea, the outer hair cells in the cochlea vibrate. This vibration emits a sound that echoes backward into the middle ear. This sound emission is not audible by the human ear. However, it can be detected by electroacoustic means. A small probe is inserted into the external auditory meatus, and the otherwise inaudible sound can be measured in this way. The significance of otoacoustic emissions in audiological assessment is that the cochleas of people who have normal hearing will produce these emissions, but the cochleas of people who have hearing losses greater than 25-30 dB do not emit these sounds. Therefore, measuring the presence or absence of OAE helps in diagnosing hearing loss and determining the degree of hearing loss.

Acoustic immittance measures

Acoustic immittance measures are determined by conducting a battery of tests that help assess outer and middle ear functionality. Three types are tympanometry, acoustic reflex, and static acoustic impedance. Tympanometry sends air into the external auditory meatus, and the air pressure causes the tympanic membrane to move back and forth. This measures the tympanic membrane's mobility. The resulting tympanogram graphs normal mobility, stiffness, or flaccidity of the tympanic membrane. Acoustic reflex is the normal reflex of the stapedius muscle in reaction to a sudden loud sound. Testing for the presence or absence of this reflex and the level of loudness that triggers it helps to find the location within the auditory system that is the source of hearing loss. Static acoustic impedance measures the actual physical volume of air present in the external auditory meatus. This measurement is helpful for diagnosing a perforated eardrum or the patency of ventilation tubes.

Balance assessment

A sense of balance requires coordination of the inner ear's vestibular system, the visual system, and muscular kinesthesia. Without this coordination, people experience dizziness. Anything disrupting the inner ear can cause this symptom. For example, Ménière's disease, calcium deposits, ototoxic drugs, or head injuries can cause dizziness. Other problems related or unrelated to the vestibular system can as well. A balance assessment may be performed to identify pathology in the vestibular system or the whole balance system. It may be conducted to determine the site of a lesion if one is already diagnosed or suspected. It may be done to monitor changes in an individual's balance functionality. It may also be done to ascertain how much the vestibular, visual, and kinesthetic systems each contribute to a functional sense of balance. It is indicated when vestibular system pathology is suspected, when a patient displays abnormal gait or nystagmus, or when a patient complains of dizziness or vertigo.

Impact of hearing loss on adults and intervention

Hearing loss is one of the most frequent causes of chronic disability in the U.S. It can be congenital, inherited, or due to aging, trauma, disease, or ototoxic agents. Hearing impairment has an impact not only on communication functioning, but also on the psychological and social functioning and overall well-being of millions of individuals. It also has an impact on those individuals' family members, friends, employers, and co-workers. A report by the National Council on Aging found that adults with no intervention for their hearing loss tend to report symptoms of depression and anxiety more often, and tend to participate in organized social activities less often than adults who have hearing aids. Hearing aids are the intervention recommended for the majority of adults with hearing loss. Unfortunately, one in five people who get hearing aids stop using them. Even those who use them show significant signs of residual disability.

Audiological rehabilitation services as they relate to hearing aids

It has been demonstrated clinically that audiological rehabilitation services assist people who have been prescribed hearing aids to accept their new hearing aids and benefit more from using them. These services also help people with hearing aids resolve many residual communication problems, as well as problems adjusting to having a hearing loss and using a hearing aid. Audiological rehabilitation services include adaptive training in amplification and other assistive devices or technologies; training in speech reading; tactile training; auditory training; individual counseling; family counseling; group counseling; and training and guidance in the development of communication strategies. Research has proven the effectiveness of such services. Audiological rehabilitation not only fosters both compliance and success with the use of hearing aids, but also enhances the psychosocial and communicative functioning of people with hearing losses. In addition, research has proven that delivering audiological rehabilitative services in coordination with fittings for hearing aids is cost-effective.

Making rehabilitative assessments for adults with hearing loss

When an individual has been diagnosed with a hearing loss, an audiologist should conduct a rehabilitative assessment before selecting or implementing any intervention. This should be done in order to establish and record the individual's rehabilitative needs, to identify which intervention procedures are most appropriate, and to aid in the selection of the intervention procedure(s). Intervention procedures that audiologists can provide to their clients include technological information, training, and assistance; educational procedures of intervention; behavioral types of intervention procedures; and counseling intervention procedures to deal with each individual's particular rehabilitative needs, and also to help the individual achieve the maximum possible benefit from treatment. When an audiologist ensures that there is continuing interaction between the client and the clinician, s/he also fosters compliance by the client with the recommendations for treatment. By monitoring and evaluating client progress, audiologists ensure the client is benefiting from treatment, and they also ensure their own professional accountability.

Auditory system disorders, audiologic assessment procedures, and normal communication development

Regarding auditory system disorders, those providing AR should be able to identify, describe, and differentiate among auditory function disorders, such as disorders of the outer, middle, and inner ear; disorders of the auditory nerve; and disorders of the central auditory system and neural pathways. With respect to audiological assessment procedures, persons providing AR must be able to administer and interpret pure-tone and speech audiometry to assess central and peripheral auditory functions. This includes taking measurements of hearing threshold sensitivity and performing differential diagnosis regarding the locations of auditory disorders. Persons providing AR must be able to identify and conduct screening

exams for problems with speech and/or language. They must be able to ascertain the need for referrals to other professionals for services. Regarding normal communication development and the effect of hearing impairment on it, they must be able to describe phonology, syntax, semantics, and pragmatics in human communication relative to comprehension and production in normal communicative development. They must be able to describe the effects hearing impairment has on these.

Assessment of persons with suspected language disorders

- Screen subjects using a formal and/or informal testing procedure to determine if a more detailed assessment is warranted.
- Obtain a description of the problem from the subject (if appropriate), caregivers, teachers, and health professionals. Determine if there have been any prior treatments.
- Interview caregivers, family members, and peers to obtain information about the nature of the speech and language ability of the subject.
- Observe the family communication style. Make note of social interactions and languages spoken.
- Obtain a health history of the mother and subject, including the prenatal and postnatal periods and childhood developmental history.
- Obtain educational history and occupational history of adults.
- Examine hearing and screen for any oral-facial defects.
- Obtain speech and language samples from the subject.

Standardized (formal) tests used for language assessment

Advantages of standardized tests
- They provide comparison data with age-matched peers.
- They provide a measurement that will be consistent across all examiners.

Disadvantages of standardized tests
- Data obtained may not be applicable to some segments of the population that are linguistically and culturally diverse.
- Certain characteristics of language may not be tested in all contexts or situations.
- They cannot be used as a single source of assessing children's language skills or assigning treatment strategies.

Nonstandardized (informal) tests for language assessment

Criterion-referenced testing: This method of assessment takes into account individual-specific context of language, such as culture. Instead of standard target goals, baseline behaviors are established for the subject, and individualized goals are established.

Authentic assessment subjects are evaluated via their performance of a given task.

Dynamic assessment is a type of authentic assessment whereby the individual is provided with directions on how to perform a task, and the ability to perform the task is assessed.

Portfolio assessment is a type of authentic assessment whereby a body of the individual's performance ability is collected over time. The subject is given directions on how to perform a task, and

the development of the performance is observed over time.

Functional or social assessment: Information on speech and language is obtained from peers, teachers, caregivers, and health professionals. The subject is examined in various social settings, and this information is used in treatment.

Type-token ratio

The type-token ratio (TTR) measures children's lexical diversity or their variety of expressive words used in conversation. Measuring TTR:
- TTR = Number of different words in a sample (a word counts only once if repeated)
- Number of words in a sample (count even if word is repeated)

The typical value of TTR for children ages 3 to 8 is 0.5, or 1:2 ratio. TTR can be applied only to children ages 3 to 8. This is in contrast to the mean length utterance (MLU) analysis of children's language, which can be applied to children of any age.

Assessment of speech and language for infants and toddlers (<3 years)

- Assess the child's readiness for speech.
- Identify any medical problems that would affect the child's attention status.
- Identify any hearing deficits.
- Assess the child's developmental milestones: cognitive, motor, social, and speech.
- Collect relevant information about the child's language from caregivers and teachers.
- Observe caregiver-child interactions. The Mother-Infant Play Interaction Scale is a standardized test that is used to assess the caregiver's interaction

style and the child's response to the interaction stimulus.
- Observe the child's play interactions with other children.

Assessing cognitive, social, and motor development of infants and toddlers

Denver Developmental Screening Test is used to assess the developmental progress of children. It encompasses many areas of development, including cognitive, motor, emotional, behavioral, and language. This test can be used to identify many learning disabilities. It is used to screen children from birth to 6 years.

The Communication Screen is used to assess auditory and verbal comprehension in children ages 2 to 5 years.

Bayley Scale of Infant Mental Development is a psychological test used to assess the mental, behavioral, and motor development of children from birth to 2.5 years.

Battelle Developmental Inventory is used to assess five areas of developmental achievements in children 6 months to 8 years. These areas are social, adaptive behavior, psychomotor, cognitive, and communication.

Vineland Adaptive Behavior Scale is used to assess the socialization skills in children from birth through 18 months. Included in this test are measures of receptive/expressive language and gross/fine motor skills.

Assessing speech and language in infants and toddlers

Preschool Language Scale is used to assess receptive and expressive language skills in children ages 2 weeks to 6 years. Both caregivers and children are interviewed to obtain appropriate data for assessment.

Early Language Milestone Scale-2 is used to determine speech and language skills in children from birth through 3 years. It can assess expressive, auditory, visual, and receptive language.

Receptive-Expressive Emergent Language Test-3 (REEL-2) is a 132-item checklist of language milestones that is provided by the child's caregiver. This test is used to assess children from birth through 3 years.

Assessing speech and language for preschool and elementary-age children

- Assess children for language disorders using nonstandardized methods or standardized screening tests.
- Determine problems with comprehension of complex language.
- Determine the presence of delay of expressive speech or poor vocabulary.
- Observe problems with word meaning, vocabulary, word structure, syntactic development, pragmatic skills, and comprehension.
- Use pictures and narratives to evoke language responses for assessment.
- Obtain information from caregivers and teachers.
- Observe family interactions and communication methods.

Denver Developmental Screening Test is used to assess the developmental progress of children. It encompasses many areas of development, including cognitive, motor, emotional, behavioral, and language. This test can be used to identify many learning disabilities. It is

- 69 -

used to screen children from birth to 6 years.

The Communication Screen is used to assess auditory and verbal comprehension in children ages 2 to 5 years.

Preschool Language and Screening Test-4 is used to assess receptive and expressive language, social communication, and voice disorders in children ages 3 to 5.5 years.

Bankson Language Screening Test is used to assess speech morphology, syntax, and pragmatics in children ages 3 to 7.

Fluharty Preschool Speech and Language Screening Test-3 is used to identify communication problems in children ages 2 to 6. Children's ability to articulate, repeat sentences, follow directions, answer questions, describe actions, and sequence events is assessed.

Assessing expressive and receptive language in preschool and elementary-age children

The Peabody Picture Vocabulary Test assesses the receptive vocabulary in children 2.5 years through adult through the ability to identify pictures and illustrations following a verbal stimulus.

The Receptive One-Word Picture Vocabulary Test provides an evaluation of children's (ages 35 months through 12 years old) receptive single-word vocabulary. The child is given a one-word stimulus and he must identify the picture accordingly.

The Expressive One-Word Picture Vocabulary Test provides an evaluation of children's (ages 35 months through 12 years old) expressive single-word vocabulary. Children demonstrate their

ability to name objects and concepts in illustrated pictures.

The Test of Word Finding-2 is used to assess children's ability to name pictures depicting objects or actions.

The Test of Auditory Comprehension of Language-3 tests children's receptive language in the categories of vocabulary, grammar, and sentence structure. This test is used for children ages 3 to 9.

The Test of Early Language Development-3 assesses the receptive and expressive language in children ages 2-7. This version of the test is reported to be applicable to all races, genders, and socioeconomic status.

The Token Test for Children is to assess the development in children aged 3 to 12.5 of receptive language. In this test, auditory reception and processing and discrimination of speech sounds are evaluated.

Assessing syntax, morphology, and semantics of language in preschool and elementary-age children

Assessment of Children's Language Comprehension tests children's comprehension of word classes in various combinations of length and complexity. This test, used for children 3 to 7 years old, measures receptive vocabulary and syntax.

Clinical Evaluation of Language Fundamentals-4 is used to assess receptive and expressive language, language structure and memory, morphology, and syntax. This test is useful for subjects from ages 5 through adult.

Multilevel Informal Language Inventory measures children's expressive ability to produce semantic relations, syntactical structures, and language morphology. It is used in children ages 4 through 12.

Test of Language Development Primary-3 is used in the assessment of multiple aspects of spoken language, including vocabulary, comprehension, grammar, and sentence structure. Both receptive and expressive forms of language are assessed. This test is used in children ages 4 to 9.

Assessing preschool and elementary-age children

Boehm Test of Basic Concepts-3 is used to assess language skills of children from kindergarten through 3rd grade. Children are asked to identify pictures of relational concepts, such as size and position.

Detroit Test of Learning and Aptitude: Primary-3 is used to assess the verbal, attention, and visual motor aspects of cognition in children ages 3 to 10.

Test for Examining Expressive Morphology is a brief test used to assess the development of expressive morphemes in children ages 3 to 7.

Test for Pragmatic Skills is used for children ages 3 to 9 who are suspected of having an impaired or absence of conversational language. In this test, illustrations of situations are presented, and children are asked to respond. This may give the examiner insight into the child's social knowledge and pragmatic language development.

Token Test for Children is a specialized test used to assess the development of receptive language in children ages 3 to 12.5. In this test, children's auditory reception, auditory processing, and discrimination of speech sounds are evaluated.

Assessing speech and language in adolescents

- Screen for any language problems with use of standardized and nonstandardized methods.
- Observe for syntactical errors or lack of speech fluency.
- Observe the child's range of vocabulary and ability to maintain conversational discourse.
- Evaluate the child's comprehension of words, figurative language, and abstract concepts.
- Determine if any reading and writing abnormalities exist. Specifically, observe letter formation, sentence structure, organization, and grammatical content.
- Interview caregivers, teachers, and peers about the child's language.
- Observe children in the classroom to identify any specific behaviors that may disrupt learning.
- Determine whether one-on-one, small group, classroom intervention, or a combination may be suitable for the child.

Screening for Adolescent Language is a rapid screening test for children ages 11 to 18 to identify abnormalities in vocabulary, auditory memory, language processing, and comprehension of figurative language.

Clinical Evaluation of Language Fundamentals is a comprehensive screening test for children ages 5 to 16. It analyzes children's receptive and expressive speech, language morphology, semantic knowledge, syntax, pragmatics, memory, logic, and attention.

Classroom Communication Screening Procedure for Early Adolescents was developed to determine the cognitive and communication skills required for secondary education. It is used to screen children ages 9 to 14 in their development of verbal expression and their ability to follow directions.

Adolescent Language Screening is used to screen children ages 11 to 17 in their development of expressive/receptive language, pragmatics, morphology, and syntactic and semantic language skills.

Assessing syntax, morphology, and semantics of language in adolescents

Clinical Evaluation of Language Fundamentals-4 is used to assess receptive/expressive language, language structure and memory, morphology, and syntax. This test is useful for subjects from age 5 through adult.

Bilingual Syntax Measure is used to measure linguistic proficiency in children at the 3rd through 12th grade level in both English and Spanish.

The Word Test: Adolescent is used to assess expressive vocabulary and semantics in children ages 12 to 18. Children are asked to demonstrate their knowledge of language and word meanings in ordinary and exceptional situations.

Test of Problem Solving: Adolescent is used to assess expressive language, cognition, and problem-solving skills in children ages 12 to 18. In this test, a series of open-ended questions is used to elicit responses.

Fullerton Language Test for Adolescents measures the receptive and expressive language skills in subjects ages 11 to adult. In this test, language morphology, syntax, and semantics are assessed.

Assessing written language in adolescents

Woodcock Language Proficiency Battery is used to assess oral vocabulary, reading, and writing proficiency in subjects ages 11 to adult.

Test of Adolescent and Adult Language-4 is used to assess expressive and written language abilities in subjects of ages 12 to 25. Specific concepts covered in this test are analogies, opposites, similarities, word meanings, sentence structure, and punctuation.

Assessimg naming and vocabulary skills in adolescents

Expressive One-Word Picture Vocabulary Test: Upper Extension provides an evaluation of receptive single-word vocabulary in children ages 12 to 16. The child is given a one-word stimulus and must identify the picture accordingly.

Receptive One-Word Picture Vocabulary Test: Upper Extension provides an evaluation of expressive single-word vocabulary in children ages 12 to 16. Children demonstrate their ability to name objects and concepts through illustrations.

Test of Adolescent/Adult Word Finding assesses the subject's ability in word finding with regard to speed and accuracy. Examinees are tested on nouns, verbs, sentence completion, descriptions, and concept categories. This test can be used to assess subjects from age 12 to adult.

Treatment of articulation-phonation disorders

The motor-based approaches to the treatment of articulation and phonation disorders presume that children have motor and perceptual defects with regard to speech sound production. These approaches are best used with children who have only several errors in phoneme production; do not have severe articulation deficits; and whose articulation disorder is based on physical insufficiencies.

The most frequently used motor-based approaches are:
- Van Riper's traditional approach
- McCabe and Bradley's multiple-phoneme approach
- Baker and Ryan's Monterey Articulation Program
- McDonald's sensory approach
- Irwin and Weston's paired-stimuli approach

Traditional approaches to articulation-phonation therapy

Van Riper's traditional approach emphasizes phonetic placement (teaching sounds of phonemes by instruction, modeling, and physical guidance); auditory discrimination/perceptual training (teaching the distinction between correct and incorrect speech sounds); and repetition of isolated speech sounds.

McCabe and Bradley's multiple-phoneme approach is based on Van Riper's traditional approach except that more than one speech sound is addressed and all problematic speech sounds are addressed in each session. Three phases are employed:
1. Establishment of the correct sound in response to a symbol for that sound
2. Transfer of target sounds to different situations
3. Maintenance of accuracy of sound production in various situations and conversation

Baker and Ryan's Monterey Articulation Program

Baker and Ryan's Monterey Articulation Program involves programmed conditioning to treat articulation disorders. This approach is based on behavioral therapy principles that speech sounds are learned motor behaviors. Sounds are targeted via a program of steps. These targeted sounds are then generalized to home and classroom, and finally maintenance therapy is employed. Since repetition of motor skills is emphasized, the approach is best for children requiring a structured motor-articulation program.

McDonald's sensory approach to articulation-phonological therapy

McDonald's sensory approach involves speech training at the level of the syllable, and not the phoneme. Perceptual training is not emphasized, but the phonetic environment is important. Practice begins with bisyllabic and trisyllabic sounds that are not in error. Correct pronunciation of sounds that are in error are trained and then moved to more varied contexts and then to natural communication.

Instrumental methods used in the visualization of the vocal folds

Indirect laryngoscopy: the use of a specialized mirror by a medical specialist to examine the larynx. Vocal cord movement can be assessed during speech.

Direct laryngoscopy: the examination of the larynx with a laryngoscope by a medical specialist. This procedure is done under anesthesia. Given that the patient cannot speak, this procedure is best when a biopsy is needed rather than for assessment of vocal cord movement.

Flexible fiberoptic laryngoscopy: the introduction of a flexible laryngoscope by a specialist through the nose to examine the laryngeal structures. Vocal movements can be viewed via a fiberoptic light system.

Rigid and flexible endoscopy: Also performed by a specialist, rigid endoscopy employs the use of a nonflexible camera that is introduced via the mouth. Unlike the flexible scope, the rigid endoscope may be passed further to the level of the laryngeal mechanism. The flexible endoscope (nasopharyngeoscope) is introduced via the nose to the velopharyngeal area. With endoscopy, fine vocal structures as well as vocal movement can be visualized.

Assessing the quality of movement of the vocal folds

Spectrography analyzes speech through measurements of amplitude and frequencies. This is most frequently used to determine the effectiveness of treatment of a voice disorder.

The videostroboscopic method uses an instrument called a videostroboscope that emits a pulsating light that creates slow-motion viewing of the vocal folds. This device can be attached to a rigid endoscope or flexible fiber-optic endoscopy. The images detail the movement of the vocal structures and can determine the presence of tumors.

Electroglottography (EGG) is used to monitor vocal vibration and closure patterns. This study is noninvasive and uses electrodes that attach to the neck.

Electromyography (EMG) assesses the activity of the muscles of the vocal folds. This is useful in diagnosing vocal cord neuromuscular disorders.

Spirometry or plethysmography is used to measure lung and breath volumes.

Hypernasality and hyponasality

Hypernasality treatment: Biofeedback is used to raise the subject's awareness of nasal resonance. A nasometer is a device that gives subjects feedback on the presence of nasality in speech production. Visual and auditory cues can be used to monitor production of nasal sounds. Therapy is directed at improving mouth opening, articulation, pitch, rate, and loudness to appropriate levels.

Hyponasality treatment: Nasometer feedback and visual and auditory cues are used to monitor correct sound production. Therapy is directed at training the subject to focus the pronunciation of appropriate words toward the nasal in an exaggerated way. Therapy also includes practicing the production of nasal and glide phonemes in combination. Feedback is then used so that the subject can determine proper nasalization.

Admission and discharge of clients within a speech pathology practice

Referrals for services may come from clinicians, educators, caregivers, family members, clients, or county agencies. Criteria for admission to services include:
- Presence of a communication deficit where there is a clear difference in communication among peers, a disruption of education, socialization, or employment, or the presence of a health and safety hazard
- Presence of a swallowing deficit in which there is a negative effect on nutrition, health, and safety
- It is appropriate to discharge clients from services under the following conditions:
- All language and communication or swallowing goals are met or the client's skills meet standards that

are comparable to his or her peers.

- The client has reached the maximum benefits of therapy or is unable to progress due to clinical or emotional reasons.
- A Request for discharge by caregivers or legal guardians or a change of provider or location has been made.
- The client is unwilling to participate or has aberrant behavior hampering continued services.

Record keeping

The speech-language pathologist has the responsibility to keep accurate records of all clients. The records should contain identifying information about the client (e.g., name, address, referring agency). Contact and pertinent information about family, clinical providers, and educators should be found in the records. The speech-language pathologist should document all issues of the screening examination, communication, speech, language and swallowing deficits. Details of all training sessions should include the date and times of sessions. Treatment plans should be included and detail all goals. Client's responses to treatment should be recorded. Records are typically the property of hospitals, clinics, referring agencies, and schools when appropriate. Records should be kept in a safe place so that confidentiality is maintained. A written consent by the client or guardian is required for outside agencies or persons to obtain the contents of these records.

Diadochokinetic rate

The diadochokinetic rate is used to assess children's oral motor skills. The ability to produce rapid speech movements using various parts of the oral structures is determined. Children who are unable to make these rapid speech movements typically have a difficult time sequencing speech sounds. A group of syllables or words is given to the child to pronounce and repeat rapidly. These syllables or words are important in that they use a combination of mouth structures (e.g., lips, tongue, palate) to pronounce. Two common groups of sounds used are *puh-tuh-kuh* and *patty cake*. These two words use syllables that require the lips, tongue, and palate to pronounce in sequence. Children are asked to repeat these words as many times as they can in a set amount of time, usually 5 seconds. A score is given based on age-appropriate standards. One of the most common tests that uses diadochokinesis is the Fletcher Time-by-Count Test of Diadochokinetic Syllable Rate.

Assessing articulation

Goldman-Fristoe Test of Articulation is used to assess the articulation of consonant sounds in children and young adults. This test is best for subjects of ages 2 to 21.

Fischer-Logemann Test of Articulation Competence is used to assess the ability to articulate all phonemes. It is used for subjects from preschool through adulthood and is practical for regional and ethnic dialects.

McDonald Deep Test is used to determine the various contexts in which sounds are misarticulated. It uses a series of pictures, which makes it suitable for children.

The Arizona Articulation Proficiency Scale is a contextual, picture-driven articulation test for children. It is like the McDonald Deep but more contemporary.

Templin-Darley Test is used to assess the articulation skills of subjects ages 3 to adult.

Assessing individuals with neurological speech disorders

Scales of Cognitive Ability for Traumatic Brain Injury (SCATBI) is used to assess the cognitive ability of individuals from adolescence to adulthood.

The Western Aphasia Battery (WAB) is used to assess the language skills of adults with aphasia due to acquired brain injury. This test is so comprehensive that it is often used to assist in the diagnosis of the type of neurological brain injury present. It contains a nonverbal component for testing as well.

Mini-inventory of Right Brain Injury (MIRBI) is used to determine the types of language deficits present in individuals with right brain injuries and can be used in individuals ages 20 to 80.

Ross Information Processing Assessment (RIPA)is used to determine the level of cognitive and language deficits present in adults with neurological brain disorders. Communication Activities of Daily Living (CADL) is used to assess functional language ability in adults with neurological-based language abnormalities.

Bedside Evaluation & Screening Test (BEST) is used to assess the language abilities in adults with aphasia.

Apraxia Battery For Adults (ABA) measures the presence and severity of apraxia in adults by way of performance assessment of a series of tasks.

Frenchay Dysarthria Assessment is used to measure the presence and severity of dysarthria in adults.

Individualized education program (IEP) for children with disabilities

The individualized education program (IEP) was developed as part of the Individuals with Disabilities Education Act (IDEA). It mandates school districts and local educational agencies to develop periodic sets of goals for the treatment of children from ages 3 to 18 and to follow the implementing of those goals. This program is usually instituted by the individual school districts of each state. It begins with the identification of any child with special needs, following a thorough evaluation. The child must meet eligibility requirements authorized by the county or state to receive services. All parties responsible for the child's care meet to plan special needs services and goals for the following months. Individuals at the meeting include school district officials, therapists, social service workers, teachers, and caregivers. The progress of the child is reassessed, and another meeting takes place in 1 year or less to adjust goals and treatment.

Reinforcers

A positive reinforcer is a reward that the child enjoys. She receives the reinforcer when she performs a desired behavior. A primary positive reinforcer is something that the child already enjoys. For a secondary positive reinforcer, the child has to learn to derive some benefit from it. The reinforcer can be provided at a fixed rate (e.g., every 10 minutes) or at a variable rate. It can also be provided via a ratio formula or a variable ratio formula whereby the child receives the reinforcer if she performs the behavior a particular number of times. The reinforcer can also be administered at random. When a reinforcer fails to stimulate the desired behavior, it is called extension. A variable schedule of reinforcement should prevent this. Negative reinforcers enhance a behavior by taking away something that

is unpleasant for the child in response to
the desired behavior.

Intervention

ASHA's checklist for working with health insurance plans and employers to assure coverage of audiological rehabilitation

(1) Have clients review their employee health plans regarding coverage. (2) Identify the workplace contact person for health benefits. (3) Contact this person and schedule a meeting to discuss audiological rehabilitation services for the client. (4) Inform the contact person about the importance of communication, about audiological rehabilitation service procedures, and about medical necessity. (5) Cite statistics about hearing loss prevalence, its educational impact, and its psychosocial impact. (6) Cite research data on early intervention in children and hearing aid benefits for seniors. (7) Quote the cost effectiveness of auditory rehabilitation according to Current Procedural Terminology (CPT) codes. (8) Explain the overlapping, interrelated, or complementary roles of audiologists and speech-language pathologists in providing communicative rehabilitation. (9) Explain how rehabilitation enables effective communication at work and home; helps one understand others and express one's needs; and contributes to one's health, which is why audiological rehabilitation should be a health benefit.

Balance disorder and the accompanying symptoms

Balance problems cause instability, a sense of movement, disorientation, a "woozy" feeling, or blurred vision. Accompanying symptoms include tinnitus, nausea, vomiting, diarrhea, faintness, anxiety, panic, fear, and blood pressure and heart rate changes. In 2003, the CDC estimated that almost half the people in the United States have had some problem with balance at some time during their lives. Balance disorders can be seriously disabling, interfering with activities like reaching for things, getting out of bed, or taking showers. Populations most at risk for balance problems are elderly people; people who have sustained head traumas; and divers, pilots, and others in jobs where motion and gravity undergo quick changes. Changes in vestibular, ocular, and proprioceptive functions due to aging make elderly people particularly at risk. In 2008, the CDC reported that a senior receives emergency room treatment for a fall every 18 seconds, while a senior dies from a fall every 35 minutes.

Epley Maneuver

The mechanism of this procedure is to move debris (canalith—literally, canal stones) from the labyrinth back into the vestibule. Debris moves from the posterior semicircular canal into the utricle. Holding the audiologist's forearms for support, the patient slowly lowers from sitting to supine position. The patient has his or her head hanging off the table's edge with the target ear downward. The patient holds this position until nystagmus stops. The audiologist manually rotates the patient's head left so the target ear is facing upward and holds this position for 30 seconds. The patient rolls onto his or her left side, rotating the head left until the nose angles toward the floor, and holds this position for 30 seconds. This maneuver is repeated until nystagmus is gone. The indication for this procedure is benign paroxysmal positional vertigo (BPPV). Contraindications to performing the maneuver are unstable heart disease because of the positions and positional changes; and cervical spondylosis with myelopathy and severe carotid stenosis, both because of the stress exerted on the neck during this procedure.

After the Epley Maneuver, or canalith repositioning procedure, has been performed, the audiologist will give the patient the following instructions. For one week afterward, the patient should turn the head and neck as one unit, avoiding twisting. For the first two nights, the patient should sleep in a recliner at a 45° angle, with pillows propping up the head. For the next five nights, the patient should not sleep on the affected side. This can be accomplished by placing a tennis ball in a pajama pocket on the affected side or pinning a pillow to the affected side to prevent rolling over in one's sleep. The audiologist will also instruct the patient to come back if the symptoms of vertigo recur, and will advise that the procedure may need to be repeated. Research (Froehling, 2000, Mayo Clinic) found this procedure works for 50% of patients. Placebos were found to work for 19% of patients.

How CPT (Current Procedural Terminology) codes for aural rehabilitation have changed since 2006

Before 2006, assessment of AR status was included in code 92506, and actual aural rehabilitation was part of code 92507. In 2006, four new codes were added for AR. The first hour of assessment of AR status is code 92626. Every 15 minutes beyond an hour is code 92627. AR for prelingual hearing losses is code 92630. AR for postlingual hearing losses is code 92633. Medicare policy limits audiology services to only diagnostic testing. For speech-language pathologists providing aural rehabilitation, Medicare stipulates they use CPT code 92507, the code formerly used by both audiologists and SLPs for aural rehabilitation. Some resources regarding reimbursement include ASHA's article "Audiologic/Aural Rehabilitation: Reimbursement Issues for Audiologists and Speech-Language Pathologists"; Bottom Line articles from the ASHA Leader, "Coding Auditory and Aural Rehabilitation Procedures" and "Coding and Reimbursement for Auditory Rehabilitation"; and ASHA's brochure, "Checklist for Audiologic Rehabilitation: Ensuring Coverage of Audiologic Rehabilitation."

Why a hearing aid wearer might also need an assistive listening device

One factor affecting speech comprehension is the distance between the sound source and the listener. The farther the listener is from the speaker, the more sound intensity fades. Every time the distance doubles, the sound's loudness decreases by 6 dB. In large lecture halls or at public events, a hearing aid alone is often insufficient. A second factor affecting speech comprehension is competition from noise in the environment. Most rooms and public places have substantial levels of background noise competing with the speaker(s)' voice(s). Combined with fading signals (1), this can necessitate a supplemental listening device. A third factor that affects speech comprehension is room acoustics. These vary widely by location. Sound waves in rooms ricochet off of walls, windows, hard furniture, and other reflecting surfaces, creating multiple sound patterns that distort the target speech signals. To those people who have normal hearing, these are simply irritating. To those people who wear hearing aids, however, they degrade their processing of speech sounds, significantly reducing the accuracy of their speech perception.

Example of a hearing aid wearer in a public situation where comprehension is still compromised

If a person wearing hearing aids is sitting in a large theater or lecture hall, s/he may find the speaker's voice audible, but may have trouble understanding what is said.

The speaker's voice is amplified yet unclear. The amplified signal fades in intensity as the distance from either the live speaker or a loudspeaker increases. Additionally, background noise such as other audience members talking or rustling papers, the sound of the air conditioning or heating system, etc. distorts the speech signal. Regardless of loudness, a distorted sound is still unclear. An assistive listening device can make a striking difference. If the speaker is wearing a wireless microphone, background noise and bad room acoustics have no effect on the speech signal because it is sent directly to the listener's ears or hearing aids with no interference. This is the same for ALDs used with movie soundtracks.

Assistive listening device that uses loop induction

Loop induction is the oldest technology for ALDs. A loop installed in the room coupled to the speaker's microphone creates an electromagnetic field. The listener in the audience has a T-switch (T for telephone or telecoil) on his/her hearing aid. Setting the aid to "T" generates a current in a coil inside the aid. This current is an electrical copy of the speech signal. The copy is undistorted by environmental factors. The "T" setting bypasses the hearing aid's microphone, so the aid does not capture echoes or background noise. For aids without telecoils, listeners can hear signals using special headset receivers. Some aids have a microphone/telephone or M/T setting, whereby the listener can hear signals from both the loop and the hearing aid microphone. This is useful if the listener wants to hear a lecture or speech, but also to hear comments his/her companion might make during the speech.

Assistive listening device that uses frequency modulation

As its name may suggest, an assistive listening device that uses frequency modulation (FM) is similar to a radio broadcasting system, but in a miniature size. The speaker wears an FM transmitter, while the listener wears an FM receiver. Unlike loop induction, which requires a special loop for generating an electromagnetic field to be installed in the room, frequency modulation sends the speech signal straight to the listener. It is analogous to the way sound signals are sent from a radio broadcast station directly to a radio. The FM transmitter's output can be received by the listener into an earphone headset; into a pair of ear buds like those used with MP3 players and portable CD players or radios; or by coupling the signal to the listener's hearing aid with the use of a neck loop, which is a small induction loop worn around the listener's neck.

Assistive listening device that uses infrared transmission

ALDs that use infrared transmission are like those that use FM in that they both send sound signals directly to listeners without an induction loop. Infrared differs from FM in that it sends signals using infrared light instead of radio waves. Infrared light is so low on the spectrum it is invisible to the unaided human eye. (Infrared cameras can capture visual images at night or in very dark conditions, whereas regular cameras cannot.) Infrared technology captures a sound signal, sending it as unseen light to a receiver with a photo detector. The detector takes up the signal and converts it back into sound. Listeners can use their hearing aids, earphone headsets, or ear buds as receivers with infrared technology. The latter two are often available in theaters and concert halls. Smaller forms of infrared, FM, or loop induction can help people hear TVs in nursing homes and senior centers, where background noise abounds.

TV closed captioning

A 1990 federal law requires that all TVs with 13" or larger diagonal screens have built-in closed captioning. Today, nearly all rental DVDs and videotapes of movies have closed captions. Decoder boxes can be used to read captions on older TVs. Two real-time captioning techniques are: (1): the text of a speech/script is inputted into a computer and projected synchronously with the broadcast; and (2): using specialized computer software, a live person with courtroom reporting transcription skills types and projects a transcription of the program's audio portion in virtual real-time. Advantages of inputting text in advance are that no live person is needed in real-time and it is more accurate if the speaker does not deviate from the script or speech. Its disadvantage is that it cannot caption unscripted programming. This is the advantage of virtual real-time captioning. The disadvantage is that it requires active involvement by a skilled transcriptionist, which is more expensive and more variable.

Note-taking method

The note-taking method is visual like closed captioning for TVs, but requires less technology ("low-tech") and is low in cost. It is obviously useful in school settings, but can also be of help in business and public settings where speeches are given. In one form of note-taking, the speaker's pre-written text is put on an overhead projector and an assistant points at the parts the speaker is reading or discussing. In another form, if there is no prepared text, an assistant takes notes by writing on the overhead projector's transparency so the notes are seen as they are being written. In a third form of note-taking, an assistant takes notes by typing them on a computer. The typed notes are projected using the overhead's projection pad, or are sent to a multimedia projector. In some schools, a student is designated the note-taker. He or she writes on heat-transfer paper that makes several copies.

Computer voice recognition

Computer voice recognition technology was originally intended as a tool to increase productivity in word processing. Instead of doctors, business people, and some authors dictating recordings which typists then transcribed, people could dictate directly to the computer, and the software would transcribe their speech into typed text. While this technology is already widely used in automated telephone systems, it is still in its infancy. Drawbacks are that its speech perception is less accurate than that of humans when there is background noise and/or the speaker's voice is unfamiliar to the system. Though designed for word processing, this technology's future potential is apparent for people with hearing loss. In any situations where closed captions or note-taking are used, voice recognition technology could be applied in the future when its ability to adjust for noise or distortion is improved to approximate the ability of normal-hearing humans.

Auditory adaptive devices used with telephones

People who have hearing loss will often need some kind of device to augment their hearing when they are using the telephone, either in addition to or without the use of hearing aids. There are auditory and non-auditory devices. For auditory devices, there are three fundamental technologies. These are: (1): a replacement handset that will amplify sound more than a regular handset and which, in some cases, also includes noise-reduction circuits; (2): an amplifier that is hard wired between the phone's base and its handset to boost the signal; and (3): a portable, battery-operated amplifier for people with hearing aids who travel and must use many different telephones. This portable amplifier can be coupled to the user's hearing aid electromagnetically if the hearing aid has a telecoil, or acoustically by using the hearing aid's microphone if the hearing aid does not have a telecoil.

TTY/TDD

TTY stands for telephone typewriter, teletypewriter, or text phone. TDD stands for Telecommunications Device for the Deaf. While people with lower levels of hearing loss may be able to communicate over the phone using auditory assistive devices, people with profound hearing loss can rarely if ever use the phone, even with amplification. TTY/TDD is a non-auditory type of assistive device. It is sometimes like a typewriter, but today it is more often digital or computer assisted. In one instance, people on both ends of the call have devices. Both parties type their messages into their units for transmission across normal phone lines. Another instance is when the person with the hearing loss has a unit but the other party does not. In this case, a relay service can be used. Live relay operators use TTY/TDD, speech, or a combination of both to serve as a middleman between the two parties.

The many protocols include EDT, DTMF, Baudot code, V.18, and V.23. The Baudot code is quite popular in the United States. This protocol runs asynchronously at either 45.5 or 50 bauds. V.18 is a very popular protocol featuring a dual standard. It can be used for V.18 transmissions, and is also an "umbrella" protocol that applies to a broad range of other TTY/TDD protocols. It is also compatible with ASCII and half-duplex modulation methods, facilitating computer and modem interfaces. There are portable TTY/TDD devices that can be used instead of landline phones. There are devices that connect to or are compatible with landline phones, making them TTY/TDD-capable. Ringer pitch or volume is adjustable on most devices. Some have visual "ringers," or can accommodate them. Some devices can be connected to hearing aids. Some devices let users speak, but also display text. Some let users hear calls, but also send text.

Telecommunications for the Deaf and Hard of Hearing, Inc. (TDI) publishes an annual directory of TTY/TDD residential and business phone numbers. It also includes fax numbers; e-mail addresses; Internet-related information; phone numbers for relay services; and mailing addresses, phone numbers, and Web site addresses for organizations and groups that serve individuals who are deaf, have hearing impairments, are deaf and blind, and/or have speech impairments. The address of TDI is 8630 Fenton Street, Suite 604, Silver Spring, Maryland, 20910. Their phone numbers are: TTY: 301-589-3006; fax: 301-589-3797; and voice: 301-589-3786. Their videophone number is: 866-970-6838. Their Web site address is: http://www.tdi-online.org/. Their e-mail address is: info@tdi-online.org. To place orders or for ordering information, the e-mail address is: orders@tdi-online.org. For those who want to advertise in the directory or contact TDI about advertising, the phone numbers are the same ones listed above for general contact. (Note: the Web site is currently under renovation.)

Advances in personal computer (PC) technology have created several communication alternatives for people with hearing loss. For those with milder hearing loss and/or hearing aids,

- 82 -

computer-based voice communication software programs such as Skype, Ventrilo, etc. allow the user to converse via PC. A telephone is not needed, and the user can easily adjust the speaker volume to be louder. Skype has a video component, which is useful for those who can speechread and/or have mild enough hearing loss that the visual information enhances their communication. E-mail is very common now, and is an excellent alternative to teletype machines. Live chat over the Internet and instant messaging on a PC or cell phone have the additional advantage of real-time communication without the need to wait for a reply, something that is necessary with e-mails. "Smart" cell phones such as BlackBerry, Palm, iPhone, etc. can send/receive text messages and e-mails, and can connect to the Internet.

Alerting devices

Many hearing aid users do not wear their hearing aids when they go to bed or shower. Electronic and other types of devices can alert them to sounds they cannot hear in both everyday and emergency situations. Electronic devices may also use airstream and kinesthetic stimuli. Other means include hearing-ear dogs trained to alert their owner to sounds. This is a good idea since dogs hear at four times the distance as humans, locate sounds faster, hear higher frequencies, and also make fine companions. Alerting devices can signal a doorbell ring or door knock, a smoke alarm, a fire alarm, or an alarm clock. Phones can have built-in lights that flash when they ring. Fire alarms can have a bright strobe light to provide a visual signal to the hearing-impaired person. Some also have transducers that shake the bed to awaken the person. Systems with sensors and feedback devices allow monitoring of a whole house from one room.

Assistive listening systems

Child care, preschool, and classroom settings are notoriously noisy and have high levels of reverberation. For children in these settings, frequency modulation (FM) systems are very helpful in terms of optimizing children's abilities to hear, to learn language, and especially to recognize speech, promoting greater educational success. Research finds the best outcomes are attained when FM systems are used early in the process of fitting the child for amplification. The enhancement of hearing afforded by the combination of the two increases attention span, decreases distractibility, and increases sound and speech awareness. Evaluation, selection, fitting, and dispensing of FM systems are functions unique to the province of a certified audiologist. FM and infrared systems can deliver enhanced speech signals in classrooms when teachers wear wireless microphones or transmitters. FM systems are more available and more widely used due to the Americans with Disabilities Act (ADA), The Individuals with Disabilities Education Act (IDEA), and Section 504 of the Rehabilitation Act.

Changes to the Rehabilitation Act that affect federal employees and the public

The Rehabilitation Act of 1973 was first amended in 1986 to stipulate that electronic and information technology created, obtained, managed, or used by the Federal Government must be accessible to people with disabilities. This updated part of the law, called Section 508, was amended in 1998, was signed that year by President Clinton, and took effect in 2001, making technology substantially more accessible to the disabled. The new standards are binding and enforceable, whereas the earlier ones were not. They specify that federal employees and members of the public with disabilities must have access to and use of information and services comparable to those available to non-disabled federal employees and members of the public. Included in the law's requirements for access to and use of information and services are compatibility with hearing aids, cochlear implants, assistive listening devices, and TTY/TDD services; adjustable volume controls for outputs; and product interfaces with available hearing technologies.

Assistive technology related to places of worship

It is often overlooked that most churches, synagogues, temples, etc. are acoustically horrible for those with hearing loss. They are often difficult even for people with normal hearing. They are usually large, open spaces with many hard, reflective surfaces that cause reverberation. Religious institutions are not bound by the Americans with Disabilities Act (ADA). Therefore, the National Organization on Disability (NOD) initiated a nationwide, multi-denominational program called "2,000 by the year 2000— Accessible Congregation Campaign." Its purpose is to remove or decrease barriers to people with hearing impairment, visual impairment, impaired mobility, chronic illnesses, and other disabilities that prevent or discourage them from participating in their religious institutions. In the area of assistive hearing technology, more and more audiologists are contributing their knowledge, training, and expertise to this and other programs to help members once again belong and contribute to their congregations if they have drifted away due to hearing loss.

Assistive technology relevant to the elderly population

Although some AT devices work with hearing aids, others stand alone, meaning they are not coupled with hearing aids. Such flexibility is most beneficial to elderly individuals. AT devices are often "gateways" to more comprehensive AR programs that could include hearing aids in the future. In other cases, the degree of hearing loss combined with the individual's lifestyle create higher listening demands, and it is seen right away that the individual will need a variety of technologies to supplement hearing aids. Elderly individuals may prefer AT devices over hearing aids sometimes or always. Those with fixed/limited incomes appreciate the lower cost of AT. Many find hearing aids stigmatizing as signs of aging, making them feel less competent and independent. Often, those successful with AT become more interested in trying hearing aids. Eventually, they find that a comprehensive AR program improves communication, increases competence and independence, decreases isolation, improves work and social life, and therefore provides a sense of empowerment.

Considerations for infants and children with hearing loss

Onset of hearing loss during infancy interferes with a normal rate and degree of language acquisition, as hearing is the main modality for learning language and speech. If parents select an auditory approach rather than signing and/or speech-reading, they must ensure the child is exposed to the highest possible quality of auditory stimulation. Giving a hearing-impaired child consistent hearing signals using only hearing aids is inadequate. Also, the child's environments of home, day-care, and school contain much noise, distorting speech sound signals. Children with even mild hearing loss usually have academic problems. FM systems in conjunction with hearing aids amplify and clarify signals. Early diagnosis and intervention

- 84 -

make big differences in a child's language development. Babies diagnosed with hearing loss by six months of age are expected to have language acquisition equivalent to their hearing peers by the age of five years. FM or sound field amplification systems provide significant benefits.

How an individual with hearing loss interested in AT can get help

The many AT applications and choices available can be confusing and intimidating, as can the technical specifications. An individual who has a hearing loss and is interested in using AT should first have a communication needs assessment conducted by an audiologist, who will consider the person's hearing loss, perception of hearing needs, and available technologies to choose the most appropriate device if the use of one is justified. A good source to find a certified audiologist is ASHA, which furthers the prevention, early identification, treatment, and rehabilitation of children and adults with hearing loss by audiologists with ASHA's Certification in Clinical Competence (CCC-A). This goal is consistent with the U.S. Public Health Services' national Healthy People 2020 initiative.

Services and procedures included in ASHA's definition of aural rehabilitation

The five components of services and procedures in ASHA's definition of aural rehabilitation include (but are not limited to):
- Identification and Evaluation of Sensory Capabilities; (II) Interpretation of Results, Counseling and Referral; (III) Intervention for Communication Difficulties; (IV) Re-evaluation of the Client's Status; and (V) Evaluation and Modification of the

Intervention Program. The details of (I) Identification and Evaluation of Sensory Capabilities are: (A) identifying and evaluating the degree of hearing loss, including assessment, regular periodic monitoring, and re-evaluation of the client's auditory capabilities; (B) monitoring non-auditory sensory capabilities relative to receptive and expressive communication; (C) evaluating, fitting, and monitoring auditory aids, and monitoring other sensory aids in various communicative environments, including all group and individual amplification systems and supplemental devices; and (D) evaluating and monitoring the acoustic properties of the communicative environments in which the person with the hearing loss interacts.

ASHA's definition of AR, and Interpretation of Results, Counseling and Referral

First, the audiologist interprets the findings of the audiological evaluation for the client, and for his or her family members, employer, teachers, caregiver(s), and significant others who communicate with the client. Second, the audiologist counsels and guides the client, his or her family members, employer, teachers, caregiver(s), and significant others about the communicative, educational, psychological, and social effects of hearing loss. Third, the audiologist counsels and guides parents and/or caregivers about available educational choices, choosing educational programs, and expediting cognitive and communicative development. Fourth, the audiologist provides individual and/or family counseling concerning understanding and accepting the hearing loss, managing problematic listening conditions, promoting effectual attitudes and strategies regarding communication, modifying communicative behavior consistent with such attitudes and strategies, and fostering the independent management of communication-related problems the client may encounter. Fifth, the audiologist makes referrals for other services that may be indicated, such as educational, medical, psychological, and social services.

Proposed Minimal Competencies for persons providing aural rehabilitation

Those who provide aural rehabilitation should show a basic knowledge of general psychology, sociology, anatomy and physiology, zoology, general physics, and mathematics. They should also show a basic understanding of communication processes, including: (A) the anatomical, neurological, and physiological foundations of normal hearing, language, and speech development and use; (B) the physical foundations and processes of hearing and speech production and perception, such as (a) acoustics, (b) phonology, (c) physiological and acoustic phonetics, (d) the processes of perception, and (e) psychoacoustics; and (C) the linguistic and psycholinguistic factors that are relevant to the normal development of hearing, speech, and language and their normal use, such as (a) descriptive linguistics, historical linguistics, sociolinguistics, and the linguistics of urban language, (b) the psychology of language, (c) psycholinguistics, (d) acquisition of language and speech, and (e) verbal learning and verbal behavior.

Evaluation of personal and group amplification and other sensory aids

Persons who provide aural rehabilitation must be able to take and analyze measurements of the properties of amplification systems. They must be able to make and interpret behavioral measurements of client performance using amplification. They must be able to fit and adjust amplification devices. They must be able to plan and deliver orientation programs addressing the use of hearing aids to improve communication. They must be able to assess and describe how the use of amplification affects communicative functioning. They must be able to evaluate and describe how environmental variables influence communication functions. They must be able to describe sensory aids and telecommunication devices available for people with hearing impairment. They must be able to devise and execute programs for the monitoring and maintenance of personal and group systems of amplification. They must be able to delineate existing alternatives for the purposes of choosing and acquiring hearing aids.

Psychological, social, educational, and vocational ramifications

Regarding hearing conservation and the prevention of communication problems, ASHA requires those providing AR to be able to devise and execute programs for the periodic monitoring of hearing abilities and communicative functioning. They must be able to describe the effects of the use of hearing aids, environmental factors, and causes of trauma on residual auditory function. They must be able to assess measurements of acoustic conditions in the environment relative to their effects on communication abilities. Regarding implications of hearing impairment for the individual's psychological, social, educational, and vocational status, they must be able to describe features of normal psychosocial development and how hearing loss affects it. They must be able to explain how hearing loss affects learning and education. They must be able to describe educational programming systems and methods in general. They must be able to identify the need for and availability of psychological, social, educational, and vocational counseling.

Communicative-rehabilitative case management

Those providing AR must be able to describe different interviewing and interpersonal communication techniques. They must possess skills related to interviewing and interacting with individuals with communication impairments and their family members. They must be able to plan and administer public information and in-service programs for professionals and other concerned parties on preventing, identifying, assessing, and managing hearing loss and ensuing communication disorders. They must be able to devise and administer parent education programs for managing hearing loss and communication disorders in their children. They must also be able to create and implement public information and in-service programs for parents, professionals, and other involved parties on preventing, identifying, assessing, and managing auditory problems alone. They must show they can communicate case information to allied professionals and others working with communicatively-impaired clients. They must be able to plan and implement service programs with allied professionals serving the hearing-impaired.

"Aural Rehabilitation" as the most appropriate terminology

First, the Committee states that their revised definition of AR renders this term less restrictive than the one found in their 1973 Position Statement. Second, the term "Audiologic Habilitation" is judged too restrictive because it refers specifically to audiology, which could limit both service delivery and supervision to audiologists alone. This is at odds with both current practice and ASHA policy. Third, the term "habilitation" implies establishing or replacing skills instead of building upon existing skills. This contradicts the research on both normal language development and language development in the hearing-impaired. The term "rehabilitation" is more accurate, as aural rehabilitation modifies communication skills that already exist in some way. Moreover, the term "habilitation" ignores the fact that many auditory disorders are sustained by adults with established communicative skill sets. Finally, third-party payers such as insurance companies and others not familiar with audiological terminology understand "rehabilitation" better than "habilitation."

Multidisciplinary nature of AR as a clinical service and its implications for training

AR services demand specialized skills, but these skills cover a wide range of disciplines. Audiologists, speech-language pathologists, teachers of the hearing impaired, physicians, counselors, and psychologists can all be involved in AR services. Thus, training should be across disciplines, and may use courses in different departments. ASHA's Proposed Minimal Competencies can be used as guidelines for evaluating, selecting, and monitoring coursework and clinical experience. Also, a competency orientation can give training programs better indices for future employers regarding what to expect of graduates, raising program credibility. It may also improve student performance because employers are less likely to have unrealistic expectations of trainers, and trainers can better meet workplace demands. This enhances service delivery, efficacy, and job satisfaction. Concerns about the time and cost of competency-based training overlook the fact that pre-service training alone is insufficient. The comprehensive service delivery reflected in the Proposed Minimal Competencies depends largely on continuing education.

Research findings related to the need for continuing education

Numerous studies have found that in-service AR training is needed and useful. A survey found that many speech-language pathologists did not receive adequate training in working with hearing-impaired children, and gained this knowledge through in-service training and outside reading. In fact, 95% of SLPs surveyed felt professional continuing education would benefit their competence in this area. While the need for continuing education is clear, ASHA's Committee on Rehabilitative Audiology feels the best delivery method(s) warrants additional study. Detailed study of this issue was also recommended by the National Commission on Allied Health Education. A study asked SLPs and teachers working with the hearing-impaired to rate their confidence in different competency areas after receiving intensive in-service training. Competencies were categorized as direct service provision or providing in-service training to others. Participants felt more confident about providing direct services after training than about training others. This supports the usefulness of providing competency-based in-service training.

Consumer and professional needs in aural rehabilitation

Three issues related to consumer and professional needs in AR identified through research are: there is not enough public information about AR services and the importance and efficacy of these services in neither urban nor rural communities; audiologists and speech-language pathologists do not always offer programs in hearing aid orientation to clients with hearing loss; and most AR programs do not specify goals and objectives related to counseling, even though research finds that counseling has a significant impact on clients' prognoses. The ASHA Committee on Rehabilitative Audiology believes that modifying their training and certification to address consumer needs and concerns about hearing aid orientation and counseling would increase the profession's credibility, and would thereby also increase customer satisfaction with its services. These outcomes would then address the professional issue of a lack of public information about the profession, its role, and its impact on health.

Training and certification standards

After examining the Association's existing standards for training and certification, the ASHA Committee on Rehabilitative Audiology has come to the conclusion that these standards do not mandate enough training for either audiologists or speech-language pathologists for them to meet the Committee's proposed minimal competencies. For example, there are many audiologists whose credentials satisfy the existing standards, but who would be hard pressed to show that they have even the most basic understanding of language development or language intervention, which have long been the province of speech-language pathologists. In the same vein, there are many speech-language pathologists who would be unable to show competence in areas such as the ramifications of audiological assessments or knowledge about amplification systems. The Committee opines that the profession is charged with the job of identifying specifically how the current standards can be made to correspond with the minimal competencies the Committee has proposed.

Recommendations the profession should study toward the end of aligning training and certification standards

The ASHA Committee on Rehabilitative Audiology has recommended that the profession study the following six issues at length and in depth toward the end of making ASHA's training and certification standards consistent with the Committee's proposed minimal competencies for aural rehabilitation: (1) aural rehabilitation's unique role as an area of service delivery that crosses disciplines; (2) the need to define roles clearly in providing aural rehabilitation to avoid service duplications and increase cost effectiveness; (3) the effectiveness of balancing expectations for training between pre-service and continuing education; (4) the needs of consumers that constitute the basis for the Committee's formulation of the proposed minimal competencies; (5) the need for ASHA to formulate an official policy to address the needs of consumers and professionals expressed herein; and (6) the possible desirability and/or usefulness of confronting the question of who should provide aural rehabilitation services by stipulating which services should be provided.

Hearing aids

Roughly 5 to 10% of hearing disorders in adults are treatable medically or surgically. In children, the percentage is higher due to the prevalence of otitis media in this age group. A hearing evaluation determines whether hearing loss is treatable medically or surgically. If not, additional testing can determine if the individual would benefit from a hearing aid(s). An ASHA-certified audiologist can find and provide the best type and model of aid for a client. For bilateral hearing loss, the audiologist may advise two aids. This improves overall hearing, facilitates listening with background noise, and helps localize sound direction. All hearing aids have a microphone, amplifier circuits, a receiver, and batteries. Styles are in-the-canal (tiny, cosmetically unobtrusive, offer some listening advantages); in-the-ear (larger than canal aids and easier for some people to handle); and behind-the-ear (connected by clear tubing to an earmold, better for children for safety and physical growth reasons).

Today, the styles of hearing aids most frequently sold are in-the-canal and in-the-ear. There is a bone conduction hearing aid for people with no outer ear or ear canal, which happens with congenital atresia. This aid has a headband and a bone vibrator, enabling hearing by bone conduction. For individuals with unilateral hearing loss, there are hearing aids that redirect sound coming to the affected ear over to the good ear. This is known as CROS, or Contralateral Routing of Sound. For people who are deaf in one ear and hard of hearing in the other, the Bi-CROS works the same way as the CROS to redirect sound from the deaf ear, but also has a regular hearing aid for the hard-of-hearing ear. It combines both signals and sends them to the ear with residual hearing. For people with hearing losses who wear eyeglasses, hearing aids can be built into the temples of the glasses.

Conventional analog, analog programmable, and digital programmable hearing aid technologies

Conventional analog hearing aids are made with a certain frequency response according to the user's audiogram. Manufacturers install settings given by audiologists. This is the least costly technology and helps many kinds of hearing loss, but does amplify all sounds, including background noise. Analog programmable aids have microchips, enabling programming of settings for various environments, such as quiet or noisy settings and small or large spaces. Using a computer, the audiologist programs the aid for different circumstances based on the individual's hearing loss profile, degree of speech comprehension, and loudness tolerance range. Some aids save several programs so users can switch settings as environments change. These cost more, but last longer and improve situation-specific hearing. Digital programmable aids convert sound waves to digital signals. A chip identifies and removes noise to produce a clear signal. Programming is more flexible to match the individual's hearing loss pattern. These are the most expensive, but offer many advantages.

Conventional analog hearing aids have the advantages of being the least expensive and having a wide range of applications in that they can address different types of hearing loss. They have the disadvantage of amplifying all sounds, meaning the competing environmental noise is amplified along with the relevant speech signals. Analog programmable aids have the advantage that their settings can be programmed for different listening situations. Analog programmable hearing aids that save several programs not only allow the user to switch channels or settings according to the particular sound environment, but can also be reprogrammed by the audiologist if the user's hearing acuity and/or needs change. Another advantage is that they tend to last longer than conventional analog aids. Their disadvantage is that they cost more than conventional analog aids. Digital programmable aids have the advantages of more precise fit, noise reduction, control of feedback (whistling noises),

management of discomfort from loudness, and better ability to be programmed.

Special optional features available in hearing aids and their advantages

One special feature that is an available option in hearing aids is directional microphones. Hearing aids normally pick up sounds at about the same level from all directions. With a directional microphone, the aid can be switched from the normal, omnidirectional setting to a unidirectional setting. For a user in a face-to-face conversation, the other speaker's voice is amplified, while sounds behind the user are minimized. This helps with background interference. A second special feature is direct audio input. Some hearing aids can be connected to a remote wireless microphone, an FM assistive listening system, a TV, a computer, a CD or tape player, a radio, or another device. This helps users hear from a great variety of sources. A third special feature is a telephone switch. This turns off the aid's microphone, eliminating both background noise and feedback (whistling) from the microphone. This facilitates telephone conversations, and can also be used in public places with FM or loop induction systems.

Procuring hearing aids, special features relevant to lifestyle, and health plan coverage

Some people are tempted to order hearing aids online or by mail to save money. This bypasses many important audiologist services. Even if an audiologist conducts an audiological and hearing aid evaluation, specifies the type and model needed, and the client orders it, s/he still misses out on fitting, hearing aid orientation and adjustment, aural rehabilitation services, and medical referral(s), if indicated. Even a rare conscientious client who had evaluation, ordered the aid, and returned to the audiologist to pursue these services could have less satisfactory results than if the certified audiologist dispensed the aid. The latter would avoid problems such as defective/damaged units, receiving the wrong model, etc. People who use the telephone a lot and people who attend many events in theaters, auditoriums, churches, etc. should get aids with telecoil/"T" switches. Medicaid must cover children's hearing aids, and it often covers adults'. Medicare does not. Some health plans cover part or all of the aid's cost, but many do not.

Adjustment to hearing aids

New users of hearing aids, especially those whose hearing loss existed for a long time before getting aids, often find all the sounds they can hear distracting. This is because they have not heard them for so long and are not used to them. Some users even hear sounds they have never heard before. Depending on the type of aid, background noises can sound distractingly loud. Users also often find that the sound of their own voice seems too loud. It can take weeks or months to adjust to hearing aids. The audiologist helps by giving the user hearing aid orientation, and also by providing aural rehabilitation if needed, optimizing communication with hearing aids. In the event that the user cannot adjust, s/he may wish to try a different make/model. Most state laws require trial periods, and most audiologists offer these even if they are not legally required. Charges for fitting and custom earmolds may be nonrefundable.

Cochlear implants

Cochlear implants can restore partial hearing to the deaf. A cochlear implant

recipient can usually understand the speech of people they know without supplemental visual information. However, cochlear implant patients do have more trouble understanding people and sounds unfamiliar to them. Children who get a cochlear implant after age two have better speech perception than those who get cochlear implants as adults. Other variables affecting perception with implants include: the patient's age at the onset of deafness; how long the person was deaf before cochlear implantation; the age of the patient at the time of cochlear implantation; how long the patient has been using the cochlear implant; whether a child's deafness was congenital or acquired in etiology; and whether a child had acquired language before becoming deaf. Children with postlingual deafness adapt more quickly to cochlear implants and have better outcomes than children with prelingual deafness.

Contrasting the acuity of speech perception by computer voice recognition systems with that of human beings

Inherent in all speech sounds is noise, or irrelevant components of the acoustic signal that can interfere with an accurate perception of the linguistically relevant parts. Computerized voice recognition systems, such as those currently used in many automated phone systems, can function quite well when they are conditioned to a particular speaker's voice and are used in a quiet environment. However, when circumstances are truer to real life and more noise is present, these systems often have trouble recognizing many words spoken by humans. In contrast, human beings listening while the same level of noise interference is present can typically understand most or all of what is being said. This is attributable to the human ability to adjust for variations in speech sounds and to use the surrounding context to deduce the correct identity of unclear signals.

King-Kopetzky syndrome

King-Kopetzky syndrome is when someone has normal hearing but has trouble understanding speech when there is background noise. It is also called Obscure Auditory Dysfunction (OAD) and Auditory Disability with Normal Hearing (ADN). Some people with no audiological knowledge may colloquially (albeit inaccurately) refer to this syndrome as "wall deafness." Researchers have found that King-Kopetzky syndrome can be attributed to a variety of conditions. Some researchers have divided patients with King-Kopetzky syndrome into subgroups based on the conditions they found. These conditions include: middle ear dysfunction; mild inner ear dysfunction; medial olivocochlear efferent system dysfunction; multiple auditory dysfunctions; psychological problems that occur in the absence of auditory defects; auditory defects and psychological problems combined; genetic factors such as autosomal dominant inheritance; and unknown conditions (researchers could not identify any conditions that might contribute to the syndrome). In 2003, researchers Stephens, Zhao & Espeso speculated that this condition could be an early stage of late-onset familial hearing impairment.

Categories of research methods used to study speech perception

Speech perception research can be behavioral, computational, or neurophysiological. Behavioral research requires active participation by the subjects, who are presented with speech sound stimuli and asked to make and report conscious decisions about these. Some examples are similarity ratings, identification tests, and discrimination tests. Computational research uses computer models to simulate speech perception. For example, computer models can help explore how the brain processes speech sounds to extract acoustic cues, and how word recognition and other high-level processes use information from heard speech. Thanks to recent technological advances, neurophysiological research can also measure brain responses to speech stimuli. Neural responses, unlike behavioral responses, do not require conscious attention to stimuli. In addition, the brain is often more sensitive to stimuli than behavioral responses indicate. Thus, a subject may not react behaviorally to a difference in two sounds during a discrimination test, but the brain will react to that difference..

Neurophysiological methods of speech perception research

Some neurophysiological methods of speech perception research include event-related potentials, near infrared spectroscopy (NIRS), and magnetoencephalography. Mismatch negativity is a significant response that can be elicited with event-related potentials when a speech stimulus varies acoustically from a previous one. An advantage is the ability to measure lower-level auditory processes separately from higher-level ones. Behavioral responses can proceed from conscious processes that developed later. They can also be influenced by factors such as spelling, and can disguise the subject's capacity to identify sounds on the basis of lower-level acoustic distributions. Brain responses, on the other hand, are more direct, and need not be conscious. Thus, infants can be tested neurophysiologically, which is an advantage when language acquisition is being studied. Another advantage of separating lower- and higher-level processes in this kind of testing is that it enables concrete evaluation of theoretical topics, such as the question of whether a human speech perception module exists or whether some acoustic invariance underlies some speech sound recognition.

Motor theory of speech perception

The motor theory of speech perception posits that the processes used to decode the articulatory encoding of speech and the ones used to produce speech are the same. This theory was pioneered by Alvin Liberman et al. They originally hypothesized that we perceive speech not by the sound patterns we hear but by the vocal tract movements made in producing them. They theorized that the speech motor system is used to both produce and perceive speech. Liberman later revised "perceptual units from articulatory movements" to "brain commands to the articulatory mechanisms," and then to "intended articulatory gestures" (movements) occurring at a linguistic, prevocal level. This theory has been modified many times. A number of hypotheses have been discarded as new research disproved them. The theory has been criticized so often on so many grounds that it has never enjoyed much success. However, the recent discovery of mirror neurons has prompted renewed interest in it. Mirror neurons connect the production and perception of motor activity, including the motor activity of the vocal tract.

McGurk effect

The McGurk effect is that when one sees one sound being produced and hears another sound at the same time, the visual information influences the auditory information. When subjects hear /ba/ but simultaneously see a video of someone producing /ga/, they may perceive neither phoneme but rather something in between, such as /da/. This supports the motor theory because this theory holds that speech is defined by its manner of production. Therefore, information that is not auditory should be included in percepts of speech, even though it may still be subjectively experienced as sound. Other support for this idea includes the finding that people can understand speech amidst surrounding noise if they can see the speaker. Therefore, visual information does make a difference. Another finding that supports this theory is that people can hear syllables better with haptic information (if they can feel the vocal apparatus during production by using their sense of touch, for example).

Direct realist theory of speech

The direct realist theory of speech perception is part of the larger direct realism theory. It maintains that perception gives us direct consciousness of our environment by accomplishing direct recovery of the distal, or far, source of what we perceive. Carol Fowler has been a primary proponent of direct realism in speech perception. This theory identifies objects of perception as vocal tract movements. Motor theory began the same way, but evolved to identifying intended movements, which direct realist theory rejects. It also rejects the abstract concept of phonemes as objects of perception. This theory contends that vocal tract movements are dictated by information within the acoustic signal, and states that this enables our perception. The motor theory postulates a specialized decoding process. Because this theory finds that articulatory gestures producing various speech sounds are units of speech perception, it eliminates the issue of lack of invariance.

Dominic Massaro's fuzzy-logical model of speech perception

Massaro's fuzzy-logical model of speech perception postulates that our memory of speech sounds is probabilistic. Massaro claims we remember prototypes (descriptions) of perceptual linguistic units such as phonemes. Prototypes contain various features. These features are not binary or digital (not "on/off" or "right/wrong," for example). Rather, their values are "fuzzy" according to the probability that they belong in a specific category. Thus, our perception of what sound we heard relative to a speech signal depends on how well it matches the values of certain prototypes. Our final perception of what sound we heard is derived from multiple information sources and features. This includes non-auditory information. For example, visual information can also have an influence. When computer models have been used to test this theory's predictions of how speech sounds will be categorized, it was found that they correlate with categorizing behaviors demonstrated by human listeners.

Speech perception theory of acoustic landmarks and distinctive features

The theory of acoustic landmarks and distinctive features was proposed in 2002 by Kenneth N. Stevens of the Massachusetts Institute of Technology (MIT). This theory focuses on the relationship between auditory characteristics and phonological features. The theory posits that listeners seek out certain elements that occur in the sound spectrum of any speech signal they hear. These occurrences give information about the articulatory movements which produced them, and are known as acoustic landmarks. The movements are limited to the articulatory abilities of human beings, and listeners are responsive to the auditory elements corresponding with these movements. In this theory, there is no such thing as a lack of invariance. Distinctive phonological features are based on the acoustic characteristics of the landmarks. Groups, or "bundles," of such distinctive features indicate specific phonetic

segments such as phonemes, syllables, and words.

Exemplar theory of speech perception

Exemplar theory differs from motor theory, direct realist theory, the fuzzy-logical model, and the theory of acoustic landmarks and distinctive features in that in these other approaches variation across speakers is considered noise, and word recognition is not related to speaker recognition. Exemplar models hold that listeners store memories of individual speech sound occurrences and compare new speech stimuli they hear against these memories for identification. In this theory, listeners also store memories of individual speakers' sounds, enabling them to identify a speaker upon hearing that person again. Research by Johnson conducted in 2005 found that listeners identify signals more accurately when they are familiar with the speaker, which supports exemplar theory. One challenge to the theory is that our memories may not have space to store every utterance we ever hear. A second challenge is the question of whether we store our own articulatory movements as well as those of other speakers when we reproduce what we hear.

Stuttering

It is estimated that 1% of persons in the United States have stuttered. The usual age of onset is 2 to 6 years old. Boys are 3 times as likely to stutter than girls are. The onset of stuttering after the adolescent years is extremely rare. An estimated 60% of those who stutter recover spontaneously without treatment. However, older children and adults may start stuttering again after an initial recovery. Stuttering tends to run in families, and the familial incidence is higher if there is a female in the family who stutters. Individuals with developmental disorders and neurological impairments have a higher incidence of stuttering. A lower incidence of stuttering is seen in hearing-impaired individuals.

Persons who stutter and their family members are not likely to have a psychiatric or personality disorder.

Stuttering is a disorder in the fluency of speech. Stuttering is diagnosed when:

- The dysfluency rate of all types of dysfluencies of spoken words exceeds 5%
- The frequency of part-word repetitions, speech sound prolongations, and broken words occurs more than in 2% of speech
- The duration of dysfluencies is more than 1 second
- The presence of associated motor behaviors, such as excessive tensing of the facial muscles, mouth tremors, grimacing, rapid blinking, hand wringing, foot stomping, or foot tapping
- Associated breathing abnormalities, such as poor breath control during speaking and abnormal breath holding
- The presence of negative emotions and avoidance behaviors: Many persons who stutter will develop a behavior to disguise or avoid stuttering. They may completely avoid certain situations, such as public speaking. They may substitute words or avoid situations in which certain words have to be used. The prospect of stuttering may produce anxiety, hostility, depression, or passive behaviors.

Dysfluencies that make up the core behaviors of stuttering

Broken words: placing unusually long pauses between words (I want to play with mom– {pause} –my.)

Incomplete sentences: production of incomplete phrases (I want to play. . . I want to . . My mommy will play with me.)

Interjections: placement of sounds, words, or phrases extraneously into speech (I want, um, to play with mommy.)

Pauses: placing unusually long gaps of silence or nonverbal gaps within sentences or phrases (I want {pause} to play with mommy.)

Repetitions: saying a word, part of a word, or a phrase more than once (I wa-wa-wa want to play with mommy.)

Revisions: changing a wording of a sentence, which does not alter the sentences meaning (I want to play: I will throw ball with mommy.)

Sound prolongation: pronouncing a sound for an unusually long duration (I want to play with mmmmmommy.)

Silent prolongation: holding the articulation position of a sound without vocal production

Stuttering is more likely to occur with consonants, the first sound or syllables of words, or the first word of a sentence or clause. Stuttering is most likely to occur with long, complex sentences. Words that are used less frequently are more likely to induce stuttering. Preschool children more often stutter on function words (e.g., conjunctions, pronouns) than content words (e.g., verbs, nouns). Older children and adults stutter more often on content words. Preschool children who stutter are more likely to produce whole-word repetitions than adolescents or adults are.

Stuttering and strong environmental controls

1. The frequency of stuttering can be reduced by repeated oral readings of printed material. This effect, called adaptation, is not sustained. If given the same material in another setting, stuttering will again occur.
2. Most persons will stutter on the same word or position of a sound when repeating oral readings. This effect is called consistency and tends to be a sustained phenomenon. This effect will be repeated among different trials.
3. Words pronounced correctly can be made to stutter. By blocking out the stuttered word of an oral reading, the adjacent word is then stuttered. This phenomenon is called adjacency.
4. The larger the audience, the more stuttering occurs.

Causes of stuttering

Genetic theory: Given that stuttering has a high familial prevalence, some researchers believe that it is genetically driven. However, given the rates of occurrences, a single-gene theory cannot yet be supported with clinical evidence.

Neurological theories: Some researchers believe that stuttering is due to a dysfunction of laryngeal muscle activity, an abnormality of the speech centers of the brain, a brain auditory processing disorder, or a dysfunction in the auditory feedback mechanism of the brain.

Learning and conditioning theory: Studies suggest that stuttering may be a product of certain environmental factors, such as: avoidance behavior, overwhelming speech expectations, or learned behaviors.

Psychosocial theory: In this theory, stuttering is thought to be a psychological disorder or neurosis, like anxiety and depression, whereby the child is undergoing a subconscious psychological conflict.

Stuttering treatment

The assessment of stuttering should include interviews with clients, caregivers, and teachers to develop a case history. Pay attention to caregiver/teacher speech interactions.

Determine the frequency, types, and variability of dysfluencies. Identify any associated motor behaviors, negative emotions, or avoidance behaviors. The Behavior Assessment Battery can be helpful in determining any negative emotional behaviors.

Treatment of stuttering employs either direct or indirect techniques. Indirect treatment involves the modification of the subject's environment, not the direct modification of speech. This is typically done by instructing parents to speak slowly and relaxed when addressing a stuttering child. Theoretically, the child will learn to modify his speech by passive listening. This technique is not effective in more severe stuttering and in older children and adults. In fact, this technique has not been favored by a consensus of speech experts in its effectiveness for even mild stuttering children. Direct treatment involves intentional alteration of speech patterns.

Stuttering modification therapy

Stuttering modification therapy: The goal with this type of therapy is not to eliminate stuttering but to reduce its frequency, avoidance behaviors, and negative emotions associated with it. This therapy encompasses four stages:
1. Identification: The subject learns to identify the characteristics of his stuttering and the behaviors and emotions connected with it in various situations.

2. Desensitization: The subject discloses that he stutters and is made to voluntarily stutter in various situations.
3. Modification: The subject is directed to use easier and more fluent stuttering. This is achieved by using cancellations (stopping after a stuttered word, pausing, and saying the word again); pull outs (stopping in midstutter, pausing, and saying the word slowly with deliberate articulation); and preparatory sets (anticipating difficult words and using more fluent stuttering).
4. Stabilization: The subject uses the first three stages of the therapy and applies them to all situations.

Fluency shaping, fluency reinforcement, and altered auditory feedback therapies

Fluency shaping therapy: This therapy focuses on production of normal fluent speech as opposed to more fluent stuttering as in stuttering modification therapy. Teaching airflow management and speech rate reduction through syllable prolongation achieves this. Once this is mastered, the subject is trained in normal speech emotional intonation (prosody) and speech rate.

Fluency reinforcement therapy: Typically used in young children, this form of therapy models slow, relaxed, and fluent speech. Through the use of pictures and play items, children are rewarded for using fluent speech.

Altered auditory feedback: Delayed auditory feedback devices delay the subjects voice to their ears by a fraction of a second. Masking auditory feedback devices produce sounds that fool the subject into thinking the vocal folds are vibrating. These techniques are very effective in reducing stuttering. However,

delayed auditory feedback appears to be more effective in producing more sustained results than masking auditory feedback is.

Cluttering

Cluttering is a fluency disorder caused by disorganized language. Speech is difficult to understand because of abnormalities of speech rhythm, rapid rate of speech, large number of dysfluencies, production of spoonerisms, disorganized thought processes, and lack of awareness of speech deficits. Reading and writing disabilities are common. There is no abnormality in the mechanism of articulation, but rather in the organization of thoughts. Although the exact cause is unclear, genetic factors and brain dysfunctions are being studied. Treatment is difficult because the subjects have little awareness, but typically focuses on reducing the rate of speech and speech planning. Treatment directed at increasing the subject's awareness of abnormal speech are employed and may include the use of auditory devices.

Disorders of voice resonance

Hypernasality refers to sounds produced with excessive nasal quality due to a dysfunction of the velopharyngeal mechanism. Air escapes through the nasal passages because of incomplete closure at the nasopharyngeal junction. The most common causes of Hypernasality is a cleft palate, velopharyngeal insufficiency due to decreased mass or weakness of the muscles of the velum (children who have had tonsillectomies may have decreased muscle functioning of the velum), and functional causes like bad habits or deafness.

Hyponasality refers to the absence of nasal sounds when appropriate. The /m/, /n/, and /ng/ sounds are pronounced incorrectly due to the absence of air

- 97 -

leaving the nose during speech. The appropriate nasal sounds are often substituted with /b/, /d/, and /g/ sounds. Hyponasality is typically caused by nasal or nasopharyngeal obstruction due to deviated septum, severe nasal congestion, nasal polyps, or enlarged adenoids.

Phonation disorders resulting from vocal abuse and misuse

Vocal nodules: small, benign growths that develop due to repeated pressure on the vocal folds. These nodules are frequently found in singers. Vocal rest will usually resolve them, and persistence may require surgical intervention.

Granuloma: benign growth that develops typically at the back of the vocal fold. Although the most frequent cause is vocal strain, it can also develop from tracheal instrumentation. These growths cause hoarseness, breathy voice, and constant coughing or clearing of the throat.

Vocal polyps: soft, pedunculated masses that develop on the vocal folds. They can form from medical conditions such as hypothyroidism as well as vocal strain. Vocal rest is the treatment of choice.

Laryngitis: inflammation of the larynx due to vocal cord strain or infections. Vocal rest and alteration of the behaviors causing strain on the folds is the treatment of choice.
Contact ulcers: caused by the forceful closing of the vocal folds. These painful ulcers may also be due to tracheal instrumentation and acid reflux. The offending phonation error can be corrected with speech therapy.

Vocal folds growths that cause phonation disorders

Hemangioma: blood-filled growth in the posterior vocal area typically caused by instrumentation or acid reflux

Leukoplakia: benign, precancerous growth on the surface of vocal structures caused by vocal overuse or irritating substances such as tobacco and alcohol. They appear as white patches in the mouth or anterior vocal folds.

Hyperkaratosis: fleshy growths that occur in the vocal folds considered precancerous. Irritants such as tobacco, alcohol, acid reflux, and vocal strain can be the cause.

Laryngeomalacia: abnormal development of the larynx leading to a floppy cartilage in the epiglottis. This causes turbulent air through the epiglottis producing a rough voice sound. This condition usually requires no treatment, as most children resolve spontaneously by age 3.

Laryngeal papilloma: vocal cord warts caused by the human papilloma virus (HPV). They primarily occur in children and resolve spontaneously around pubescence.

Laryngeal web: a membrane over the glottis. This typically forms due to the consequence of tracheal instrumentation, infection, or injury.

Laryngeal tumors: Both benign and cancerous can cause phonation disorders.

Laryngectomy

Laryngeal cancer is the most common reason for the surgical removal of the voice box. Without vocal cord vibration, the production of well-articulated sounds is very difficult. There are a number of modalities used to restore phonation. External devices are used to produce sounds. The most common external device is the artificial larynx. This is a hand-held apparatus that is pressed against the neck and produces articulated sounds.

Esophageal speech is a method that uses the resonation of the esophagus to produce sounds. Patients recovering from laryngectomies are taught to produce sounds by passing air through the mouth via a method similar to burping or belching. Several words can be produced at a time.

The surgical implantation of speech devices is also done. The most common procedure is the Blom-Singer tracheophageal puncture (TEP). A device is inserted between the trachea and esophagus. When occluded by the patient's finger, the esophagus resonates to produce sounds.

Craniofacial anomalies

Craniofacial anomalies are a group of disorders characterized by the abnormal development of skull and facial bones. These anomalies are most likely caused by genetic defects. The two most common craniofacial anomalies are cleft lip and cleft palate. In these abnormalities, either the top lip or palate does not close completely. There are various levels of severity. Although this abnormality can be surgically treated, children may have significant speech articulation, phonation, and resonance problems. Children with clefts are susceptible to ear infections that may lead to hearing loss and thus causing speech delays. Treatment of resonance disorders when there is an incomplete velopharyngeal closure is difficult and should be considered after surgical intervention. Treatment of clefts should be a part of a multidisciplinary approach with clinicians, caregivers, and teachers.

Craniosynostosis

Craniosynostosis is the abnormal premature fusing of the bones of the skull.

This leads to developmental abnormalities of the head and face bones. Genetic defects cause this anomaly. Children with this abnormality typically have a flat midfacial structure and protruding eyes. The most common disorders associated with craniosynostosis are Apert syndrome and Crouzon syndrome.

Apert syndrome is characterized by a sunken midface, webbed feet and hands, occasional hearing loss, and possible cleft palate with hyponasality.

Crouzon syndrome is characterized by widely spaced eyes, underdevelopment of the maxillary area and jaw, and possible cleft palate. These children typically have hearing loss and hypernasality due to abnormal palatal structures.

Surgical treatment is directed toward advancement of the midface structures and correction of any dental abnormalities. Speech therapy may be best following surgical correction.

Emotional distress

Conversion aphonia: Lack of muscle control of the vocal folds leads to the inability to speak. Persons with this disorder may whisper or produce no sounds at all. After a thorough clinical work up ruling out physical causes, psychotherapy is recommended.

Ventricular dysphonia: The false vocal folds interfere with phonation. The false vocal folds are composed of portions of the arytenoid muscles. There are four known causes of ventricular dysphonia that include obstruction, congenital abnormalities, and overuse syndromes. The fourth cause, the most rare, is due to emotional stress. When the cause is emotional, behavior therapy and psychotherapy are the treatments of choice.

Vocal hyperfunction: Excessive force in the closure of the vocal folds causes hoarseness and vocal fatigue. This disorder is caused by abnormal contraction of the muscles that close the vocal folds and is induced by emotional stress. Yawn-sigh therapy is a technique used to relax the structures of the vocal tract and is used to correct vocal hyperfunction.

Professional Issues

Certification

The current requirements for certification for speech-language pathology were implemented in 2005. All applicants applying after January 1, 2006, must adhere to these requirements regardless of when the coursework for certification was completed. Applicants must possess a master's, doctoral, or appropriate postbaccalaureate degree to apply for certification. Graduate course work and clinical participation must be attended at a program that is approved by the Council on Academic Accreditation in Audiology and Speech-Language Pathology. The graduate degree may be in any area of study, but the applicant must complete a minimum of 75 semester credits in areas pertinent to speech and language pathology. The graduate program will determine which courses are appropriate for study. A transcript will be required from the academic facility to demonstrate that these requirements have been met.

Postgraduate certification

The candidate for certification for speech-language pathology must pass the PRAXIS speech-language certification examination with a passing grade of at least 600. For scores to be considered for certification, the examination must have been taken within 5 years of applying for certification. Candidates must also complete a speech-language pathology clinical fellowship following the completion of all course work and practical supervised hours. There must be 36 weeks of completed full-time clinical practice that includes direct patient contact and all administrative duties. There should be 35 hours per week of clinical work under the auspices of a certified speech-language pathologist. A mentor must directly observe 18 hours of the clinical fellowship. The mentor then uses this observation to submit the candidate's assessment. The candidate should be prepared to verify the clinical hours submitted.

Course work and practical requirements

All applicants are required to complete a minimum of 75 semester or 115 quarter hours of appropriate course work. These hours must include at least 36 semester or 47 quarter hours of graduate level course work. There are four areas of course work required: behavioral science, mathematics, biology, and physiology. The academic program will determine the specific subjects that are required in each area. Candidates for certification must also complete 400 hours of supervised clinical experience in speech-language pathology. The requirement is that 25 hours be observation and 375 hours direct client contact. At least 325 of the required 400 hours must have been completed at the graduate level. The applicant may use 75 hours obtained as an undergraduate to complete the requirements. Supervision of clinical experience must be with a certified speech-language pathologist.

Scope of practice

The practice of speech-language pathology involves:
- Screening, assessment, diagnosis, treatment, and prevention of the following disorders: speech (articulation, fluency, resonance, and voice disorders), language (morphology, phonology, syntax, semantics, and pragmatics) both oral and written, swallowing, and the cognitive aspects of communication

- Screening for hearing loss and providing services to individuals with hearing loss
- Establishing needs for communication and swallowing devices and assisting in the use of those devices
- Client advocating in community and educational programs to promote improvement in speech, language, or swallowing deficits
- Cooperating with families, educators, and other health professionals to provide consultative services on behalf of the client
- Providing specialized services, such as accent training, voice training to transgender clients, and voice training to improve professional standards
- Using instruments to visualize the oral and vocal structures

American Speech-Language-Hearing Association (ASHA)

The American Speech-Hearing-Language Association (ASHA) was formed to adopt and maintain standards of excellence in the practice of speech-language pathology and audiology. Its organization provides credentialing in these two areas of practice. The Certificate of Clinical Competence is required to practice speech-language pathology and audiology in most states. The intention of ASHA is to prepare competent candidates to provide services to speech- and hearing–impaired individuals. It seeks to encourage scientific study to assist in the diagnosis, treatment, and prevention of communication disorders. Practicing speech pathologists rely on ASHA for updated practice standards. The organization advocates for the speech and hearing impaired and works with those organizations that have similar goals. ASHA acts as a legal and administrative supportive body for those within the profession.

The American Speech-Language-Hearing Association (ASHA) has a strict code of behaviors with regard to providing services in speech, language, and hearing. This standard is expected of all certified and noncertified members of ASHA as well as all applicants and candidates for certification.

The four principles of ethics are as followed:
1. Speech pathologists shall maintain the highest regard for the welfare of their clients. They shall not discriminate on any basis, including race, sexual orientation, or gender. Research shall be conducted in a humane and ethical manner.
2. Pathologists should maintain the highest level of clinical competence.
3. Pathologists should not misrepresent the profession to the public by making inaccurate representations about credentials or making false statements in assessment of clients.
4. Pathologists should maintain truthful and honorable relationships with colleagues and clients.

Health Insurance Portability and Accountability Act of 1996 (HIPAA)

The federal government adopted a set of rules protecting the privacy of patients' medical information while allowing the necessary flow of medical information needed to provide adequate care. Although the statue was written in 1996, the final modifications took effect in April 2003. The law sets standards for health plans and health care providers to provide privacy of patient records that are oral, electronic, or paper. Patients may have access to copies of their medical records upon request and be allowed to add corrections when appropriate. Access must be granted within 30 days. Providers must give patients written notification of how their records will be used. Health practitioners are allowed to share medical information among themselves in the treatment of patients. Signed consent must be obtained to share information with third parties. Medical information may not be shared for marketing purposes. All communication with the patients must be private.

Evidence-based practice in treating communication disorders

There is a continuous amount of clinical research in the area of communication disorders. Institutions use research to provide the best methods of practice in speech pathology. It is important to be able to adequately interpret the large amount of research available and to determine which body of evidence is best applied to clinical practice. There are several important factors important in reviewing the validity of a study. The results of the study should be able to stand up to independent confirmation based on the evidence provided. The study should contain experimental controls and should be unbiased. The size of the samples in the study should be large enough that the results did not occur just by chance. The study should provide information that is relevant and practical to the targeted population.

Experimental design

Experiments in medicine and speech pathology are designed to determine the effect of some treatment or procedure. The dependent variable of a design is that effect that has been altered by some factor, namely the independent variable. The experimenter must test the treatment or independent variable in an

environment free of outside biases. These biases are called confounders. For example, when determining the effect of a speech therapy, a subject's lack of ability to understand English may bias the study. The two main categories of experimental designs are group and single-subject designs. Group designs involve randomizing a group to receive the treatment and one that does not. The two groups are then compared for cause and effects. If used properly, group designs are very accurate. However, it can be very difficult to randomize the two groups accurately. Single-subject designs do not use controls. Instead, they follow the extensive effects of treatment on individuals. It is easier to integrate this design into clinical practice; however, it may be difficult to generalize the results to the general population.

Assessing data from a clinical study

A clinical trial or clinical experiment should be assessed for internal and external validity. Internal validity is present if a causal relationship is established between a treatment and an effect. External validity is present if the causal relationship established can hold up among different settings and groups. Evidence-based practice relies on establishing levels of evidence to interpret clinical studies. There are three general categories of clinical evidence.

Class I evidence refers to data obtained from a randomized controlled experiment. This is considered the best category of evidence.

Class II evidence refers to data obtained from nonrandomized trials or case studies. The lack of randomization limits reliability of the data from this class.

Class III evidence refers to data obtained from expert opinions or committees. Data from this class is the weakest because of the lack of control group comparisons.

Scales of measurement used to characterize data in a clinical study

Ordinal scale rates a variable of study based on its classification into ordered qualitative categories. Examples of variables on an ordinal scale are restaurant star rankings and numeric perceptions of pain.

Nominal scale contains categories of variables that have no rankings. Examples of nominal variables are political affiliation and country of origin.

Interval scale classifies variables into quantitative categories; however, the variables are compared on a finite interval scale of measurement. Since there is no true zero point, one cannot make a conclusion of how many times higher a variable is compared to another. An example of an interval measurement is temperature on the Fahrenheit scale.

Ratio scale is similar to an interval scale except that it has true zero points, and with it is possible to make mathematic comparisons of the data. An example of a ratio measurement is the Kelvin scale of temperature.

Descriptive (observational) studies

In quantitative research, the goal is to assess the relationship between a set of variables. In descriptive or observational studies, the variables are not changed or manipulated. The measurement of an outcome is made on an observational basis. Types of descriptive studies are:
- Case study: a collection of data on single subjects
- Prospective/cohort study: a measurement of data at the start of a study and after its conclusion;

for example, studying the effects of cholesterol in a high-fat diet
- Case control/retrospective study: study of a particular attribute in a group and then comparing variables with a group without the attribute (control group)

Experimental or longitudinal studies.

In experimental or longitudinal studies, data are quantified following some intervention. Types of longitudinal studies are:
- Time series: A variable is measured before and after an intervention.
- Crossover design: This is similar to time series except there are two groups compared for the study. One group receives the treatment while the other receives a reference or placebo treatment. This design is to minimize the effect of other variables that may change the outcome of treatment as is often seen with the time series studies.
- Randomized control design: This is like the crossover design. Two groups are used, but the participants of the two groups are randomized.
- Single-blind study In this study, the subjects do not know the group to which they have been randomized.
- Double-blind study: Here, neither the subjects nor the experimenters know which groups are receiving the real treatment and which are receiving placebo.

Validity and reliability that standardized tests should meet to ensure the absence of test bias

Construct validity is the ability of a test to accurately measure an observable trait.

Concurrent validity is the ability of a test to obtain the same measure of results compared to other tests that are already deemed valid.

Content validity is the ability of a test to measure all aspects of an observable trait.

Predictive validity is the ability to predict behavior based on the results of the test.

Test-retest reliability is the consistency of the test to perform the same when given multiple times.

Parallel forms reliability refers to the presence of pretest and posttest forms so that measures of successfulness of a treatment are not biased by memory of test material.

Inter-rater reliability refers to the use of multiple observers to rate the data obtained on a test. This affords more reliability of the data obtained.

Using standardized tests in order to minimize their inherent disadvantages

Attempt to use standardized tests that are norm-referenced. Norm-referenced tests are those in which scores from a sample group of subjects is analyzed such that the individual being tested is compared to a sample of his peers.
- Evaluate the standardized test for validity and reliability.
- Give details for all incorrect responses on the test.
- Use nonstandardized methods to detail language skills if the test demonstrates areas of deficiency.
- Quantify correct and incorrect responses for a particular language skill.
- Devise a specific treatment goal based on information provided by the test.

Follow the progress of the treatment based on targeted language skill goals.

Counseling in audiological services

Traditionally, audiologists never had counseling classes in their graduate courses. Most persons with hearing impairment were not likely to ask about getting hearing aids on their own. Those seeking amplification help from audiologists would often complain of dissatisfaction with their interactions. Researchers (English et al., 1999) suggested this dissatisfaction was related to audiologists' lack of counseling training. They conducted a preliminary study to develop an audiology counseling course. They looked at two learning objectives. The first was to distinguish between content messages and affect messages, and the second was to know the appropriate responses for each. Their results showed that before instruction, students were more likely to respond to affective messages with informational content, which authors dubbed "...a type of 'communication mismatch.'" After counseling instruction, they were more likely to mirror clients' affective messages with affective responses. This research demonstrates that training audiologists in counseling may improve client satisfaction.

Evolution of counseling

Historically, audiologists stuck to the medical model, and were told to refer clients to social workers for anything emotional. This is somewhat unrealistic. When a person is told their child has hearing loss, they get upset even when they expected the news. Being upset, they do not retain information. In 2006, Luterman wrote that he found it more helpful to give emotional support first, and then gradually introduce information. Trying to make clients feel better "invalidates their experience."

Audiologists should allow them to grieve. In the past, many audiologists equated "counseling" with teaching. Luterman states that the ability to differentiate the two is the "hallmark of the complete professional." He notes that a parent asking, "What causes hearing loss in a child?" does not usually want information, but feels guilty and afraid s/he caused the loss. Asking the person if s/he thinks s/he caused it makes it safe to express guilt and other feelings, which may help more than information.

Relationship for speech and hearing professionals and their clients

Most speech and hearing professionals view counseling as outside their scope of practice. Avoiding the emotional realm, however, limits the ability to help clients. Communication disorders generate feelings of loss, grief, anger, anxiety, confusion, vulnerability, and loss of identity. Clients also often do not expect speech and hearing clinicians to deal with emotional issues, and are reluctant to talk about their feelings with them. The clinician can invite the client to share feelings. When they are given permission and invited to share, they may do so. If they are unwilling, the clinician should accept this. Some experts advocate incorporating counseling as well as teaching responses into their interactions in such a way that clients are not conscious of being "counseled" (Luterman, 2006). A counseling relationship can transform emotions into constructive behaviors. Confusion can create an impetus to learn more; awareness of vulnerability stimulates reprioritization; anger provides the energy to change; guilt becomes commitment; and grief becomes compassion for others.

Counseling approach that has been used in conjunction with communicative rehabilitation

A study by Wolter et al. in 2006 found that adolescents and adults with communication disorders often have accompanying problems such as lowered self-esteem and self-efficacy, which interfere with the remediation of the communication problems. The author states that language-based rehabilitative practices, no matter how sound, may not attain the best outcome if counseling is not integrated into the treatment. The researchers described the narrative therapy approach for clients with reduced self-esteem and conducted a literature review on this topic. They focused on clients with language-literacy deficits (LLD). This may sound more like speech-language pathology, but it is important to remember that people with hearing losses often suffer such deficits. Audiology and SLP are interrelated fields, while communicative rehabilitation is cross-disciplinary in nature. Narrative therapy is based on constructivist theory. Clients externalize problems by making them into narratives. They can then "rewrite" and reconstruct their life stories.

Informational counseling by audiologists to families of infants with hearing loss

According to ASHA's Joint Committee on Infant Hearing (JCIH, 2007), informational counseling is imparting information to families throughout the affected family member's childhood about a broad range of topics. Five examples of topics included are: (1) interpretation of what the child's audiogram means; (2) the options for amplification and associated technologies; (3) the educational choices available; (4) the options available for modes and techniques of communication; and (5) public health policies, education policies, and advocacy regarding hearing loss. Audiologists face many challenges related to counseling families. One is giving enough information, but keeping it clear and succinct. Misleading or confusing communication can affect the family's acceptance of the hearing loss and delay intervention. A second challenge for audiologists is constantly maintaining a balance between their role of teaching and guiding families and their role of advocating and facilitating informed decision making by families.

Adjustment to hearing loss counseling by audiologists for families of children with hearing loss

Adjustment to hearing loss counseling is defined as the support audiologists provide to families when they are informed that their child has a hearing loss and are trying to achieve recognition, acknowledgement, and understanding of what the realities are of having a child with hearing impairment. According to ASHA's policy on scope of practice for audiology (2004b), it is within audiology's scope of practice to incorporate emotional support in their interactions with families, so this becomes the audiologist's responsibility. An additional responsibility of audiologists is to pay attention to a minority of parents who display acute emotional reactions to the diagnosis of their child's hearing loss. The audiologist should observe them carefully. If such extreme feelings are ongoing for long periods of time and/or they become worse with time, these parents' needs may go beyond the audiologist's scope of practice. The audiologist should refer the family to mental health professionals.

EHDI

EHDI is Early Hearing Detection and Intervention, which ASHA advocates. The 2007 position statement by ASHA's Joint Committee on Infant Hearing (JCIH) includes these benchmarks: (1) all infants should have hearing screenings using physiological measurement by one month old; (2) all infants not passing initial hearing screenings and/or re-screening should be evaluated medically and audiologically to establish a diagnosis of hearing loss by three months old; and (3) all infants with confirmed diagnoses of permanent hearing loss should receive intervention as early after diagnosis as possible, but at least by six months old. Real-life challenges for families in terms of meeting these benchmarks include: medically fragile infants, cultural differences, family systems, and individual coping styles. Limitations to family resources such as support systems, effective communication skills, spiritual beliefs, and financial stability can also hinder timely achievement of these benchmarks. Audiologists should help by being sensitive to what these challenges mean for families, and by providing support services and effective counseling.

Family-focused service provision with respect to EHDI

Family-focused service provision aims to find a balance between systems-driven and technology-driven approaches to EHDI. Although the importance of timely intervention is documented by research and advocated by public policy, the JCIH acknowledges that, in reality, not all families can meet age criteria for intervention. The rates and correctness with which families process new information and adjust to it vary. Thus, intervention should proceed at an acceptable pace for the family, regardless of the child's age of diagnosis. As the primary agents of change and decision makers for children, families must have their needs and wants acknowledged and met. Another consideration is the family's cultural background. Assessment and treatment services should address culture and language differences with effective communication modes and interpreters as needed. Reasonable needs, expectations, and preferences and family rights must be considered when providing services. Family socioeconomic, cultural, racial, and ethnic diversity must be honored by EHDI systems.

Unbiased information

According to ASHA's guidelines, the term "unbiased" implies that families are the only parties who can decide the results they want for their children. "Unbiased" also implies that information is delivered to families without editing or spinning, in a clear and direct fashion. The clinician must be aware of and acknowledge his or her own biases and opinions, must communicate those biases to families, and must give bases for their opinions. "Unbiased" does not imply that the audiologist should not express his or her expert opinion to families. The professional has, understands, and can explain information related to a child's specific hearing loss. The clinician can also describe available amplification and communication choices. This is valuable for families navigating the proliferation of decisions possible in EHDI systems. When families are prepared to make informed decisions in an attempt to achieve the results they desire, audiologists are responsible for informing them how best to attain those results.

Areas of knowledge audiologists must be familiar

According to ASHA's guidelines for audiologists giving informational and adjustment counseling services to the families of children with hearing loss, audiologists must have current, direct (i.e. firsthand) knowledge of the following areas:
- (1) published research studies, including those on outcomes and

those with guidelines in support of evidence-based practice; (2) a broad range of hearing loss in children, a knowledge of which an audiologist can gain via clinical experience covering a wide spectrum of hearing loss; (3) the hearing opportunities and development conferred by hearing aid and cochlear implant technologies; (4) opportunities and practices in early intervention and education; and (5) legislation pertaining to public health and education. When counseling families of children with hearing loss, audiologists are responsible for distinguishing between the professional communication of current knowledge and the expression of biased viewpoints, and for making sure that families understand the difference between the two.

Family stress related to having a child with hearing loss

Studies have shown family situations characterized by stress correlate with inadequate emotional adaptation and higher rates of behavioral problems in children. Researchers have also found that the stress experience of parents correlated positively with deficiencies in social competence of youths with hearing impairment. A frequent response to stress is depression. Based on research findings, mothers appear more likely than fathers to become depressed in response to hearing loss in their children. Maternal depression hampers the emotional accessibility of the mother to the child and the potential for effective interactions between the mother and the child. This increases the child's risk for difficulties with communication, cognitive deficits, and emotional problems. For many years it has been known and shown by research that some parents of children with chronic conditions will overprotect and overindulge them, fostering dependency and stunting development. Grief is also common, and is chronic throughout the active parenting years.

Best practice principles for informational counseling regarding newborn hearing screening

(1) Three principles for informational counseling are: (A) keeping parental communication confidential and family-focused; (B) keeping communications clear and succinct rather than using technical terminology; and (C) encouraging and allowing parents to ask questions. (2) Initial information, spoken and written, includes: (i) why newborns' hearing should be screened; (ii) screening procedures and possible results; (iii) reasons for not passing screening and the associated ramifications; (iv) significance of timely follow-up; and (v) why more tests may be indicated. (3) There are additional considerations for parents. For example, if screening information is only presented to a mother after she is in labor and admitted to the hospital, it is likely she will find it difficult or impossible to absorb this information. Therefore, ASHA recommends: (a) information/materials be given during hospital programs for prenatal instruction and/or outreach programs by public health facilities; (b) information be at a 4th-5th grade reading level; and (c) information be available in the family's preferred language.

Audiological follow-up services for newborn hearing screening

Audiological follow-up services include second-stage re-screening on an outpatient basis and/or a direct referral to an audiologist for testing. There are many considerations for information counseling regarding follow-up. Follow-up recommendations should be given to parents personally by the audiologist.

ASHA recommends not using the negative word "failure" regarding screening results, but rather using the phrase "referral for further testing." Delivering information using a positive, constructive attitude while also conveying how important the screening results and follow-ups are is advised to increase the likelihood of family compliance with follow-ups. Informational counseling to families when their babies are in the NICU will differ from when they are in a well-baby nursery. When follow-up is indicated, families should be given (1) specific advice on testing, including names, addresses, and phone numbers of facilities; (2) access to an audiologist who can answer questions in the meantime; and (3) local, state, and national resources providing information about ensuing steps in the EHDI process.

Considerations that remain after an infant passes newborn hearing screening or when no screening is done

The purpose of newborn hearing screening is to find all developmentally significant hearing loss in all newborn infants. However, professionals realize that some babies may pass the screening even if they have minimal or mild hearing loss. Some may pass the screening because they have hearing loss with uncommon configurations. Others will pass the screening as infants, but will subsequently develop late-onset hearing loss. Later diagnoses of permanent hearing loss in babies who passed their newborn screenings can make it more difficult for some families to accept such diagnoses. Even if an infant passes the initial newborn hearing screening or the family opts to forgo the newborn hearing screening, informational counseling is still indicated. The professional must instruct the family that the child still needs to be watched, and that his or her hearing, speech, and language skills and development should be checked regularly and often throughout the early childhood years.

Adjustment counseling related to newborn hearing screening results

With respect to universal newborn hearing screenings, professionals must remember that parents may receive screening results during an emotionally vulnerable period. Ethical guidelines regarding informed consent dictate that parents must receive spoken and written communication that their baby's hearing will be screened before hospital discharge. Some families may decline screening, and this option must be disclosed. Parents should receive emotional support, regardless of their choices. They should also be informed that in some states data on babies who are not screened are reported to state governments. Parents who put off screening medically fragile babies should be informed about screening, hearing loss, developmental milestones, and how to get post-discharge screening. Adjustment counseling for failed screenings includes listening to and addressing parental feelings/concerns and expediting follow-up to alleviate anxiety. The timing and presentation of screening results affect parent-child bonds crucial to children's psychological health and parental compliance. Minimizing false positives and negatives and orchestrating optimal delivery of screening results are paramount.

Family informational counseling when hearing loss in an infant has been confirmed

Confirmation of a hearing loss is the stage in service delivery wherein an audiologist's individual continuity of care is established. Audiologists must provide both accurate knowledge and emotional support during testing and follow-up.

Initially, the audiologist may explain: (1) why having babies sleep is helpful in some tests but not in others; (2) why moderate sedation can ensure the best testing conditions; (3) why it is necessary to monitor the baby's health; (4) the different types of procedures and the significance of each; and (5) why some tests must be repeated at intervals. Explanations are best conveyed not as technical information (the implications of which parents may not be able to interpret), but in functional terms. In other words, the audiologist should explain what concrete effects the hearing loss will have on their baby's development rather than talking about the frequency and decibel levels of the hearing loss.

Parental collaboration in the service delivery process for their hearing-impaired baby

Some cons of parental collaboration are: because 90% of hearing-impaired babies are born to normal-hearing parents, most will be uninformed about children's hearing losses; and first-time parents often feel insecure with a new baby, and even parents with other children may feel uncertainty about integrating the new child into the family. Pros of parental collaboration include: parents have parenting instincts; and since parents are actively involved in parenting their children, services related to hearing loss should be included among the activities requiring their participation. Collaborative roles parents can take on include:

- (1) establishing and prioritizing a visit's objectives; (2) supplying spoken or written descriptions of the child's auditory behaviors; (3) communicating their observations of the child's behavior and development; (4) facilitating the child's cooperation with testing and/or demonstration of skills;

and (5) giving feedback on how typical their child's behavior was during audiological testing. Parental collaboration and presence lets audiologists explain each step, facilitating understanding.

Parental informational counseling that ASHA recommends audiologists do during the process of confirming a child's hearing loss

ASHA recommends that audiologists do the following during informational counseling with parents when confirming hearing loss in their child. First, when a failed screening and/or other factors give an initial impression of hearing loss, audiologists should schedule follow-up testing as soon as possible to mitigate parental anxiety. Whenever possible, audiologists must contact the families in advance to explain the next tests to be performed. Second, diagnostic tests should all be given by the same audiologist. This furthers rapport and trust, ensures individualized continuity of care, and avoids variation in interpretation, which can happen when various audiologists interpret test results. Third, the amount of information given and the degree of detail in which it is given should be determined by listening to the questions and remarks made by the parents. Fourth, audiologists must allow sufficient time for parents and/or family members to talk about their concerns and/or any problems they are experiencing.

Considerations for audiologists related to providing adjustment to hearing loss counseling to families of newly-diagnosed children

An initial requirement for successful counseling is to establish rapport with the family. To do this, the audiologist must respect the family's socioeconomic status;

any cultural differences; less typical or traditional family structures; and varying opinions, whether they are informed or not and regardless of whether all family members agree with them. Respect and rapport engender trust. Even if the process of establishing trust slows diagnosis somewhat, the audiologist should allow time for this prerequisite foundation. Components of adjustment counseling include: acknowledging family vulnerability during diagnosis; acknowledging that diagnosis affects siblings, grandparents, and other extended family members; determining social supports such as friends, relatives, clergy, etc., and advising families to avail themselves of these as necessary; concentrating on the family's value and cultural systems and their advantages and needs in these contexts; distinguishing acute grief from clinical depression and making referrals as needed; and giving families emotional support.

Balancing informational and adjustment counseling of families of children with hearing loss

The most effective hearing loss counseling balances informational and adjustment aspects. Unlike professional clinicians, family members are not normally trained to separate the two, so their communications often combine both content and affective components. Audiologists should differentiate between the two and respond accordingly, answering content components with informational content and recognizing and respecting affective components. Benefits of adjustment counseling include the fact that it can help families be more receptive to new information, and can enable them to make more informed decisions. One caution is not to try to protect families from stressful information. An example of such protection would be suggesting that success is ensured by the audiologist's intervention methods. This can encourage dependency. Each family goes through the adjustment process at its own rate. Another caution is not to assume that grief over hearing loss progresses in the same manner as grief over death. The two reactions differ (Luterman, 2006). With death there can be closure, while hearing loss and the grief over it are chronic.

Parental grief over a child's hearing loss

Because hearing loss, unlike death, is chronic, even parents who appear to have adjusted very well to their child's hearing loss can experience reactivations of their initial reactions due to various triggering events. These could include the anniversary date of the diagnosis, follow-up audiology visits, birthday parties, IEP meetings, etc. Untrained individuals may mistake acute grief for clinical depression. It is important for an audiologist to know the difference in order to determine if referral to a mental health professional is indicated, and to decide what the most appropriate referral is. Seven signs of clinical depression are:

- (1) missing appointments; (2) expressing or showing feelings of profound sadness; (3) difficulty with cognitive tasks such as concentrating, remembering, making decisions, or thinking clearly; (4) feeling pessimistic and/or hopeless; (5) heightened fatigue and/or diminished energy; (6) having trouble sleeping; and (7) isolation or withdrawal from the rest of the family members.

Skills audiologists need to provide adjustment to hearing counseling to families

Audiologists must use different communication skills for adjustment counseling than for informational counseling. They will need to talk less than when giving information, listen more, and use active and reflective listening to give emotional support. Crying should be expected, as it is a normal expression of grief. Audiologists should let parents cry, tacitly showing understanding and support by allowing time and simply offering tissues. Silent intervals are expected as parents process their emotions. Audiologists should allow for this silent time without interrupting. Expressions of anger should also be expected, as parents feel a lack of control, feel as though their expectations have been destroyed, and experience fear. These reactions do not necessarily reflect a rejection of the audiologist's competence, so audiologists should not personalize them. Families with more stressors need more time to process information and emotions to accept hearing loss, and audiologists must be sensitive to this. The severity of parents' stress reactions corresponds not to the amount of hearing loss, but to parents' perceptions, which determine the amount of support they need.

Informational counseling services audiologists may provide to families during intervention and habilitation

Depending on the needs of the individual family, audiologists may provide informational counseling that includes information about: choices for communication based on the family's preference for speech or visual methods; technological possibilities, including the appropriateness of and eligibility for cochlear implants; all educational choices applicable to the child's developmental requirements and hearing status, including inviting parents to observe on-site intervention programs; communicating the necessity to check and confirm the child's amplification on a continuing basis; hearing aid orientation and instruction in upkeep and troubleshooting for the child (when possible), families, caregivers, teachers, and therapists; long-term audiological follow-up, including issues related to progressive hearing loss; making educational transitions and processes related to them; legislation and advocacy related to public education and public accessibility; and other informational resources, such as Web sites, DVDs, printed materials, physical and/or online tutorial demonstrations, classes, etc.

Responsibilities of audiologists to families as informational counselors

As providers of unbiased information, recommendations, and informed choices for communication and education, audiologists are, as ASHA states, "...responsible to...and not for families." Audiologists should maintain communication with parents and allied professionals to assure suitable services are procured and to prevent confusion from conflicting information sources. They should help parents notice and enjoy their children's abilities, not just their special needs, and should include children in decision-making and feedback as soon as they are old enough, beginning with steps such as selecting hearing aid color and learning to check its batteries. This will help foster autonomy and enhance self-esteem. Audiologists are also responsible to advocate for the establishment of educational choices in the community if these are lacking. Communication/education options are often limited to what is available rather than what is best for the child. Audiologists should participate on multidisciplinary teams and in IFSP and IEP development. As parents' empowerment as advocates grows, audiologists shift roles from care coordinators to facilitators.

Adjustment to hearing loss counseling for families during intervention and habilitation

Due to the proliferation of modes of communication, educational choices, and technological advances, parents must make complicated decisions early in intervention. Therefore, they will need support. Some families bring strong coping skills and support systems to hearing loss intervention, while some are deprived in these areas. Others are somewhere in between. Therefore, the ability of families to move forward with intervention varies in terms of ease and speed. Audiologists must realize some families' failure to follow their recommendations is not a sign of neglect, but of limited ability to cope. Therefore, in providing services, audiologists must take into account the quantity and quality of their demands on families. Four variables essential to understanding coping are: (1) family variables (composition, SES, resilience, cohesiveness, roles, responsibilities, creativity/problem-solving, etc.); (2) parent variables (marriage quality, maternal locus of control, time concerns, etc.); (3) child variables (temperament, age, gender, extent of disability, etc.); and (4) external variables (social stigma, social support, collaboration with professionals, etc.).

Maternal coping skills and development in their hearing-impaired children

Researchers have found that the more successfully mothers developed useful coping strategies with their deaf children, the better the children's development was in reading, problem-solving behaviors, cognitive flexibility, emotional awareness, and social competence. These children also demonstrated less impulsive behavior. Research has also shown a correlation between parental stress and parental behavior. The more stress parents reported, the more often they used punishment, constraint, and discipline in everyday parenting. With respect to hearing technologies, audiologists must dissuade parents from viewing these as a "cure," despite many innovations. This view leaves parents unprepared for future challenges and is unrealistic. However, audiologists must give parents information and support about available and appropriate technologies to engender hope and an optimistic outlook, and to help avoid fearfulness and withdrawal. Audiologists and parents should also remember that while research documents continuity of intervention as important to successful results, parents can always change their minds over time.

Diagnostic teaching approach

Intervention plans for hearing-impaired children may be revised over time according to various changes in status. Information pertinent to the specific changes to be made can be gathered from the child through a diagnostic teaching approach. The audiologist will still establish individual goals applicable to the child. However, the audiologist will also monitor factors that are conducive or prohibitive to learning on an ongoing basis. This approach emphasizes asking which methods, techniques, strategies, and supports will promote the specific child's most efficient learning. Diagnostic teaching can help the audiologist identify which technologies may be most effective for the child, such as hearing aids, assistive listening devices, and cochlear implantation. Diagnostic teaching can also help the audiologist identify a communication method that is preferred and consistently used by all family members. This communication method should also be the most effective for the child. It can also help identify disabilities in addition to hearing loss that were not previously diagnosed.

Intervention and habilitation stage of adjustment to hearing loss counseling

Many families of children with hearing loss will find it supportive to meet with other families going through the same thing. If a family is interested, the audiologist should provide information and opportunities for them to attend family support groups. Adjustment to hearing loss counseling includes: giving families formal and informal occasions to meet and interact with other families with hearing-impaired children; and giving families a chance to meet adults who are hard of hearing, adults who are deaf and oral, and/or adults who are culturally deaf and use different modalities and technologies for communicating. Families may also wish to observe and/or interact with children who employ different methods and technologies to communicate. Developing and expediting support groups is also included in adjustment to hearing loss counseling. Benefits for families include knowing they are not alone, sharing experience, validating one another's perceptions and experiences, learning new information, benefiting family/extended family members, and enabling empowerment. The audiologist's role is a facilitative rather than an instructional one..

Ongoing support by audiologists

An important thing to remember is that families not only need supportive counseling after their child is diagnosed with hearing loss, but also throughout their years of active parenting. Because some types of hearing loss can be progressive, the audiologist must realize that some families will feel fear every time their child has another audiological evaluation that might show the hearing loss has progressed. They will need reassurance if the loss has not progressed and emotional support if it has become worse. Families will also need support during times of transition and when decisions must be made regarding interventions. Because grief responses and stress related to hearing loss are both chronic, as is the disability itself, families will need counseling at various times during parenting. Specifically, they will require counseling whenever some event triggers a reactivation of their original feelings. Audiologists also need to support families as their children move from early intervention programs to preschool, and then to school.

Changes in recent years that have had an impact on the field of audiology

In recent years, the importance of early detection of hearing loss and early intervention has been demonstrated by research. As a result, universal hearing screening for newborns has become a mandate. Another change is that audiology was traditionally based on the medical model. As such, it concentrated on giving information but not on counseling. This is changing as experts in the field explain the necessity of emotional support and how it can lead to positive outcomes in aural habilitation and remediation. Experts are also touting the importance of family-centered counseling. However, according to research, only a distinct minority of schools require or even offer counseling courses in audiology programs. This shortcoming will be partly helped by the change in requirements for beginning audiologists. They now require a Clinical Doctorate as opposed to a Master's degree, and more coursework is required beyond the degree. ASHA remarks that it and similar organizations must still monitor counseling coursework and post-professional education.

Education and experience needed to prepare audiologists to counsel families

ASHA recommends that audiology program curricula be expanded to include specific courses relevant to the emotional repercussions of diagnosed hearing loss in children on families. Such courses should cover knowledge of: childhood development; parenting skills; the grieving process; the role of affective states on acceptance of hearing loss; counseling to aid in personal adjustment; family systems theory (cf. Murray Bowen); cultural diversity; and how limited financial, social, and emotional resources affect the coping capacities of families in response to the stressor of childhood hearing loss. ASHA also recommends that audiology students have supervised work experience with, and practical observation of: families with hearing-impaired children of differing ages, in both clinical and more informal environments; families who are at different stages in the process of accepting the hearing loss; families who are at differing points on the continuum of the delivery of services; established family support groups; and mentor counselors.

Future research that is needed about effective methods of counseling families

ASHA recommends further research in several areas, including: the psychosocial impact of newborn hearing screenings on the child and family; the effects of false positive and false negative screening results on families, including stress, coping, and quality of life; parents' comprehension and retention of information on screening, comparison of medical vs. family-focused approaches and their integration, use of assistive devices, and speech and language development; parents' follow-up compliance, including written vs. oral recommendations, family SES and educational profile, diversity in language and culture, and the influence of NICU vs. well-baby clinic placement on complying with follow-up recommendations; variables influencing family satisfaction with and transitions between services, especially early intervention, preschool, and school systems; behavioral indicators and status of support systems that influence families' vulnerability; predictors of successful results for families; and innovations in methods for delivery of support and counseling services to families lacking the resources to fully participate in EHDI systems.

Referral for Otologic Examination for Patients with Congenital or Traumatic Deformity of the Ear

This quality measure is based on the percent of patients aged newborn and older who present with an inborn or acquired ear deformity, have an audiological evaluation, and are then referred to a physician, preferably one with training and experience in ear disorders. The measure is to be reported at least once for patients seen in each reporting period to ensure referrals. Clinicians making the defined quality actions may report this measure. Patients not eligible for this measure include those already under a physician's care for congenital or traumatic ear deformities and those patients who have received an evaluation by a physician for a congenital or traumatic ear deformity within the past six months. Care settings that apply in this measure are Medicare Part B outpatient settings, but not hospital outpatient and skilled nursing facility outpatient settings. Audiologists enrolled as private practitioners in Medicare Part B are designated as eligible providers.

Referral for Otologic Evaluation for Patients with a History of Active Drainage from the Ear within the Previous 90 Days

This quality measure is based on the percent of patients aged newborn and older with diseases of the ears and mastoid processes who present with a history of active aural drainage within the past 90 days, receive an audiological evaluation, and are then referred by the audiologist to a doctor (preferably one specializing in ear disorders) for an otologic evaluation. To see that these patients get referrals for suitable care, this measure is to be reported at least once in each reporting period when patients were seen. Clinicians taking the quality actions defined may report this measure. Patients already under the care of a physician for aural drainage are not eligible for this quality measure. Applicable care settings are defined as Medicare Part B Outpatient settings, but not hospital outpatient and/or skilled nursing facility outpatient settings. Audiologists enrolled in Medicare Part B as private practitioners are defined as eligible providers.

Referral for Otologic Evaluation for Patients with a History of Sudden or Rapidly Progressive Hearing Loss

This quality measure is based on the percent of patients aged newborn and older who receive an audiological evaluation confirming and documenting a sudden or rapidly progressing hearing loss and are immediately referred by the audiologist for an otologic evaluation by a physician, preferably one who specializes in ear and/or hearing disorders. To see that these patients receive the care they need, this measure is to be reported at least once in each reporting period when patients are seen. Clinicians taking the quality actions defined may report this measure. Any patient already under the care of a physician for a sudden or rapidly progressive hearing loss is not eligible for this quality measure. Applicable care settings are defined as Medicare Part B Outpatient settings, but not hospital outpatient and/or skilled nursing facility outpatient settings. Audiologists enrolled in Medicare Part B as private practitioners are defined as eligible providers.

Accepting Referrals for Private Practice From Primary Place of Employment

Ultimately, this document refers to the medical model wherein physicians cannot refer patients from their primary employers to their own private practices. More directly, it is grounded in ASHA's Code of Ethics, Principle of Ethics III, Rule B: "Individuals shall not participate in professional activities that constitute a conflict of interest." ASHA's Board of Ethics gives three guidelines for professionals intending to take cases from their primary employers for their own private practices. First, people receiving professional services must be informed of services accessible from the provider's primary employer, private practice, or other practice. People are free to choose whether, where, and from whom they procure services. Second, differences between costs of services at the primary employer and in the private practice must be made clear to prospective recipients. Third, practitioners intending to take cases in their private practices from their primary places of employment must inform their primary employer's administrator of their intention.

Accepting Referrals for Private Practice From Primary Place of Employment

In this illustration, public school SLP "Jones" had offered summer services and charged students' parents for years. Her school offered only limited services during summer, and "Jones" always informed the superintendent of her intention to offer summer services. When the school district increased its summer services, it had another SLP, "Smith," run its program instead of "Jones." Some parents elected to pay "Jones" in the summer rather than use the school district's free services. "Smith" complained to ASHA's Board of Ethics that "Jones" was "spiriting away" clients from the school to her private practice, violating the Code of Ethics. "Jones" responded that parents were informed of the school's free services and of her charges for private services; she had informed her superintendent, who did not object; and according to ASHA's guidelines, clients are free to choose their service providers. The ASHA Board of Ethics confirmed what "Jones" stated.

Accepting Referrals for Private Practice From Primary Place of Employment

Ms. "West" supervised graduate students part-time at a university clinic and also had a private practice. The university hired her without a contract or a non-compete agreement. "West" offered a few clients additional therapy at competitive rates in her private practice. They were happy, benefited, and found the cost justified. Confronted by the clinic director, "West" stated the following points in her defense. She provided continuity of care; clients requested more time than was possible to provide at the clinic; she declined other clients with different diagnoses requesting private services who had insurance coverage she did not accept; she only took clients that would benefit from increased treatment, of which she had proven expertise; charges were similar; and clients were not leaving the clinic and were benefiting. A true conflict of interest, however, existed. "West" did not inform her employer about seeing clients privately, and clients had not signed an informed consent form for private treatment. "West" was terminated, and the director filed a complaint with ASHA's Board of Ethics.

Accepting Referrals for Private Practice From Primary Place of Employment

"Amanda" had a private practice at home working with school-aged children. She also worked for an agency that supplied temporary therapists to long-term care facilities. She told this employer about her private practice, in which she followed the rules regarding informed consent and disclosure. At a state professional convention, in an ethics panel, she was asked whether her situation could constitute a conflict of interest. Considering ASHA's Code of Ethics, she suspected it might, and reported herself to the state licensure board and ASHA's Board of Ethics. Both approved of her self-disclosure. They found she did not violate the Code because she informed her primary employer of her private practice in advance, and also because her employer's population was geriatric, while her private population was pediatric. They also found that she could see geriatric clients in her home provided the agency was informed, the agency approved, and she did not recruit geriatric clients from the agency.

Advantages and benefits of referrals to professionals in private practices

As Plesh (ASHA Leader, 2003) notes, the general public finds mass marketing techniques overwhelming and off-putting. Nearly 50% of consumers' choices of services are based on someone's recommendation. "Referral marketing" establishes credibility, gets rid of obstacles of mistrust that may be present when a professional is unknown, and can grow a professional's practice. Referral

marketing accomplishes these cost-effectively and time-efficiently. Referrals from clients are advantageous because they come from people who have first-hand experience with the professional's services. Many consumers are encouraged by good reviews from fellow consumers. Referrals from colleagues are advantageous because consumers may trust a professional's judgment of another professional, and because a professional's willingness to risk his/her reputation by endorsing someone shows his/her confidence in his/her colleague. As referrals usually cost no money and take only the time required to ask for them, Plesh recommends not being afraid to ask, but cautions that existing clients must be satisfied for referrals to help.

Research study on rates of compliance with referrals for testing to follow up on newborn hearing screenings

Lieu et al. (American Journal of Audiology, 2006) investigated infants in NICUs to determine compliance with diagnostic testing following NHS referrals; timeliness of follow-ups; and usefulness of multi-level auditory brainstem response (ABR) for screening high-risk babies. It was found that 69% of the babies had follow-ups. Of those, 37% had normal hearing, 38% had hearing loss, and 25% of parents were unsure of test results. Diagnostic follow-ups by 6 months of age more than doubled from 1999-2002, from 13% to 31%. It was found that 56% of infants failing screening bilaterally had confirmed hearing loss, while 25% of those passing screening unilaterally had confirmed hearing loss. Of infants passing screening bilaterally at 90 dB nHL/above, 67% had confirmed hearing loss, while 32% of all other participating infants did. The author concluded follow-ups had improved in her program* from 13% to 31% over three years, and that multi-level ABR could help monitor and assure follow-ups on high-risk infants. *(Washington University School of Medicine, Dept. of Otolaryngology – Head and Neck Surgery)

Considerations related to cochlear implants

Michael Stinson, a professor at the Rochester Institute of Technology's (RIT's) National Technical Institute for the Deaf (NTID) in Rochester, N.Y., led the development of the C-Print speech-to-text system. Stinson grew up with progressive hearing loss. In 2001, he received a cochlear implant. Based on his experiences, he makes recommendations for clinicians. Stinson reports he hears speech from a greater distance with the implant, helping him to understand conversations in small groups. However, he notes that hearing acuity varies according to the situation, and that many cochlear implant recipients still find group communication and background noise challenging. Therefore, teachers must evaluate student communication in school hallways, classrooms, lunchrooms, auditoriums, etc. — anywhere other than a quiet room. Clinicians must talk to peers and teachers about student problems with group conversations and role plays; give students communication strategies; encourage students to assert themselves regarding their communication needs; discuss identity issues; and encourage deaf culture awareness.

Current practices in cochlear implantation; social and cultural aspects of the informed consent process; age of implantation; and bilateral implants

In 2007, Berg et al. surveyed cochlear implant centers and teams regarding pediatric cochlear implantation. They found 100% of teams informed parents about audiological information, medical/surgical risks, and communicative/educational options. Only 45% gave parents information on autonomy/identity issues and deaf culture. The majority of centers found the ideal implantation age was 10 to 15 months. Most centers, even those affiliated with teaching hospitals, never or rarely did bilateral implantations, and few talked to parents about bilateral implants. The researchers concluded audiologists are the only non-surgical professionals always included on cochlear implant teams. They also concluded that graduate programs should increase coverage of the genetics of hearing impairment and of deaf culture, and that audiologists should discuss with parents research evidence on optimal implant age, bilateral implants, and educational audiology. Berg remarks that audiologists should pay attention to their part in the informed consent process because they play such a crucial role in informing parents and coordinating care.

Changes from the mid-1990s to 2010 that have influenced detection, testing, and intervention for hearing loss in children

Since the mid-1990s, legislation of the Newborn and Infant Hearing Screening and Intervention Act of 1999 and IDEA 2004 (the Individuals with Disabilities Education Improvement Act) have enabled better services for babies, preschoolers, and families. Research and technological progress have led to universal newborn hearing screenings; improved appreciation of the importance of early development; and more available information on hearing, hearing loss, hearing disorders, and deafness. Services have improved due to advances in audiology, genetics, and neurobiology, and because of increased consciousness and involvement by the medical community. Linguistics research advances have spotlighted the significance of early language development and the correlation between developmental language milestones and speech and/or signing. The attributes of children with HL receiving services have also changed. Due to NHS, children are younger, may have mild losses or unilateral loss, may have auditory dyssynchrony or neuropathy, or may come from families with cultural and language differences. Significant proportions also have other disabilities.

Contrast the progress in newborn hearing screenings with follow-up rates

Since newborn hearing screenings began, the average age when hearing loss is confirmed has gone from 24-30 months to 2-3 months. However, according to the CDC (2008), nearly half of newborns referred for follow-up do not receive it. One reason for this is that methods and procedures that should get families to follow up are chosen or implemented in such a way that they are not effective. A second reason is that there are not enough qualified professionals to deliver services to babies and families. Families at the highest risk for lack of follow-up are those with inadequate health care services; insufficient financial resources; or cultural, language, or literacy differences that hamper their access to comprehensive information. The ramifications of lack of follow-up are serious. The advantages of newborn hearing screenings are wasted if their results are not followed up for confirmation and early intervention, and if professionals and families do not become involved early in the process.

Research findings supporting the importance of family involvement in providing intervention services

In 2007, Calderon and Greenberg identified factors common to all successful intervention programs they studied. These included parents' self-efficacy in interacting with children, quality of relationships between parents and professionals, hopefulness of parental attitudes, and how realistically positive their expectations were. In 2000, Moeller found that children enrolled in early intervention programs before one year old with strong familial support had superior verbal reasoning skills and vocabulary development. Also in 2000, Calderon found that communication between parents and children strongly predicted social-emotional development and early reading skills, and that family involvement also predicted children's social and academic outcomes. In 2003, Meadow-Orlans et al. found that parents of hearing-impaired children value hearing-impaired adults as support sources. Thus, in 2005, Marge & Marge recommended that hearing-impaired adults and deaf organizations should be vital components of EHDI systems. Professionals create bases for families to engage in intervention processes. Family-centered approaches promote families' active participation and fulfillment of their capacity to form their children's futures.

Legislation and professional organization guidelines for the interdisciplinary model of early intervention in hearing loss

IDEA 2004, Part C, identifies the IFSP (Individual Family Service Plan) as the center of the early intervention program, and mandates that its development and application be strongly family oriented and involve a collaborative team approach. In 2008, ASHA also advocated collaboration, finding that team resources promote optimal childhood development and family support. Professionals on early intervention teams may include (but are not limited to): the core of the team (pediatric audiologist, deaf education teacher, speech-language pathologist, and service coordinator); early childhood special educator; sign language specialist; listening and spoken language specialist; cued speech specialist; deaf-blind specialist; occupational therapist; physical therapist; psychologist; counselor; social worker; physician(s) (family practitioner, otologist, pediatrician, etc); and geneticist. Because of a shortage of professionals qualified to serve hearing-impaired children and their families, ASHA recommends regional service delivery to pool available professional resources and create a sufficient population of children.

Collective expertise required of an interdisciplinary team providing services

Members of an interdisciplinary team providing intervention services to children with hearing loss and their families should collectively demonstrate expertise in all of the following fields: childhood development; hearing loss; disorders of the auditory system; language development in spoken language; language development in sign language; development of auditory skills; assistive hearing technologies; assistive visual technologies; developmental disabilities (e.g. intellectual disabilities, giftedness, cerebral palsy, autism spectrum disorders, childhood mental illness, personality disorders, mood disorders, physical disabilities, and many more); other (non-developmental) disabilities; blindness; visual impairment; cognitive development; emerging literacy; social development and emotional development; counseling and family support; deaf culture and deaf communities; cultural diversity and linguistic diversity; advocacy and empowerment; and transitional planning. Team members should also possess knowledge of the most current research in all of these fields. For the planning and implementation of services for hearing-

impaired children and their families to be comprehensive, findings of evaluations from all disciplines must be incorporated.

ASHA's Joint Committee on Infant Hearing's (JCIH's) 2007 revised position statement

Areas updated include: definition of targeted hearing loss, hearing screening and rescreening protocols, diagnostic auditory evaluation, medical evaluation, early intervention, surveillance and screening in the medical home, communication, and information infrastructure. The definition of targeted hearing loss has been expanded to include neural hearing losses like auditory neuropathy/dyssynchrony in NICU infants. Medical evaluation has also been updated. The revised position statement states that genetic consultation should be offered to families of babies with confirmed hearing loss. It states that infants with confirmed hearing loss should have evaluations by otolaryngologists experienced with pediatric hearing loss and pediatric ophthalmologists. In the revised statement, risk factors for congenital and acquired hearing loss are grouped together instead of grouping losses by onset time. Information infrastructure is also an area that has been updated. It now states that states should have child health information systems to track and manage data. This will allow professionals to check EHDI service quality and recommend improvements. It also states that health and educational professionals should be connected to assure transitional success and ascertain hearing-impaired children's results that will inform public health policy.

Diagnostic auditory evaluation section

Audiologists qualified to evaluate neonates and infants should deliver diagnostic evaluations and amplification services. To confirm permanent hearing loss in children under three years of age, at least one ABR test should be included in a complete diagnostic audiological evaluation. The matter of when and how many hearing re-evaluations should be done for at-risk children should be customized to individuals according to their risk of developing late-onset hearing loss. At least one diagnostic audiological evaluation should be made between 24-30 months for babies who pass newborn hearing screenings, but have risk factors. Evaluation beginning earlier and repeated more often may be required for babies with cytomegalovirus (CMV), progressive hearing loss symptoms, traumas, culture-positive postnasal infections associated with sensorineural hearing loss, neurodegenerative disorders, chemotherapy, extracorporeal membrane oxidation (ECMO), a history of familial hearing loss, or caregivers with hearing concerns. Amplification should be fitted within one month of diagnosis of permanent hearing loss in infants whose families choose amplification.

Early intervention and surveillance and screening in the medical home sections

Several updates were made to the early intervention section of the position statement by ASHA's JCIH. One is that all families of babies with any degree of permanent hearing loss, whether it is unilateral or bilateral, are eligible for early intervention services. To assure specialized services for babies with confirmed hearing loss, centralized entry points for referrals should be established and identified. Babies with confirmed hearing loss should receive early intervention services from hearing loss professionals, including audiologists, speech-language pathologists, and deaf educators. Addressing earlier emphasis on "natural environments," the JCIH recommends offering both home-based

and facility-based intervention. Updates were also made to the surveillance and screening in the medical home section of the position statement by ASHA's JCIH. One is that regular surveillance of developmental milestones, parents' concerns, auditory skills, and middle-ear status should be done for all babies in their medical homes following AAP's pediatric periodicity schedule. Global development of all babies should be screened at 9, 18, and 24-30 months (or anytime concern exists) using a valid, objective, standardized instrument. Babies failing speech-language parts of screenings or those with hearing and/or language concerns should be referred for SLP and audiological evaluations.

Hearing screening and rescreening protocols and communication

Several updates were made to the hearing screening and rescreening protocols section of the position statement by ASHA's JCIH. One is that the JCIH recommends separate protocols for well-baby nurseries and NICUs. Screening babies in NICUs for more than five days should include ABR. NICU babies failing automated ABR should be referred directly to audiologists for rescreening and/or comprehensive evaluation including ABR as needed. Bilateral rescreening is recommended, even for babies failing initial screenings unilaterally. Repeat screenings are recommended before discharge of readmitted babies having conditions with the potential to cause hearing loss. Several updates were also made to the communication section of the position statement by ASHA's JCIH. One is that birth hospitals and state EHDI coordinators should collaborate to assure NHS results are communicated to parents and medical homes. Hospitals should assure babies have medical homes. Parents should be given information on follow-up and resources. Throughout

EHDI processes, information must be communicated to families with cultural sensitivity and clarity. Information from individual NHS, audiological evaluations, and aural habilitation should be conveyed promptly to medical homes and state EHDI coordinators. Families should be informed without bias of all available options for communication and hearing technologies.

Challenges to future EHDI success

The challenges identified by ASHA's JCIH are as follows: there is excessive attrition from screening failure to rescreening, and from rescreening failure to diagnostic evaluation; there is a shortage of professionals experienced with both pediatrics and hearing loss; referral for diagnosis and intervention is often not timely; program maintenance requires stable, regular federal and state funding; pediatric services in all specialties are reimbursed more poorly than adult services; there is insufficient access to uniform Part C services among and within states; integrated state systems for data tracking and management are lacking; demographics are changing quickly and cultural diversity is increasing; funding is needed for hearing aids, cochlear implants, FM systems, and loaner programs; specialized services for hearing-impaired children with multiple disabilities are lacking; state Part C guidelines may render children ineligible for services until language is delayed; children may be ineligible for assistive technology; in-service education for professionals is lacking; regulations hinder information exchange across providers and states; OAE and ABR equipment calibration lack national standards/uniform performance standards.

Practice Test

Practice Questions

1. For which of the following instruments/apparatus do national standards or uniform performance standards for calibration exist?
    a. Pure-tone audiometers
    b. Otoacoustic emissions
    c. Auditory brainstem response
    d. All have calibration standards.

2. Which of these is MOST likely to be introduced *deliberately* by the examiner during an audiometric examination?
    a. A distorted tone
    b. Switching transients
    c. A masking noise
    d. None of the above

3. One component required in the production of sound is a hearing mechanism to receive it. The other three necessary components include all of the following EXCEPT
    a. vibration.
    b. medium.
    c. force.
    d. velocity.

4. The outer ear is classified as which kind of device?
    a. Mechanical
    b. . Acoustic
    c. Hydraulic
    d. Biological

5. The middle ear is classified as which kind(s) of device(s)?
    a. Acoustic
    b. Mechanical
    c. Both of these
    d. Neither of these

6. The inner ear is classified as which kind(s) of device(s)?
    a. Mechanical
    b. Hydraulic
    c. Biological
    d. All of the above

7. Without the middle ear, if sound were to reach the inner ear, to the hearer it would be
    a. virtually nonexistent.
    b. so loud it caused nerve damage.
    c. distorted in its frequencies.
    d. impossible to interpret.

8. Which of the following is MOST likely to cause a conductive hearing loss?
   a. Presbycusis
   b. Otitis media
   c. Noise exposure
   d. Birth trauma

9. Which of these is MOST likely to cause a sensorineural hearing loss?
   a. A foreign object
   b. Impacted cerumen
   c. Ménière's disease
   d. Serous otitis media

10. Which of the following is NOT a true statement about conductive and sensorineural hearing losses?
   a. Conductive hearing losses are often reversible.
   b. Sensorineural hearing loss is usually permanent.
   c. Sensorineural losses also impair discrimination.
   d. Conductive loss does not affect threshold levels.

11. A person with hearing loss who suffers from recruitment will have
   a. a different hearing threshold in one ear than in the other ear.
   b. less distance between threshold and uncomfortable loudness.
   c. more distance between comfortable and uncomfortable loudness.
   d. overcompensation of the better ear for the more affected ear.

12. Which condition is MOST often associated with normal hearing?
   a. Hyperacusis
   b. Diplacusis
   c. Presbycusis
   d. None of the above

13. The relationship of Hertz (Hz) to sound waves to cycles per second equals
   a. 1:10:100
   b. 1:2:3
   c. 1:1:1
   d. 1:100:10

14. The human voice typically has a frequency range of approximately
   a. 50 Hz – 500 Hz.
   b. 6000 Hz – 11,000 Hz.
   c. 30 Hz – 30,000 Hz.
   d. 80 Hz – 6000 Hz.

15. In general, the frequency range of human hearing is roughly
   a. 20 Hz to 20,000 Hz.
   b. 10 Hz to 30,000 Hz.
   c. 1 Hz to 10,000 Hz.
   d. 200 Hz to 5000 Hz.

16. When using manual pure-tone audiometry as part of a hearing loss prevention program, the frequencies that should be tested are
    a. 250, 500, 1000, 2000, 3000, 4000, and 5000 Hz.
    b. 500, 1000, 2000, 3000, 4000, 6000, and 8000 Hz.
    c. 1000, 2000, 3000, 4000, 6000, 8000, and 10,000 Hz.
    d. 800, 1000, 1200, 1400, 1600, 1800, and 2000 Hz.

17. If an individual has a low-frequency hearing loss, which frequencies should be tested for diagnostic purposes, in addition to the usual frequencies tested for monitoring purposes (#16)?
    a. 125 Hz
    b. 250 Hz
    c. Both
    d. Neither

18. Extended high-frequency audiometry, when used for specialized purposes, is done at frequencies of
    a. 9000 to 16,000 Hz.
    b. 4000 to 8000 Hz.
    c. 15,000 to 25,000 Hz.
    d. 900 to 1600 Hz.

19. When testing at the usual prevention audiometric frequencies (#16), the examiner should additionally test inter-octave frequencies if the subject's first audiogram shows a difference between any two adjacent octave frequencies of
    a. 10 dB or more.
    b. 20 dB or more.
    c. 30 dB or more.
    d. 40 dB or more.

20. In routine air conduction testing using conventional pure-tone audiometry, the initial frequency to test should be
    a. 500 Hz.
    b. 8000 Hz.
    c. 125 Hz.
    d. 1000 Hz

21. Which of the following is true about air conduction vs. bone conduction hearing testing?
    a. Testing bone conduction shows only conductive hearing loss.
    b. Testing air conduction shows only sensorineural hearing loss.
    c. Testing bone conduction shows both types of hearing losses.
    d. Testing air conduction shows both types of hearing losses.

22. Which of the following statements is correct regarding air-bone gaps when testing hearing by air conduction and by bone conduction?
    a. An air-bone gap in the two tests' results indicates purely sensorineural hearing loss.
    b. Matching air and bone conduction results indicate purely sensorineural hearing loss.
    c. An air-bone gap in the two tests' results means there is only conductive hearing loss.
    d. Matching air and bone conduction results indicate that there is a mixed hearing loss.

23. Measurement of otoacoustic emissions will
    a. indicate levels of ototoxic vehicle exhaust emissions in the air.
    b. diagnose a sensorineural hearing loss if emissions are detected in the ear.
    c. indicate a sensorineural hearing loss if emissions are absent from the ear.
    d. diagnose the presence of otorrhea if emissions are coming from the ears.

24. Which of these is NOT an acoustic immittance measure?
    a. Otoacoustic emissions
    b. Tympanometry
    c. Acoustic reflex testing
    d. Static acoustic impedance

25. The proportion of children with only minimal hearing loss who fail at least one school grade compared to the proportion of normal-hearing children who similarly fail is approximately
    a. twice as many.
    b. five times as many.
    c. nine times as many.
    d. 18 times as many.

26. How much of a teacher's speech can a child who has a hearing loss of 20 dB hear?
    a. 80 percent
    b. One half
    c. One quarter
    d. One third

27. Reducing hearing by 10 dB will reduce a person's subjective perception of the loudness of speech sounds by
    a. one tenth.
    b. one half.
    c. one third.
    d. one fifth.

28. According to research studies, approximately how much of young children's learning of language and speech is incidental, occurring via conversations around them in their environments?
    a. 90%
    b. 75%
    c. 50%
    d. 25%

29. The embryonic outer ear forms from the
    a. mesoderm.
    b. ectoderm.
    c. endoderm.
    d. All of the above

30. The embryonic middle ear forms from the
    a. endoderm.
    b. mesoderm.
    c. Both of the above
    d. Neither of the above

31. The embryonic inner ear forms from the
    a. ectoderm.
    b. mesoderm.
    c. endoderm.
    d. All of the above

32. A person with a conductive hearing loss riding in a car with open windows is likely to hear conversation
    a. less well than normal-hearing individuals in the car.
    b. better than normal-hearing individuals in the car.
    c. the same as normal-hearing individuals in the car.
    d. with similar acuity but poorer discrimination than others.

33. Which hearing frequencies are most commonly affected worst by presbycusis?
    a. Lower frequencies
    b. Middle frequencies
    c. Higher frequencies
    d. All of the above equally

34. Which of the following can cause tinnitus?
    a. Ménière's disease
    b. Middle ear fluid
    c. Any hearing loss
    d. All of the above

35. Gradenigo's syndrome consists of hearing loss, plus all of the following symptoms EXCEPT
    a. earache.
    b. otorrhea.
    c. vesicles.
    d. diplopia.

36. Which of the following statements about etiology is true of microtia and congenital atresia during fetal development and prognosis for treatment?
    a. A microtic pinna and congenital atresia of the canal reflect earlier etiology and more involved prognosis for reconstruction.
    b. Congenital atresia of the canal with a normal pinna reflects earlier fetal etiology and a better prognosis for reconstruction.
    c. A microtic pinna and congenital atresia of the canal reflect later fetal etiology and a better prognosis for reconstruction.
    d. Congenital atresia of the canal with a normal pinna reflects later fetal etiology and a more difficult reconstructive prognosis.

37. Which of the following statements about otosclerosis is correct?
    a. This condition causes only a conductive hearing loss.
    b. This condition causes only sensorineural hearing loss.
    c. Otosclerosis occurs more often in black populations.
    d. Otosclerosis occurs more often in white populations.

38. When indicated, a stapedectomy can
    a. resolve or minimize a conductive hearing loss.
    b. cause or exacerbate sensorineural hearing loss.
    c. cause both of the outcomes above at the same time.
    d. be held responsible for none of the above results.

39. Which of the following is true regarding a myringoplasty?
    a. Ossiculoplasty should be performed.
    b. Stapedectomy should be performed.
    c. Neither of these should be performed.
    d. Both of these may be performed.

40. Which of the following can cause reversible sensorineural hearing loss?
    a. Aspirin
    b. Old age
    c. Diabetes
    d. Ménière's

41. Noise exposure can cause hearing loss that is
    a. temporary from short-term exposure.
    b. permanent from long-term exposure.
    c. permanent, regardless of duration.
    d. Both answer (a) and answer (b)

42. Which statement is correct regarding the acoustics of speech sound production and the speech perception of listeners?
    a. Speech production is linear but listeners' perception runs the sounds together.
    b. Speech production and listener perception are both linear.
    c. Speech sounds are coarticulated but the listener's perception of them is linear.
    d. Neither the production nor the perception of speech sounds is linear in nature.

43. Which of the following is NOT a type of perceptual constancy in speech perception?
    a. Vocal tract normalization
    b. Categorical perception
    c. Speech rate normalization
    d. All are types of constancy.

44. VOT is an acoustic cue in speech sound waveforms signaling the difference between
    a. vocalization and devocalization of stops.
    b. nasalization and denasalization of vowels.
    c. fricatives/affricates and stops of consonants.
    d. front and back articulatory tongue placement.

45. The phonemic restoration effect is most analogous to
   a. perceiving discrete movie images as continuous.
   b. perceiving a word missing a letter as complete.
   c. perceiving a word with extra letters as correct.
   d. perceiving a tiny detail in a very "busy" picture.

46. Researchers have found that infants can discriminate among
   a. vowels in their native language by the age of 11-12 months.
   b. consonants in their native language by the age of 6 months.
   c. consonants in their native language by the age of 9 months.
   d. vowels in their native language around the age of 6 months.

47. Japanese learners of English as a second language (ESL) commonly have difficulty with the /l/ sound in English words such as "little" because the sound does not exist in their first language. At what level is this example?
   a. Syntactic
   b. Morphological
   c. Phonemic
   d. Semantic

48. Chinese learners of English as a second language (ESL) often leave out articles like "a/n" or "the" and plural "-s" word endings because these do not exist in their first language. At what level is this example?
   a. Semantic
   b. Phonemic
   c. Syntactic
   d. Morphological

49. German learners of English as a second language (ESL) might put the verb at the end of an English sentence after all its modifiers, as is done in German, while in English the modifiers tend to follow the verb. For example, German learners might say something like, "We last week at that café downtown spoke." At what level is this example?
   a. Syntactic
   b. Semantic
   c. Phonemic
   d. Morphological

50. Among the following, who are more likely to have better results understanding speech with cochlear implants?
   a. People who received implants as adults
   b. People with postlingual onset of deafness
   c. People with prelingual onset of deafness
   d. None of the above; people vary individually with no patterns.

51. Which is a factor LEAST likely to determine whether a child with hearing loss will acquire spoken language?
   a. The clinician's skill in giving the parents guidance
   b. The parents' understanding of language acquisition
   c. The severity and nature of the child's hearing loss
   d. The status of the child's brain and nervous system

52. According to OSHA, when audiometric tests are given to employees in a workplace, the employee must have access to these test records. Others who must have access to these records do NOT include

a. former employees.
b. designated representatives.
c. the Assistant Secretary (Labor).
d. any of the employee's relatives.

53. What is the distribution of deaf children born into hearing families versus those born into deaf families?

a. Many more are born into hearing families.
b. About the same number are born into hearing families as into deaf families.
c. Many fewer are born into hearing families.
d. Slightly more are born into hearing families than into deaf families.

54. Which frequency is NOT normally used in calculating a pure tone average?

a. 2000 Hz
b. 4000 Hz
c. 1000 Hz
d. 500 Hz

55. According to the CDC, how many people in the U.S. have had some sort of problem with their balance at some time in their lives?

a. Almost half
b. Nearly 1/3
c. Almost 3/4
d. Over 2/3

56. When senior citizens fall, it is often related to balance problems. The CDC finds that a senior citizen receives emergency room treatment for a fall

a. every 23 minutes.
b. every 57 seconds.
c. every 18 seconds.
d. every 16 minutes.

57. The CDC reports that a senior citizen dies as the result of falling

a. every 45 minutes.
b. every 35 minutes.
c. every 25 minutes.
d. every 15 minutes.

58. Which of the following is NOT a contraindication to performing the Epley maneuver or canalith repositioning procedure?

a. Any unstable heart condition
b. Severe stenosis of the carotid
c. Cervical spondylosis with myelopathy
d. Benign paroxysmal positional vertigo

59. For a person wearing hearing aids and attending a lecture in a large audience, which environmental factor would NOT interfere with speech comprehension?
    a. Distance from speaker to listener
    b. Competition of noise in the room
    c. A wireless microphone for speaker
    d. The room's acoustic quality

60. Which of these things that help deaf and hearing-impaired people to communicate is NOT a recent digital technology?
    a. Skype
    b. TTY/TDD
    c. Live chat
    d. IM

61. Which of the following is NOT used as an alerting device for hearing-impaired people?
    a. Flashing lights; strobe lights
    b. Transducers to shake beds
    c. Trained hearing ear dogs
    d. All the above are used to alert.

62. Children with hearing loss diagnosed by the time they are ____ old can, with early intervention, be expected to have language development equivalent to that of their normal-hearing peers by the time they are ____ old.
    a. Six months; five years
    b. One year; three years
    c. Three months; six years
    d. This cannot be predicted.

63. Which of the following is NOT a current issue for providers and recipients of aural rehabilitation (AR) services?
    a. There is not enough public information available about aural rehabilitation.
    b. There is not an identified body for professional certification of audiologists.
    c. There is not always a hearing aid orientation provided by audiologists/SLPs.
    d. There is not counseling included in most AR programs' goals and objectives.

64. Which of the following is correct regarding insurance coverage of hearing aids?
    a. Medicare always covers hearing aids for children and adults.
    b. Medicaid is required to cover hearing aids for children and adults.
    c. Medicaid must cover child hearing aids and often can cover adults'.
    d. Private health insurance plans always cover child/adult hearing aids.

65. Which of the following is NOT included in the scope of an audiologist's practice when working with families of hearing-impaired children?
    a. Providing emotional support and counseling
    b. Observing parents for acute emotional reactions
    c. Referring parents to mental health professionals
    d. Providing mental health counseling services

66. "Microtic" means
    a. a microscopically small tic.
    b. an abnormally small pinna.
    c. an otic type of microphone.
    d. None of the above

67. A person's eustachian tubes must function normally in order for
    a. myringoplasty to work.
    b. the person to breathe.
    c. the person to swallow.
    d. the individual to hear.

68. Eustachian tube function can be tested by using
    a. the Valsalva maneuver.
    b. catheterizing the tube(s).
    c. impedance audiometry.
    d. Any or all of these tests

69. When conducting an otolaryngology exam, an otologist should test the functioning of the auditory/vestibular (VIII) nerve, the facial (VII) nerve, and other cranial nerves as well. Which of the following groups are NOT other nerves whose function the otologist should test?
    a. Trigeminal (V), Abducens (VI)
    b. Glossopharyngeal (IX), Vagus (X)
    c. Olfactory (I), Oculomotor (III)
    d. Accessory (XI), Hypoglossal (XII)

70. If an examiner finds a patient has a missing or decreased corneal reflex in one eye, which of the following cranial nerves is affected that could indicate acoustic neuroma?
    a. Optic nerve
    b. Trigeminal nerve
    c. Oculomotor nerve
    d. Abducens nerve

71. The auditory nerve has
    a. a cochlear branch.
    b. a vestibular branch.
    c. Both these branches
    d. No kinds of branches

72. Which of the following growths in the external auditory meatus is the LEAST serious?
    a. Osteoma
    b. Carcinoma
    c. Epithelioma
    d. None is less serious than the others.

73. Which of the following can cause chronic serous otitis media?
    a. Mucus in the middle ear
    b. Lymph in the middle ear
    c. Enlargement of adenoids
    d. All of the above

74. Which of these is NOT a complication of chronic suppurative otitis media?
    a. Facial nerve paralysis
    b. Brain abscess
    c. Meningitis
    d. All of the above

75. If someone was born without an oval window, it is advisable to
    a. create an opening and construct a membrane where it should be.
    b. perform a surgical fenestration of the horizontal semicircular canal.
    c. conduct either one of these procedures.
    d. conduct neither one of these procedures.

76. Which of the following is MOST involved in hearing loss counseling provided by audiologists to families of hearing-impaired children?
    a. Audiogram interpretations
    b. Options for communication
    c. Emotional and grief support
    d. Advocacy for hearing losses

77. According to ASHA, which of the following is NOT included in the principles for best practice in informational counseling about newborn hearing screening?
    a. Confidentiality and focusing on family
    b. Communicating clearly and concisely
    c. Using accurate technical terminology
    d. Encouraging and answering questions

78. Approximately how many children in the United States have hearing losses?
    a. More than a million
    b. Almost five million
    c. One-half of a million
    d. One-quarter million

79. At least what proportion of children through age 18 has hearing loss?
    a. 2%
    b. 3%
    c. 4%
    d. 5%

80. Approximately one out of how many babies born in the U.S. has some kind of hearing problem?
    a. 32
    b. 22
    c. 42
    d. 12

81. Of all the babies in the U.S. born with some degree of hearing loss, what proportion is born with severe or profound hearing losses?
    a. One sixth
    b. One tenth
    c. One third
    d. One half

82. How many U.S. children out of 1000 have educationally significant hearing loss?
    a. 103
    b. 93
    c. 83
    d. 73

83. How many U.S. children <u>of school age</u> have *bilateral* hearing loss deemed educationally significant?
    a. 11 of every 1000
    b. 7 of every 1000
    c. 14 of every 1000
    d. 4 of every 1000

84. Of school-aged children in the U.S., what range has *unilateral* hearing loss considered educationally significant?
    a. 12 to 15 of every 1000
    b. 13 to 16 of every 1000
    c. 16 to 19 of every 1000
    d. 18 to 21 of every 1000

85. About how many of every 1000 *school-aged* children in the U.S. have severe to profound hearing losses?
    a. Three
    b. Five
    c. Seven
    d. Nine

86. How many of every 1000 school-aged children in the U.S. have permanent sensorineural hearing loss?
    a. Ten
    b. Five
    c. Eight
    d. Twelve

87. About what percentage of children in the U.S. with hearing losses have another disability in addition to the hearing loss?
    a. 20%
    b. 30%
    c. 40%
    d. 10%

88. Speech audiometry can obtain hearing thresholds for speech rather than for pure tones. It can also be used to corroborate or check pure-tone audiometry results. Which of the following is NOT another way speech audiometry can be used?
    a. To aid differential diagnosis of the etiology of a hearing loss
    b. To measure an individual's capability for auditory processing
    c. To measure the ability to recognize sub-threshold speech levels
    d. To estimate the communication functionality of an individual

89. The type of a hearing loss is
    a. locational.
    b. qualitative.
    c. quantitative.
    d. None of the above

90. The severity of a hearing loss is
    a. locational.
    b. qualitative.
    c. quantitative.
    d. None of the above

91. The configuration of a hearing loss is
    a. locational.
    b. qualitative.
    c. quantitative.
    d. None of the above

92. According to research, which statement is correct about the role of counseling in aural and communicative rehabilitation?
    a. Communicative rehabilitation programs are not as successful without counseling.
    b. Communicative rehabilitation programs are equally effective without counseling.
    c. Communicative rehabilitation programs are less effective with added counseling.
    d. Communicative rehabilitation programs are not studied in relation to counseling.

93. A consideration in adjustment to hearing loss counseling is the family's relative ability to cope. According to ASHA, to understand the family's coping skills, family variables are one necessary factor to learn. Which of the following is NOT one of three other essential factors?
    a. Parent variables
    b. Child variables
    c. External variables
    d. Internal variables

94. Which statement is NOT true about a diagnostic teaching approach to intervention with hearing-impaired children?
    a. It can reveal other disabilities that were not previously diagnosed in a child.
    b. It helps audiologists find the best assistive technologies for a specific child.
    c. It evolves over time with changing needs, so it does not involve goal-setting.
    d. It helps audiologists find the family communication method best for a child.

95. Relative to support groups for families of hearing-impaired children, the role of the audiologist is that of a(n)
    a. leader.
    b. instructor.
    c. facilitator.
    d. All of the above

96. The rules of ASHA's Code of Ethics prohibit behavior creating conflicts of interest by audiologists and other professionals, as do principles of ethical practices in general. If an audiologist has a primary employer and a private practice and wants to see a client in private practice whom he has been seeing at his primary employer, ASHA provides guidelines for doing this without a conflict of interest. Which of the following is NOT one of those guidelines?
    a. Requiring the client to sign a "non-compete" agreement
    b. Informing clients of all services; they are free to choose
    c. Informing clients of any fee differences between the two
    d. Notifying the primary employer of private practice plans

97. Researchers have found that cochlear implant teams and centers do not always inform families of
    a. audiological information.
    b. autonomy/identity or deaf culture.
    c. the medical and/or surgical risks.
    d. education/communication options.

98. Since the inception of newborn hearing screenings, the average age at confirmation of hearing loss is
    a. one tenth of what it used to be.
    b. one fifth of what it used to be.
    c. one half of what it used to be.
    d. essentially unchanged.

99. According to the Centers for Disease Control and Prevention (CDC), how many newborns who are referred after failing hearing screenings actually receive follow-up?
    a. 85%
    b. 75%
    c. Two thirds
    d. About half

100. Which statement is correct regarding validity and reliability of assessment instruments?
    a. Validity and reliability are both specific to each situation.
    b. Where one of these exists, the other does, and vice versa.
    c. Reliable instruments are repeated with consistent results.
    d. Instruments need either validity or reliability but not both.

Answer Key

Question	Answer	Question	Answer	Question	Answer	Question	Answer
1	A	26	C	51	C	76	C
2	C	27	B	52	D	77	C
3	D	28	A	53	A	78	A
4	B	29	B	54	B	79	D
5	C	30	C	55	A	80	B
6	D	31	A	56	C	81	A
7	A	32	B	57	B	82	C
8	B	33	C	58	D	83	B
9	C	34	D	59	C	84	C
10	D	35	C	60	B	85	D
11	B	36	A	61	D	86	A
12	A	37	D	62	A	87	B
13	C	38	C	63	B	88	C
14	D	39	B	64	C	89	A
15	A	40	A	65	D	90	C
16	B	41	D	66	B	91	B
17	C	42	C	67	A	92	A
18	A	43	B	68	D	93	D
19	B	44	A	69	C	94	C
20	D	45	B	70	B	95	C
21	D	46	D	71	C	96	A
22	B	47	C	72	A	97	B
23	C	48	D	73	D	98	A
24	A	49	A	74	D	99	D
25	D	50	B	75	B	100	C

Answer Explanations

1. A: Pure-tone audiometers (a) have established standards (e.g., ANSI) for their calibration. However, there are no national standards or uniform performance standards for otoacoustic emissions (OAE) testing (b) or for auditory brainstem response (ABR) testing (c) equipment. Therefore, not all of these have national or uniform standards, so (d) is incorrect.

2. C: A masking noise (c) is most likely to be introduced purposely by the examiner during an audiometric examination, under some circumstances (for example to aid in differential diagnosis of conductive vs. sensorineural hearing loss, as noise will mask bone conduction). A distorted tone (a) is an error in the audiometer that should not exist. By definition, pure tones are "pure." Distortion is a malfunction. Switching transients (b) are clicking or popping sounds resulting from suddenly turning a tone on or off. Having subjects respond to these rather than the pure tones would confound test results, so audiometers have circuits creating gradual, smooth transitions that eliminate these noises. Audible switching transients are also a malfunction of the audiometer. Since (c) may be used deliberately, answer (d), none of the above, is incorrect.

3. D: Velocity (d) is not one of the required components for producing sound. It is rather a characteristic of one of the components, the medium (b) through which sound waves travel. Velocity or speed of the molecules that sound waves displace within the medium is related to the medium's relative pressure and its other physical properties. Required components for producing sound are a source of vibration (a) to generate sound waves; a medium (b) whose molecules the sound waves displace, allowing the waves to travel through space; and force (c), or the relative pressure of the sound waves, which determines the intensity of the sound.

4. B: The outer ear is (b) an acoustic device in that it collects acoustical energy. It is not mechanical (a) in that it does not perform any movements to transmit sound as the ossicles do. It is not a hydraulic device (c) in that it does not contain any fluid as the inner ear does and is not involved in moving fluid as the inner ear is. It is not a biological device (d) in that it does not analyze sound energy for its properties and does not transmit it to nerves or the brain as the inner ear does.

5. C: The middle ear is (c) both of these – acoustic (a) and mechanical (b). It is an acoustic device (a) in that it collects sound energy, like the outer ear. It is a mechanical device (b) in that sound energy causes the tympanic membrane to vibrate, which in turn moves the malleus, which moves the incus, which moves the stapes, which moves the oval window. The movements of the ossicular chain represent a mechanical process. Since (c), both of these, is correct, answer (d), neither of these, is incorrect.

6. D: The inner ear is (d) all of the above. It is mechanical (a) in that the hair cells inside the cochlea are moved by incoming sound energy, and this movement is mechanical. It is hydraulic (b) in that the inner ear is full of fluid, which is agitated by incoming sound energy, and this movement of fluid is a hydraulic process. It is biological (c) in that it analyzes incoming sound energy for its properties, including frequency (which will be perceived as pitch), intensity (which will be perceived as loudness), complexity (e.g.,

number of frequencies, formants) and temporal features (duration, continuity vs. interruption); it transmits the energy along the auditory nerve to the brain.

7. A: Without the middle ear, sound reaching the inner ear would be (a) virtually nonexistent to the hearer. An estimated 99.9% of sound would be reflected back to the atmosphere from the inner ear without middle ear mediation because the impedance, or resistance, of the inner ear is higher than that of the air. Sound pressure is magnified roughly 17 times by the middle ear mechanism by the tympanic membrane, being roughly 17 times bigger than the stapes footplate. Pressure is force per unit area, so the smaller stapes receives greater pressure from the larger eardrum. The hearer would likely not even be aware of the remaining 0.1% of the sound. Therefore it would not be so loud as to cause nerve damage (b), which would only result from over-amplification. Its frequencies would not be distorted (c), as intensity, determined by sound pressure, has nothing to do with frequency, determined by number of cycles per second. It would not be impossible to interpret (d), as the inner ear analyzes sound energy and the brain, using this information, interprets or perceives it (the middle ear is not involved in these tasks).

8. B: Otitis media (b) is most likely to cause conductive hearing loss. A middle ear infection can cause swelling and fluid buildup in the middle ear. This interferes with the conduction of sound energy through the middle ear into the inner ear. If fluid buildup causes enough pressure, it can perforate or rupture the eardrum, also disrupting conduction. Presbycusis (a), or hearing loss associated with the aging process, is due to death and/or destruction of the hair cells and/or nerve tissue and as such is a sensorineural hearing loss. Noise exposure (c) can also destroy hair cells and neural tissue, causing sensorineural hearing loss if the noise is loud enough and exposure is continual or repeated enough. Birth trauma (d) can also cause sensorineural hearing loss.

9. C: Ménière's disease (c) is most likely to cause sensorineural hearing loss. This disease has symptoms of tinnitus (ringing in the ears), vertigo/balance problems, and/or dizziness, as it affects the vestibular system and sensations of aural fullness or pressure, as well as sensorineural hearing loss. Foreign objects in the ear (a) cause conductive hearing losses, as does impacted cerumen (b) or wax buildup. Removal of the offending body/substance typically remediates the conduction problem. Serous otitis media (d) is middle ear infection, which also can cause a conductive hearing loss. Treatment of the infection and removal of fluid will typically alleviate the conduction problem.

10. D: It is not correct that (d) conductive hearing loss does not affect threshold levels; it does. Both conductive and sensorineural types of hearing loss reduce hearing acuity, i.e. the patient's threshold, or the lowest (quietest) decibel (dB) level at which the patient can hear sounds half of the time. It is correct that conductive hearing losses are often reversible (a) through medical and/or surgical treatment. It is correct that sensorineural hearing loss, unlike conductive hearing loss, is usually permanent. It is also correct that sensorineural hearing loss, in addition to impairing acuity, impairs hearing discrimination, or the ability to differentiate among fine differences in speech sounds. With impaired discrimination, the listener might be able to hear the sounds, but not clearly enough to recognize every word.

11. B: A person with recruitment will have (b) less distance (in dB) between hearing threshold and uncomfortable loudness level (UCL). People with recruitment also experience less distance between their hearing threshold and their most comfortable

loudness (MCL), and between their MCL and UCL. Normal-hearing people have a wide range of loudness they are able to hear without discomfort, from very soft, e.g. 0 dB, to quite loud, e.g. 80 dB. Recruitment narrows this range such that the individual will often demand speakers to repeat, but when the speaker (almost inevitably) speaks much louder, the hearer will recoil and complain that the other is "shouting." Thus recruitment causes a very small window of loudness that is both audible and not painful to the listener. Having differing thresholds in each ear (a) has nothing to do with recruitment and is quite common in hearing loss. More distance from MCL to UCL (c) is the reverse of what happens in recruitment. Recruitment does not cause the better ear to overcompensate for the more affected ear (d).

12. A: Hyperacusis (a) is most often associated with normal hearing. Hyperacusis is hypersensitivity to loud sounds or noise. Lesions of the facial (VII) nerve, causing paralysis of the stapedius muscle, can result in hyperacusis. This condition can also occur with hearing loss, as from Ménière's disease; however, of the choices given, it is the only one often (or ever) associated with normal hearing levels. Diplacusis (b) is hearing the same sounds at different frequencies (pitches) in each ear due to distortion of the sound's actual frequency in the affected ear; this condition always accompanies hearing loss. The loss is either unilateral (explaining the distortion in only one ear) or bilateral but with much greater loss on one side. "Presbycusis" (c) is the term for hearing loss associated with advancing age in adults. As (a) is correct, answer (d), none of the above, is incorrect.

13. C:The relationship of Hz to sound waves to cycles per second is (c) 1:1:1. Sound is made by vibration; vibratory motion is oscillation, meaning movement up and down in cycles. One cycle generates one sound wave. Frequency is determined by the number of cycles per second. A frequency of one cycle per second equals 1 Hz. Therefore, 1 Hz equals one sound wave and one cycle per second, or 1:1:1. Answers (a), (b), and (d) all represent incorrect ratios.

14. D: The human voice typically has a frequency range of approximately (d) 80 Hz to 6000 Hz. The majority of the sound energy is between 125 Hz and 6000 Hz. The energy tends to peak around the area between 1000 and 3000 Hz. Answer (a) is incorrect because 50 Hz is lower than the lower limits of the human voice range and 500 Hz is much lower than its upper limits. Answer (b) is incorrect because 6000 Hz is the upper limit, not the lower limit, of the human voice, and 11,000 Hz would be a higher voice than humans could hear (though dogs can hear frequencies this high—up to around 60,000 Hz). Answer (c) is incorrect because 30 Hz is lower than the human voice's lower limits and 30,000 Hz is much higher, as in answer (b).

15. A: The range of frequencies that human ears can normally hear (allowing for individual variability) is (a) from 20 Hz to 20,000 Hz. Answer (b) is incorrect because 10 Hz is lower than the lower limits of human hearing and 30,000 Hz is higher than its higher limits. Answer (c) is incorrect because 1 Hz is lower than the human ear's lower frequency limits and 10,000 Hz is lower than its upper limits. Answer (d) is incorrect because 200 Hz is higher than the lower frequency limits of human hearing and 5000 Hz is lower than its upper limits. Obviously the normal human ear can hear frequencies below and above the range of the human voice (see #14).

16. B: The frequencies normally tested using manual (or conventional) pure-tone audiometers in hearing loss prevention programs are (b) 500, 1000, 2000, 3000, 4000, 6000, and 8000 Hz. Answer (a) is incorrect because 250 Hz is not tested unless the individual has a low-frequency hearing loss (#18), and the 8000-Hz frequency is not included, which is important due to the prevalence of high-frequency hearing losses, especially in aging adults, even when lower frequencies are not impaired. Answer (c) is incorrect because the 500-Hz frequency level is omitted at the lower end and 10,000 Hz is wrongly added at the high end. Over-the-ear/supraural and insert earphones are not recommended by ASHA (American Speech and Hearing Association) for measuring frequencies above 8000 Hz; around-the-ear/circumaural earphones are used for extended testing of higher frequencies. Answer (d) includes frequencies not representing octaves and not used in standardized audiometric testing (800, 1200, 1400, 1600, and 1800 Hz).

17. C: Both (c) 125 and 250 Hz should be tested in the event of a low-frequency hearing loss. 250 Hz (b) should be tested in any individual for diagnostic purposes, while testing begins at 500 Hz for monitoring purposes (#16). 125 Hz (a) should be tested in addition to 250 Hz for diagnostic purposes if the individual has a low-frequency hearing loss. Therefore answer (d), neither, is incorrect.

18. A: Extended high-frequency audiometry is done at frequencies of (a) 9000 to 16,000 Hz. Answer (b) is incorrect as 4000 to 8000 Hz are frequencies included within regular audiometry. Answer (c) is incorrect as 25,000 Hz is beyond the normal range of human hearing (see #15). Answer (d) is incorrect as 900 Hz is neither a very high frequency for human hearing, nor is it a standard frequency tested in audiometry; 1600 Hz is also not a standard frequency.

19. B: Testing inter-octave frequencies to pinpoint a hearing loss of narrower range that exists only at one frequency or a few frequencies close together is indicated according to ASHA if the subject has a difference between any two adjacent octave frequencies of (b) 20 dB or more. A difference of 10 dB (a) is not considered large enough to test frequencies between the octaves, as variability within 10 dB is common and not usually significant. 30 dB (c) and 40 dB (d) are both within the "or more" designation, but are differences too large for beginning further diagnostic testing; 20 dB is enough of a difference to warrant looking for a more frequency-specific hearing loss.

20. D: In routine audiometry the first frequency to test should be (d) 1000 Hz. Then the audiologist should test at 3000 to 8000 Hz in ascending order; then re-test at 1000 Hz; then test at 500, 250, and 125 Hz. Re-testing at 1000 Hz should be done in the first ear, which should be the better ear if known, but is unnecessary in the second ear. Frequency order is unlikely to affect test results in most cases, but according to ANSI and ASHA, following the same order promotes the tester's consistency among subjects and reduces the chance of accidentally omitting frequencies. While 500 Hz (a) is the lowest frequency tested in many screenings, 1000 Hz is the recommended first frequency. 8000 Hz (b) is the highest frequency tested in routine audiometry, and the sequence of frequencies is ascending, not descending. 125 Hz (c) is the very lowest and last frequency usually tested. (250 and 125 Hz are often not tested in screenings but are used in complete audiological evaluations and/or where a low-frequency hearing loss is known or suspected.)

21. D: It is true that (d) testing air conduction will show both types of hearing losses—conductive and sensorineural. It is not true that bone conduction testing will reveal conductive hearing loss (a). Bone conduction testing reveals only sensorineural hearing loss. It is not true that air conduction testing shows only sensorineural hearing loss (b); it will reveal both types. Since bone conduction can identify sensorineural hearing loss but not conductive hearing loss, it is not true that bone conduction testing shows both types (c).

22. B: If the air conduction test and bone conduction test results match, the hearing loss is sensorineural (b), not mixed (d). Because bone conduction testing works via vibration of the skull bones, it bypasses the air conduction of sound through the outer and middle ears, where conductive hearing losses originate. Thus bone conduction testing will reveal only hearing losses originating in the inner ear, cranial nerves, or brain—all sensorineural. If including the outer and middle ear by air conduction testing produces the same results as bone conduction testing, hearing is not reduced in the outer or middle ear, so conductive hearing loss is ruled out and the loss must be sensorineural. If there is a difference between air conduction and bone conduction test results, this is called an air-bone gap. An air-bone gap can indicate mixed (both conductive and sensorineural) hearing loss, not purely sensorineural (a) and not necessarily only conductive (c). If the air conduction threshold is abnormal but the bone conduction threshold is normal, there is a conductive hearing loss. If air and bone conduction thresholds are both abnormal, with air conduction being worse by 10 dB or more, the hearing loss is mixed.

23. C: Otoacoustic emissions (OAE) testing will indicate a sensorineural hearing loss if they are not identified during the test (c). Otoacoustic emissions are tiny sounds, inaudible to human hearing, emitted by the vibrations of the cochlea's outer hair cells, which rebound back into the middle ear and can be detected by an electroacoustic probe. With normal hearing, the cochlea's outer hair cells vibrate in response to incoming sound. However, with hearing loss of more than 25 to 40 dB, they do not vibrate, indicating the cochlea is compromised. Thus OAE testing can help to diagnose hearing loss and its extent. OAE has nothing to do with vehicle exhaust emissions in the air, which are toxic but have not been found to be ototoxic (a). The detection of emissions identifies normal hearing, not sensorineural hearing loss (b). OAE are sub-audible sounds, not substances, coming from the ears; otorrhea is fluid, mucus, or pus discharging from the ears, and is not diagnosed by the presence of OAE (d).

24. A: Otoacoustic emissions (a) or OAE testing is not an acoustic immittance measure. Acoustic immittance measures assess outer and middle ear function, while OAE assesses inner ear function (see #24). Tympanometry (b) is an acoustic immittance measure that tests the mobility of the tympanic membrane by blowing air into the ear. Acoustic reflex testing (c) is an acoustic immittance measure that determines whether the normal acoustic reflex is present, wherein the stapedius muscle reflexively pulls the stapes footplate slightly away from the oval window in response to sudden loud sound, reducing transmission of the sound's full intensity to protect against hearing damage. Testing for this reflex can help localize the origin of hearing loss within the auditory system. Static acoustic impedance (d) is an acoustic immittance measure of the physical amount or volume of air inside the ear canal, which helps to diagnose perforation of the tympanic membrane, or whether inserted ventilation tubes are open.

25. D: Approximately (d) 18 times as many children with only minimal hearing losses fail at least one school grade as normal-hearing children. In fact, the number is slightly more: 37% of children with minimal hearing loss compared to 2% of children with normal hearing. Thus twice as many (a) children or five times as many (b) both grossly underestimate these proportions, and even nine times as many (c) is slightly less than half the actual proportions.

26. C: A child with hearing loss of 20 dB (i.e., with a hearing threshold around 20 dB rather than 0) will actually hear only (c) one quarter of the teacher's speech. This allows comprehension of the majority of speech, but with much greater effort, strain, and fatigue, with additional negative results of poorer grammatical understanding, loss of interest due to the difficulty, and behavior problems. A 20 dB hearing loss does not allow the child to hear as much as 80% (a) of the teacher's speech, or as much as half (b), or even as much as one third (d). Thus even a hearing loss considered mild has significant negative educational impact.

27. B: Reducing hearing by 10 dB will reduce a person's subjective perception of the loudness of speech sounds by (b) one half. This is why even minimal hearing loss has such a strong unfavorable impact on education and social functioning. Because it is subjective, the listener's perception of reduced speech loudness does not correspond to the actual reduction of 10 dB. Thus, how much quieter speech seems with a 10 dB loss cannot be estimated as one tenth (a) by considering that a reduction of 100 dB represents a profound hearing loss and 10 is 1/10 of 100. The perception of speech as half as loud with a 10 dB loss is a greater reduction than one third (c). Similarly to (b), one also cannot guess that the perceived reduction would be by one fifth (d) or 20%, twice the actual dB of loss; a perceived reduction of twice the actual reduction might sound plausible, but the difference in the listener's perception of speech is actually much greater—1/2 or 50%, five times the number of dB of the actual hearing loss.

28. A: Research studies find that approximately (a) 90% of young children's learning of language and speech is incidental, from conversations surrounding them in their environments. This figure might sound astounding to some but is accurate, emphasizing the crucial nature of early intervention in childhood hearing loss and its implications for speech and language development. 75% (b), 50% (c), and 25% (d) are all incorrect figures, underestimating the actual proportion of incidental, environmental speech/language learning by young children.

29. B: In the human embryo, the outer ear parts form out of the (b) ectoderm, the outer embryonic layer that is first to develop. Skin (epidermis), teeth, and nervous system tissue also develop from ectoderm. The ear canal forms from the first pharyngeal cleft (ectodermic). Mesoderm (a) is the middle embryonic layer, which differentiates into middle ear parts as well as other bones, cartilage, connective tissue, blood, and tissues of the heart, kidneys, lymphatic vessels, and smooth muscles. Endoderm (c), the inner embryonic layer, develops into epithelium lining most of the gastrointestinal tract, liver, pancreas, trachea, bronchi, the lungs' alveoli, bladder and part of the urethra, and the follicles of the thymus and thyroid glands. As only (b) is correct, answer (d), all of the above, is incorrect.

30. C: The middle ear in the human embryo forms from (c) both of these, i.e. both the endoderm (a) and mesoderm (b). The middle ear cavities, as well as the eustachian tubes,

develop from the first pharyngeal pouch. The lining of this pouch, epithelium, forms from endoderm; therefore the epithelial linings of the middle ear cavities and eustachian tubes are endodermically derived. Of the ossicles, the malleus and incus form from the first pharyngeal arch, and the stapes forms from the second pharyngeal arch. The pharyngeal arches are formed from mesenchyme, or unspecialized cells of the mesoderm. Thus the middle ear's linings are from endoderm, and its other parts are from mesoderm. As (c), both of the above, is correct, answer (d), neither of the above, is incorrect.

31. A: In the human embryo the inner ear develops out of the (a) ectoderm or the outer embryonic layer. Otic placodes are thickened ectodermal depressions that form into otocysts, which differentiate into two compartments, the cochlear pouch (which will hold the cochlea) and the vestibular pouch (which will hold the vestibular system). The inner ear parts do not develop out of (b) mesoderm, the middle embryonic layer. They do not form from (c) endoderm, the inner embryonic layer. As (b) and (c) are incorrect and (a) is correct, answer (d), all of the above, is incorrect.

32. B: A person with a conductive hearing loss riding in a car with open windows is likely to hear conversation (b) better than normal-hearing individuals in the car. This is because ambient noise coming in the car windows interferes with normal hearing, but the conductive hearing loss masks some of this interfering noise. Also, the normal-hearing individuals who can hear the noise will raise their voices over it. Thus the person with conductive hearing loss benefits from the others' raised voices, and also hears less of the interfering noise, so that person hears conversation better than those who can hear all of the noise. For these reasons, the person with the conductive hearing loss will not hear (a) less well than the others. This person will also not hear (c) the same as the others. Such a person will not have (d) similar acuity but poorer discrimination than the others: impaired discrimination is a symptom of sensorineural hearing loss, not conductive, and those with sensorineural losses have both poorer discrimination and poorer acuity. Conductive losses typically cause poorer acuity but not poorer discrimination.

33. C: Presbycusis, or the hearing loss that accompanies aging in adults, most commonly affects (c) higher frequencies the worst and also the earliest. The loss might occur only in the higher frequencies, or there might be higher hearing thresholds at other or all frequencies, with the worst losses occurring at the highest frequencies. Usually middle frequencies (b) are the next to be affected. Noise-induced hearing loss (not presbycusis) can affect middle-high frequencies such as 3000 Hz. Lower frequencies (a) are the least likely and/or the latest to be affected by presbycusis. Since hearing loss at higher frequencies (c) is sustained most in presbycusis, answer (d), all of the above equally, is incorrect.

34. D: All of these (d) can cause tinnitus, a ringing or other noise in the ears. Ménière's disease (a), which affects the vestibular system, causes balance problems, vertigo, dizziness, hearing loss, tinnitus, and a feeling of fullness or pressure in the ear(s). Fluid in the middle ear (b), which can result from otitis media (middle ear infection), can also cause tinnitus. In fact, any type and degree of hearing loss (c) from any etiology can cause the symptom of tinnitus.

35. C: Gradenigo's syndrome is a name for the grouped symptoms of (a) severe earache; (b) otorrhea, or discharge from the ear; and (d) diplopia, or double vision. This group of

symptoms can be caused by suppurative otitis media, a middle ear infection producing pus, when it involves the petrous apex and the abducens nerve. Gradenigo's syndrome does not include (c) vesicles. Vesicles, or small cysts, on the outer ear and/or in the ear canal, are symptoms of the herpes zoster oticus virus, also called Ramsey Hunt syndrome.

36. A: The correct answer is (a): If the pinna is microtic, or severely underdeveloped, with congenital atresia of the external auditory meatus (that is, if the external auditory canal is malformed or not formed), this indicates that the defect occurred earlier in the fetus's development, and reconstruction will involve more work to rebuild both the outer ear and canal. Congenital atresia of the canal with a normal pinna indicates that the defect occurred later in the fetus's development, giving a better reconstructive prognosis—not only because the outer ear is normal and does not need to be created or modified, but also because this raises the probabilities of both the ossicles and the eardrum being intact, giving a better prognosis for hearing. Answer (b) correctly states the better prognosis, but incorrectly states earlier etiology rather than later. Answer (c) incorrectly states both etiology and prognosis, the opposite of correct answer (a). Answer (d) correctly states later etiology with a normal pinna, but incorrectly states the prognosis for reconstruction as more difficult.

37. D: The correct answer is that otosclerosis occurs more often in white populations (d). Histological research has found more than eight times as many cases of otosclerosis in white people than in black people. Therefore answer (c) is incorrect. Otosclerosis does not cause only conductive hearing loss (a) or only sensorineural hearing loss (b). It can cause either or both. Its abnormal bony growth most often affects the middle ear, causing conductive hearing loss; but it can also extend into the vestibule and labyrinth in some cases, and when it encroaches on the inner ear in this way it causes sensorineural hearing loss. A patient with otosclerosis in both the middle ear and inner ear will have mixed hearing loss.

38. C: When a stapedectomy is indicated, as with otosclerotic fixation of the stapes or its footplate, this surgery can (c) cause both of these outcomes: It can resolve or minimize a conductive hearing loss (a), either by freeing the stapes to move again, or by removing an overly compromised stapes and replacing it with a prosthetic one to serve the same function; it can also cause sensorineural hearing loss or make existing sensorineural loss worse (b). These are a major pro and con of stapedectomy. Therefore answer (d), that this operation cannot be held responsible for either or both results, is incorrect.

39. B: A stapedectomy (b) should *not* be performed at the same time as a myringoplasty because creating an opening to the inner ear while the eardrum is not intact carries too high a risk of resulting in sensorineural hearing loss. If the stapes is fixated, a stapedectomy should be performed later, after the eardrum has had a chance to heal from the myringoplasty. Ossiculoplasty (a), on the other hand, is usually performed to repair the malleus, incus, or both, at the same time as myringoplasty when indicated. Therefore it is not correct that neither procedure should be performed (c) with myringoplasty. It is also incorrect that both procedures should be performed (d) at the same time as the myringoplasty.

40. A: Aspirin (a), taken in very large doses, is known to cause a sensorineural hearing loss which, unlike most sensorineural hearing losses, is reversible upon discontinuing the drug.

Some other ototoxic drugs, such as other nonsteroidal anti-inflammatory drugs (NSAIDs), some antibiotics, and some potent diuretics, can have similar effects. The SNHL caused by old age (b), called presbycusis, is irreversible. Diabetes (c) tends to cause a progressive but gradual bilateral high-frequency SNHL that is irreversible. Ménière's disease (d) causes permanent SNHL, as well as vertigo and tinnitus.

41. D: Noise exposure can cause hearing loss that is (d): both (a), temporary from short-term exposure, and (b), permanent from long-term exposure. Noise exposure does not necessarily cause permanent hearing loss regardless of duration (c) of the exposure. Short-term exposure to noise, such as that from guns or explosives such as firecrackers, can cause what is known as a "temporary threshold shift." People with this noise exposure typically have tinnitus following the noise. Long-term exposure to noise causes a permanent impairment known as noise-induced hearing loss. A typical feature of this loss is a dip in the audiogram around 3000 Hz, although some people also have higher-frequency hearing loss as well.

42. C: The correct statement is (c): Speech sounds are coarticulated, meaning the individual phonemes actually run together and even overlap, but when we hear them, our perception separates them into discrete units heard in a linear fashion. This enables us to differentiate among speech sounds to understand what is said. Our visual perception does the opposite of this when viewing movies: they are really a series of separate images, but our perception runs them together into what seems like continuous movement. Answer (a), like visual perception of movies, is the reverse of the correct answer regarding auditory perception of speech. It is not true that both speech production and speech perception are linear, so answer (b) is incorrect. Since our perception of speech sounds is linear, answer (d), that neither production nor perception is linear in nature, is incorrect.

43. B: Categorical perception (b) is not a type of perceptual constancy. Perceptual constancy is our ability as listeners to recognize speech sounds across different individual speakers. Vocal tract normalization (a) is a type of perceptual constancy wherein the listener can identify the same speech sounds despite differences in resonance and pitch from one person's voice to another's. Speech rate normalization (c) is a type of perceptual constancy wherein the listener can identify the same speech sounds despite differences in individual speakers' speed or tempo of speaking and the duration of the speech sounds they produce. Categorical perception (b) is our trait as listeners of perceiving speech sounds discretely although they are not produced this way (see also #42); we even hear sounds in a continuum as discontinuous, by differentiating among their distinctive features, such as vocalized vs. devocalized features. Since (b) is not a type of perceptual constancy, answer (d), all are, is incorrect.

44. A: VOT, or voice onset time, is an acoustic cue in speech sound waveforms signaling the difference between (a) vocalization and devocalization of stops (for example, /b/ vs. /p/, /d/ vs. /t/, or /v/ vs. /f/). The difference between nasalized and denasalized vowels (b); between friction and plosion in consonant production (c); and between front and back (or middle) articulatory placement (d) are all signaled by various other acoustic cues present in the waveforms of the individual speech sounds.

45. B: The phonemic restoration effect is most analogous to (b) perceiving a word that is missing a letter as complete. The phonemic restoration effect is our tendency as listeners to

"fill in" a phoneme in a word even when it is omitted, distorted, or replaced by an incorrect phoneme, by using the phonemic context of the rest of the word. This effect has been demonstrated in research experiments. Subjects did not even know which phoneme was missing; the same is true in everyday listening. Visually, we do the same thing when we read a word that is missing a letter and automatically correct the error, filling in the missing letter by seeing it the way we normally expect it to appear. Seeing separate movie images as connected (a), not seeing extra letters in a word (c) so it conforms with our expectation of correct spelling, and isolating a small detail or figure from a complex ground (d) are all other phenomena of visual perception that are real, but not as analogous in vision to the phonemic restoration effect in hearing as answer (b).

46. D: Researchers have found that infants can discriminate among (d) vowels in their native language by about 6 months in age. Additionally, they have found that infants can discriminate among consonants in their native language by the time they are 11-12 months old. Thus they can identify the phonemes for vowel sounds earlier than 11-12 months and answer (a) is incorrect. Infants learn to recognize vowel sounds earlier than consonant sounds, as vowels are more resonant and have broader differentiations than consonants. Therefore answer (b), that infants can discriminate consonants by 6 months of age, is incorrect. Even by 9 months, as in answer (c), they will still lack the full capability of telling the difference among consonant sounds; so, this answer is also incorrect.

47. C: This example is at the (c) phonemic level. A phoneme is a representation of an individual speech sound unit, such as /l/. Many Japanese ESL learners will pronounce /l/ more like /r/ because they have no /l/ sound in Japanese but do have the /r/ sound, so they assimilate the unfamiliar phoneme by substituting the most similar sound in their existing repertoire. The syntactic (a) level involves sentence structure and word order. The morphological (b) level involves grammatical structure and structural changes to words reflecting grammatical categories. The semantic (d) level involves the meanings of words.

48. D: This example is at the (d) morphological level. In English, articles like "a/n," "the," "this," "that," "these," etc., indicating number, definiteness vs. indefiniteness, etc. and noun endings indicating plurality vs. singularity, are structural "function words" that have no counterparts in Chinese, whose grammatical word structure is different. The semantic (a) level is related to the meanings of words. The phonemic (b) level is related to individual speech sounds, or phonemes, which represent various individual vowel and consonant sounds. The syntactic (c) level is related to sentence structure and word order within a sentence.

49. A: This example is at the (a) syntactic level. Syntax is word order or sentence structure. Because the grammatical structure of German differs from that of English, German ESL speakers may place verbs at the ends of English sentences, as speakers do in German. The semantic (b) level has to do with the meanings of words and how they may be interpreted. The phonemic (c) level has to do with individual units of speech sounds that we associate with particular vowels and consonants. The morphological (d) level has to do with the internal structures of words and structural changes indicating various grammatical functions and relationships.

50. B: People with postlingual onset of deafness (b) are more likely to understand speech better with cochlear implants. Having learned language before losing hearing gives the

postlingually deaf advantages of better original learning and understanding of language, accomplished optimally through hearing rather than other modalities. Their earlier experience with hearing also facilitates adaptation to hearing again with cochlear implants. People with prelingual onset of deafness (c) did not learn language through the normal, optimal auditory sense, so their foundation of speech and language learning is not the same. Also, they do not have the previous experience of learning and understanding language through hearing, so hearing with implants will not correspond to their past prelingual hearing of sounds. People who received implants as children have better results than people who received them as adults (a), as they have fewer changes to adapt to, less interference from competing behaviors learned earlier, are more open to learning new skills, learn them more deeply and permanently, and have much more time to adjust to and learn about hearing with implants. While there is individual variation, it is not true that these patterns do not generally exist (d).

51. C: The factor least likely to determine whether a child with hearing loss will acquire spoken language is (c) the severity and nature of the child's hearing loss. Although more profound deafness can affect the ultimate quality and clarity of the child's speech, many methods and technologies exist to promote learning speech, such as deaf education teaching strategies, hearing aids, cochlear implants, FM systems and other assistive listening devices, speech reading and other visual supplementation, etc. Regardless of issues of speech quality, the type and extent of hearing loss do not determine whether a hearing-impaired child will or will not learn spoken language. Among the most influential factors determining whether the child will learn to speak are (a) how skillful the clinician is in guiding the parents to use effective strategies for spoken language learning with their children; (b) how well the parents are able to understand and apply the principles of early language learning; and (d) the condition of the child's brain and central nervous system, which indicate the child's capacity to learn spoken language.

52. D: Any of the employee's relatives (d) are not included in OSHA's specifications as to who must have access to workplace audiometric test records. The only circumstance wherein a relative or family member would be given access to these records would be if the employee designated that person as his representative (b). Anybody the employee designates as that employee's representative must be given access to the records. So must any former employees (a). (Note: while former employees are included, OSHA requires the records to be kept at the workplace as long as the employee works there. Therefore, employees would be well advised to request these records before or upon leaving the company's employ, as the records might not still be there after the employees have been gone for a while. Such records could be important in cases of noise-induced hearing loss if the company did not comply with OSHA hearing conservation standards and the employee files a claim to receive benefits.) The Assistant Secretary of the Department of Labor (c), the department under which OSHA operates, must also have access to these records.

53. A: The proportion of deaf children born into hearing families versus deaf families is (a) the vast majority. The estimate is that around 93% of deaf children are born to hearing parents and families, while only about 7% of deaf children are born to deaf parents or families. Thus the incidence of deaf infants being born to hearing and deaf families is not about the same (b) at all. Deaf children born to hearing families are not the vast minority (c) but the exact opposite. With such a great difference in percentages, the proportion of deaf children born into hearing families is not just slightly more (d) than those born into deaf families, but is rather over 13 times as many.

54. B: 4000 Hz (b) is not a frequency used to calculate a pure tone average. Pure tone average is obtained separately for each ear by averaging a person's audiometric hearing thresholds at three frequencies: 500 Hz (d), 1000 Hz (c), and 2000 Hz (a). These frequencies are chosen because they are the most relevant to the frequency ranges for the hearing and perception of speech. If a person's thresholds for one ear are, for example, 30 dB at 500 Hz, 45 dB at 1000 Hz, and 65 dB at 2000 Hz, the pure tone average would be (rounded up from 46.67) 47 dB, indicating a moderate hearing loss.

55. A: The U.S. Centers for Disease Control and Prevention (CDC) finds that almost half (a) of all U.S. citizens have had some kind of balance problem at some point in their lives (2003). Balance problems can significantly interfere with basic activities of daily living. They can also lead to falling, especially in the case of older adults. Falling is a serious problem in the elderly population (see #56, #57). Answer (b), nearly 1/3, underestimates the number of people who have ever experienced any problem with balance. Almost 3/4 (c) overestimates the number, as does over 2/3 (d).

56. C: The CDC reports (2008) that a senior citizen receives emergency room treatment for a fall (c) every 18 seconds in the United States. Every 23 minutes (a), every 57 seconds (b), and every 16 minutes (d) are all inaccurate figures, underestimating how often senior citizens in this country are injured seriously enough for emergency room visits. Although muscular weakness, gait problems unrelated to balance, visual impairments, and cognitive impairments all contribute to falling, a major cause of falls by elderly people is balance problems. Many balance disorders also involve hearing loss. Because of the intimate relationship of the vestibular system, ocular system, and cranial nerves, visual, hearing, and balance problems can coexist, especially in aging populations.

57. B: The CDC reports (2008) that in the U.S., a senior citizen dies as a result of falling (b) every 35 minutes. This is more frequently than every 45 minutes (a), but less frequently than every 25 minutes (c) or every 15 minutes (d). Although elderly people also fall due to unstable gait, poor vision, weak muscles, and impaired judgment, a significant factor causing older people to fall is problems with the sense of balance and proprioception; these are controlled by the vestibular system in the inner ear and can be disrupted by compromise of the cranial nerves. Thus many balance problems in the elderly are accompanied by hearing losses.

58. D: Benign paroxysmal positional vertigo (d) or BPPV is not a contraindication to performing the Epley maneuver. BPPV is the primary indication for performing this procedure. The Epley maneuver or canalith repositioning procedure involves the audiologist rotating the patient's head into different positions while the patient lies on a table with the head hanging over the edge. The procedure moves debris or canalith backward out of the labyrinth and into the vestibule. Research finds this maneuver is effective for 50% of patients versus 19% receiving placebo treatment. Performing the Epley maneuver is contraindicated where there is any unstable heart condition or disease (a), as it could trigger cardiovascular incidents; severe carotid arterial stenosis (b); or cervical spondylosis with myelopathy (c), because of the procedure's stress on the neck/cervical spine, its blood supply, and its nerves.

59. C: A wireless microphone for the speaker (c) to wear would not interfere with speech comprehension but would greatly improve it if the room has an FM system, infrared system, or induction loop system and the listener has either hearing aids with T (telephone/telecoil) or M/T (microphone/telephone) switches, a headset designed to use with the room system, earbuds, or a neck loop. Such assistive listening devices (ALDs) as FM, infrared, and induction loops send electronic copies of the speaker's speech sounds directly to the listener's hearing aids, headset, or earbuds and ears, free of distortion and background noises. This alleviates the environmental factors that interfere with comprehension: (a) distance between the speaker (either the live person or the loudspeaker amplifying the person's speech) and listener, as the intensity of the signal fades over distance; (b) competition of noise in the room, such as audience members talking and rustling papers, noise from air handling systems, etc., all of which cause much greater comprehension problems for the hearing-impaired than for the normal-hearing; and (d) room acoustics. If the room has many smooth, hard surfaces, these reflect sound waves so they bounce all around the space, creating distortion.

60. B: TTY/TDD (b) is not a recent digital technology. It is a much older technology of using teletype machines. "TTY" stands for teletype or telephone typewriter and "TDD" stands for telecommunications device for the deaf. Profoundly deaf people cannot use the telephone, even with amplification. Before the Internet existed, TTY/TDD was the only way deaf people could use the phone—either by having a TTY/TDD machine or by using a relay service with live operators. The Internet, the proliferation of personal computers (PCs) in the home, and the development of many software programs have changed this. Skype (a) allows communication over a PC; the quality is good, the audio volume can be turned up, and the video component helps people who can speechread. Live chat (c) allows people to communicate over a PC without video. They can receive nearly instantaneous replies, unlike with e-mails, and interact in real time. IM (d) or instant messaging is another recent technology that allows people to communicate either via PCs or via cell phones with texting capabilities, without video but also without delays.

61. D: All of the options named are used to alert (d) hearing-impaired people. Many people with hearing aids do not use them when sleeping or bathing, and many others cannot hear certain sounds well even with amplification. Various electronic devices use existing amplification, special signals, airstream stimuli, or kinesthetic stimuli to alert the deaf to sounds they cannot hear. Flashing lights (a) can be mounted on telephones to signal when they ring, or can be used to signal ringing doorbells, someone knocking, smoke alarms going off, etc. Strobe lights (a) can be used to signal fire alarms or alarm clocks. The University of Rochester (N.Y.)'s National Technical Institute for the Deaf (NTID) has dormitories where the majority of residents are deaf; fire alarm systems in these dorms use strobe lights to awaken and alert students. Transducers causing beds to shake (b) are used, especially for people who are also blind/visually impaired or sleep too soundly to be awakened by bright lights. Hearing ear dogs (c) have been trained to alert their owners to certain sounds. Dogs hear four times as far, hear frequencies three times higher, and can localize the origins of sounds faster than normal-hearing humans. They provide added benefits of pet companionship and can also often get help or alert others in emergencies. Dogs do not trigger seizures in people with seizure disorders as strobe lights or shaking beds can, and some dogs even recognize incipient seizures and alert their owners to prepare for them and avoid injuries.

62. A: Children with hearing loss diagnosed by the time they are six months old can, with early intervention, be expected to have language development equivalent to that of normal-hearing peers by the time they are five years old (a). Diagnosis by one year old is not early enough to be optimal, as babies normally begin to develop speech and language before this age; and three years old is too soon for hearing-impaired children to equal normal language development with early intervention (b). While ASHA (2007) does recommend comprehensive audiological evaluations by the age of three months for any infant failing newborn hearing screening, it recommends intervention in the case of confirmed hearing loss "...no later than 6 months of age." Although three months old might be even better for types of intervention feasible at that age, six years old is still incorrect as the age when children's language development catches up with norms, according to research findings (c). Since researchers have found evidence of these ages, answer (d), this cannot be predicted, is incorrect.

63. B: Current issues for providers and recipients of AR services do not include the lack of an identified body for professional certification of audiologists (b). The American Speech and Hearing Association (ASHA) certifies both audiologists and speech-language pathologists (SLPs), awarding its Certificate of Clinical Competence (CCC) to those who qualify by meeting its requirements for educational courses, supervised clinical work experience, test scores, etc. (It should be noted that ASHA's Committee on Rehabilitative Audiology has proposed minimum competencies for these professions, states that ASHA's own standards for certification do not currently meet these minimum competencies, and recommends changing its training and certification.) ASHA's Committee on Rehabilitative Audiology finds that three primary issues in AR are (a) insufficient public information on AR; (c) insufficient numbers of audiologists and SLPs including hearing aid orientations for their clients; and (d) omission of goals and objectives for counseling in a majority of AR programs, despite research evidence that counseling benefits client prognoses.

64. C: The only wholly correct statement is (c): Medicaid is required by law to pay for hearing aids for children, and while it often covers adults' hearing aids as well, it is not required by law to pay for adults' hearing aids as it is for children's (b). Medicare does not cover hearing aids at all, for children or adults (a). Private health insurance plans do not always cover hearing aids (d); some plans cover all of the cost, some cover part of the cost, and some do not cover any of it. This depends on the insurance company and the specific policy issued.

65. D: It is not within the scope of an audiologist's practice to provide mental health counseling services (d) to families of hearing-impaired children. Audiologists are not mental health professionals. However, ASHA deems it within the scope of practice for audiologists to provide emotional support and adjustment counseling (a). This is not the same kind of counseling a mental health professional can give, which is indicated in the event of mental health problems beyond the normal emotional reactions to a child's diagnosis of hearing loss. To distinguish between these, it is within the audiologist's scope of practice, and recommended, to observe parents closely for more acute emotional reactions (b), and if these continue for a long time without improving or become worse, to refer parents to mental health professionals (c).

66. B: "Microtic" means (b) an abnormally small pinna or outer ear. This happens with cases of congenital atresia when the pinna did not form correctly in utero. The pinna might

be entirely absent, or it might be abnormally small in size, to varying degrees. "Microtic" (the adjective) or "microtia" (the noun) do not refer to a tiny tic (a), or an otic type of microphone (c). Since (b) is correct, answer (d), none of the above, is incorrect.

67. A: A person's eustachian tubes must function normally in order for (a) myringoplasty, or repair of the eardrum(s), to work. The eustachian tubes must be able to be inflated with air if they are functioning normally. People can have eustachian tube dysfunction and still be able to breathe (b), to swallow (c), and to hear (d), so these answers are all incorrect.

68. D: Eustachian tube function can be tested by using (d) any or all of these tests. The Valsalva maneuver (a) is pinching the nostrils shut and "blowing" with the mouth closed, forcing air into the eustachian tubes. The Politzer maneuver uses apparatus to clamp one nostril shut and force air into the other nostril while the person swallows water; this maneuver can be used to test eustachian tube function. Catheterizing the tube/s (b) is sending air into the eustachian tube(s) via a cannula inserted through the nose. Impedance audiometry (c) tests the amount of resistance to sound pressure and is another way to get information related to eustachian tube patency. If these measures fail, the eustachian tubes do not function normally.

69. C: The nerves the otologist need not test in a routine otolaryngology exam are (c): The Olfactory nerve (CN I), which transmits sense of smell to the brain, and the Oculomotor nerve (CN III), involved in eye movements, as well as the Optic (II) nerve, which transmits visual input to the brain. The otologist should test the functioning of cranial nerves V through XII, i.e. the trigeminal and abducens (a); facial, auditory/vestibular, glossopharyngeal, and vagus (b); and accessory and hypoglossal (d) nerves. Tumors affecting these nerves can affect structures (pharynx) and muscles involved in speech. This falls under the field of otolaryngology, and it is the otologist who should test these neural functions in addition to evaluating other hearing and voice mechanisms.

70. B: The corneal reflex, involuntary blinking caused by touching the edge of the cornea, objectively identifies facial sensation. If it is missing in an unconscious patient, it can diagnose brainstem dysfunction. If an examiner finds this reflex missing or diminished in a conscious patient, the nerve affected is either the facial nerve CN VII (efferent) or the trigeminal nerve (b) CN V (afferent). If the patient has a larger acoustic neuroma affecting the trigeminal nerve, it will cause a decrease or absence of the corneal reflex on one side. If the abducens (d) nerve (CN VI) is affected, one eye will stop moving at the midline rather than the corneal reflex being affected. This can be caused by nasopharyngeal tumors or infections in the petrous bone's apex. The optic nerve (a) and the oculomotor nerve (c) are not implicated by a lack or reduction of the corneal reflex.

71. C: The auditory nerve (CN VIII) has (c) both these branches: a cochlear branch (a), which carries impulses for hearing from the cochlea, and a vestibular branch (b), which carries impulses for balance from the vestibule and labyrinth. It is the only cranial nerve with these two separate kinds of branches. Since (c), both, is correct, answer (d), no kinds of branches, is incorrect.

72. A: The least serious type of tumor listed that grows in the ear canal is (a) osteoma. This is a benign bony tumor that is not uncommon. Osteomas are usually small and do not interfere with the patient's hearing. If they grow large enough to obstruct the canal and

cause conductive hearing loss, the offending bone can be removed. Thus these are not serious, as they are not malignant, usually do not affect hearing, and can be surgically excised if they do. Carcinomas (b) and epitheliomas (c), however, are much more serious. These are malignant cancers that can result in death if not treated. Unlike osteomas, they do not grow only in the bony portion of the canal, and they can affect soft tissues (e.g. squamous cell carcinoma, the most common; basal cell carcinoma; adenoid cystic carcinoma; adenocarcinoma, etc.) As (a) is much less serious than (b) or (c), answer (d), that none is less serious than the others, is incorrect.

73. D: All of these can cause chronic serous otitis media (d). This condition can have various etiologies. If the eustachian tubes are obstructed, the air they will not admit builds up in the middle ear, causing negative pressure. This pressure causes mucus to get into the middle ear (a). If the eustachian tubes are able to receive air, another cause is drainage of lymph into the middle ear (b). If there are repeated episodes of infection, even though antibiotics control the infection, the middle ear may remain filled with fluid in between episodes; this is often caused by enlarged adenoids (c). Another source of chronic middle ear infection, especially in adults, is nasopharyngeal neoplasms (tumors or growths).

74. D: All are (d) complications of chronic suppurative otitis media. Chronic suppurative otitis media is a recurring middle ear infection that produces pus. It can be caused by a cholesteatoma, which should be diagnostically ruled out or in before treatment. If there is no cholesteatoma needing surgical removal, treatment is with antibiotics and regular cleaning; but if these do not work, surgeries such as mastoidectomy and myringoplasty are indicated. If not treated, chronic suppurative otitis media can lead to complications including paralysis of the facial (seventh cranial) nerve (a); abscesses in the brain (b); and inflammation of the meninges, the protective membranes covering the brain and spinal cord, called meningitis (c). Thus this type of middle ear infection is more serious than it might seem and must be diagnosed and treated as promptly as possible.

75. B: If the oval window is congenitally absent from the middle ear, fenestration of the horizontal semicircular canal (b) is preferable over surgically constructing an oval window (a). This is because the oval window underlies the facial nerve; operating on that location carries too great a risk of damaging that nerve. Creating a window in the horizontal semicircular canal can afford a similar function to that of the oval window when that structure is missing. Thus it would not be equally preferable to do either one of these (c). Without doing anything, there is a conductive hearing loss, as there is no oval window to send sound impulses from the ossicular chain to the cochlea, so doing neither procedure (d) is an incorrect answer.

76. C: Providing emotional support and grief counseling (c) is most involved in family adjustment to hearing loss counseling to be provided by audiologists. Interpreting audiograms (a), explaining the options for communication (b) for their child, and discussing advocacy for hearing loss (d) are all part of informational counseling to be provided by audiologists to families of hearing-impaired children. Other topics included in informational counseling are available educational options, available options for amplification, public health policies, and educational policy.

77. C: Using accurate technical terminology (c) is not included in ASHA's best practice principles for informational counseling about newborn hearing screening. Although the

- 154 -

neophyte audiologist might consider it instructionally valuable to use the proper technical terms, ASHA advises against using jargon that parents and families are not likely to understand. ASHA recommends keeping communication clear and concise (b) to avoid confusion that could delay or interfere with screening, re-screening, diagnostic evaluation, and treatment. ASHA also advises that informational counseling communications should be kept confidential and be family-focused (a) in orientation. The Association also advocates encouraging family members to ask any questions they have (d), as well as answering such questions.

78. A: According to HelpKidsHear.org, more than a million (a) children in the U.S. have hearing losses. Almost five million (b) is an overestimate of the number of children with hearing loss in America. Half a million (c) and a quarter million (d) are both underestimates of the numbers of children in the United States who have hearing losses.

79. D: Out of children through the age of 18 years in the United States, roughly 5% (d) are found to have hearing loss. 2% (a), 3% (b), and 4% (c) are all figures that underestimate the proportion of children in the United States who have hearing losses. Note: The estimate is reported as "at least 5%," so it could be more than this percentage. This might not sound like a large number, but when one considers that the total population of children in America—just through age 17, not even through age 18—is estimated by the U.S. Census Bureau to be around 75 million, 5% would equal 3.75 million—even more than the estimate of more than a million children (#78).

80. B: Approximately one out of every 22 (b) babies born in the United States has some kind of problem with hearing (not necessarily hearing loss alone—see #81). One out of every 32 (a) is an underestimate of the frequency with which babies are born with hearing problems in this country. One out of every 42 (c) is also an underestimate, but by a larger degree. One out of every 12 (d) would be a greater incidence of babies born with hearing problems than is actually the case in the United States.

81. A: One sixth (a) of babies born with hearing loss in the United States have severe or profound degrees of hearing loss. Six out of every 1000 babies in the U.S. are born with hearing loss; one out of every 1000 is born with severe or profound degrees of hearing loss. Therefore, of the six out of a thousand born with hearing loss, one has a severe or profound level of hearing loss, so this equals one in six, or one sixth. One tenth (b) is a smaller proportion than is actually the case in this country. One third (c) would be twice as many with severe or profound degrees of loss than is actual. One half (d) would be three times as many with severe or profound hearing loss out of those born with any hearing loss than in reality.

82. C: 83 out of every 1000 U.S. children have hearing loss considered educationally significant (c). 103 out of 1000 (a) and 93 out of 1000 (b) are larger proportions than is actually the case. 73 out of every 1000 children (d) is an underestimate of the proportion of all children in the United States who have hearing loss that is considered educationally significant (i.e., the hearing loss is sufficient to have a negative impact upon educational progress, outcomes, and success).

83. B: Seven of every 1000 school-aged children have bilateral hearing loss deemed educationally significant (b). 11 of every 1000 (a) is an overestimate by more than 50% of

this population. 14 of every 1000 (c) is double the actual proportion of children of school age with educationally significant hearing loss in both ears. Four out of every 1000 (d) is a considerable underestimate of the actual proportion of school-aged children with bilateral hearing losses that are educationally significant (i.e., the hearing loss will have a negative impact on their education).

84. C: The range of the estimated proportion of school-aged children in the U.S. identified as having educationally significant hearing loss in one ear is (c) 16 to 19 of every 1000. The range of 12-15 of every 1000 (a) and the range of 13-16 of every 1000 (b) are both underestimates of the actual range. A range of 18-21 of every 1000 (d) is an overestimate of the estimated proportion of school-aged children with such a diagnosis. Note: When considering such things as surgery, unilateral hearing loss might be considered not an emergency because the child can hear and communicate with one ear. However, this consideration is only with respect to performing surgery immediately versus scheduling it for a later date and does not relate to educational significance or impact. Research has found that even unilateral hearing losses can have significant educational impacts on children.

85. D: About nine (d) of every 1000 school-aged children in the United States have severe to profound hearing losses. Three (a), five (b), and seven (c) of every 1000 school-aged children all under-represent the proportion of school-aged children in the United States who experience severe to profound degrees of hearing loss. Severe levels of hearing loss, according to ASHA, are hearing thresholds of 71 to 90 dB, and profound levels of hearing loss are 91 dB and above. In other words, children with these diagnoses need pure tones 71 to 91 dB louder, or more, than normal-hearing children in order to hear them, since normal hearing thresholds are around 0 dB.

86. A: Ten (a) of every 1000 school-aged children in the United States have permanent sensorineural hearing loss. Five (b) of every 1000 is only half the actual estimated proportion. Eight (c) of every 1000 is an underestimate of the actual number, and twelve (d) of every 1000 school-aged children is an overestimate of how many have permanent sensorineural hearing losses.

87. B: It is estimated that about 30% (b) of children in the United States with hearing losses also have another disability. 20% (a) underestimates how many hearing-impaired children in this country have multiple disabilities. 10% (d) severely underestimates the proportion of this population. 40% (c) is an overestimate of how many hearing-impaired children are multiply disabled. These figures reflect the overall prevalence of hearing loss in the child population. In addition, since less than a third of hearing-impaired children have other disabilities, more than two-thirds of them have only hearing loss; this shows that the incidence of hearing loss alone in children is greater than the incidence of hearing loss combined with other disabilities.

88. C: Speech audiometry cannot measure the ability to recognize speech at levels below the person's hearing threshold, or sub-threshold levels (c). It can, however, measure an individual's ability to recognize speech at levels *above* the individual's hearing threshold, or supra-threshold speech. It can also help an examiner differentially diagnose the etiology of a hearing loss (a) when similar symptoms can have different causes. Speech audiometry can measure the auditory processing ability of the individual (b). Some people have the

ability to process and hence recognize pure tones as sound, but their ability to process the much more complex sound signals of speech might be compromised. When auditory processing of speech is impaired, the person's ability to communicate is affected. Thus speech audiometry can also help the examiner estimate how functional an individual's communication is (d).

89. A: The type of a hearing loss is (a) locational. In other words, the type of loss is defined by the location within the auditory system where the cause of the hearing loss occurred or exists. Thus a conductive hearing loss is caused somewhere in the outer ear or middle ear, such as by foreign objects, cerumen (wax), a perforated, ruptured, absent, or otherwise dysfunctional eardrum, lesions in the pinna or ear canal, otosclerotic bony growth, otherwise dysfunctional or absent ossicles, a missing oval window, etc. A sensorineural hearing loss is caused by dysfunction in the cochlea, vestibule, labyrinth/other parts of the inner ear, and/or nerve tissue. Central auditory processing disorders have their etiology in the brain. Mixed hearing loss has etiologies in both areas of the outer and/or middle ear, plus the inner ear. Types of hearing loss are not classified by quality (b) or quantity (c). Since (a) is correct, answer (d), none of the above, is incorrect.

90. C: The severity of hearing loss is (c) quantitative. It is measured in numbers of decibels (dB) above 0, the normal hearing threshold. According to ASHA, normal hearing is considered to be between -10 dB and 15 dB. A "slight" hearing loss is a loss of 16 to 25 dB. A mild hearing loss is a loss of 26 to 40 dB. A moderate hearing loss is a loss of 41 to 55 dB. A moderately severe hearing loss is a loss of 56 to 70 dB. A severe hearing loss is a loss of 71 to 90 db. And a profound hearing loss is a loss of 91 dB or more. Severity is not locational (a), i.e. it is not determined by the place its cause occurred, as is type of hearing loss (#91). Severity of hearing loss is not qualitative, i.e. it is not determined by a non-numerical description. Since (c) is correct, answer (d), none of the above, is incorrect.

91. B: The configuration of a hearing loss is (b) qualitative. The configuration or shape of the hearing loss is visualized on the audiogram. Hearing loss configuration is described according to its characteristics. For example, if the audiogram curve shows abnormal thresholds for only the highest frequencies, the configuration will be described as a high-frequency hearing loss; the same is true for a low-frequency hearing loss. Many people with noise-induced hearing losses have audiograms with an isolated dip, "notch" or "cookie bite" at the 3000 Hz frequency, or sometimes at the 4000-6000 Hz frequencies. When someone's hearing loss is uniform at every frequency, the line plotted on the audiogram is described as "flat," as it does not go up or down at different frequencies. When the line curves, it can be ascending or descending. An ascending curve indicates hearing that gets progressively worse with higher frequencies, and a descending curve indicates hearing that gets progressively worse with lower frequencies. Configuration of hearing loss may be described as gradual or precipitous; i.e. the changes in acuity occur in small dB increments, or there is a sudden, sharp difference at a given frequency. Configuration is not locational (a), i.e. it does not refer to the place of origin of the hearing loss within the auditory system. It is not quantitative (c), i.e. its qualities are described rather than measured in numbers. Since (b) is correct, answer (d), none of the above, is incorrect.

92. A: Research studies have found that communicative rehabilitation programs that are only language-based and do not incorporate counseling are not as effective (a) as programs that do include counseling as an integrated component. It is thus incorrect that such

programs are just as effective without counseling (b) or that they are less effective when it is included (c). It is also incorrect that researchers have not studied this topic (d). Despite the importance of counseling to rehabilitative success, the majority of graduate programs in audiology and SLP do not offer counseling courses, and ASHA recommends that this be changed.

93. D: ASHA does not name (d) internal variables as essential to understanding family coping ability. Understanding internal variables for every family member would not be feasible without intensive psychological analysis of, and disclosure by, each member, which in turn would not be practical (or even necessarily desired or allowed by family members). ASHA does name family variables, which include socioeconomic status, family composition, family roles and family responsibilities, cohesiveness, resilience, problem-solving ability, and creativity. It also names parent variables (a). These include the quality of the parents' marriage, issues related to time, and the mother's relative locus of control (internal/external). Another factor is child variables (b). These include the child's age, gender, degree of disability, and temperament type. The fourth factor ASHA lists is (c) external variables. These include absence, presence, and/or extent of social support; absence, presence, and/or extent of social stigmatization; and whether and to what extent the family can and does collaborate with professionals.

94. C: It is not true that a diagnostic teaching approach does *not* involve setting goals (c). While it is true that this approach does evolve over time with changing needs, the audiologist will still set individual goals for the child; these can be revised as needed. This approach can uncover disabilities other than hearing loss that were not previously diagnosed (a). It does help audiologists determine which assistive technologies will work best for the individual child (b). And it does help the audiologist to ascertain which communication method both works best for the specific child, and will be preferred and used consistently by all family members (d).

95. C: The role of the audiologist relative to support groups for families of hearing-impaired children is that of a (c) facilitator. The group members share their experiences, exchange information, and give one another social and emotional support. Thus the audiologist should not lead the group (a), as more control should not reside with the audiologist but with the group's members. According to ASHA, the audiologist's role is not "instructional" (b) with support groups but "facilitative" (c). The audiologist is not there to teach a support group; this is better done during informational counseling of an individual family. Rather, the audiologist should supply only what is needed to make the group's functioning easier and more effective, by giving feedback, information, help, services, or encouragement as needed or requested. Since only (c) is correct, answer (d), all of the above, is incorrect.

96. A: It is not one of ASHA's guidelines that the professional require the client to sign a "non-compete" agreement (a). This is mainly a practice among businesses when they make a deal or sign a contract to ensure companies do not infringe on copyrights, use the same packaging or labeling, appropriate intellectual property, duplicate trademarked information, etc. (This is not the same as having the client sign informed consent for private treatment, which should always be done.) ASHA's guidelines do include informing the client of all services available from both the primary employer and the professional's private practice, and state that once so informed, the client is free to choose between the two (b). The guidelines also require the professional to inform the client of any differences in fees

between the two (c). ASHA also stipulates that the professional must notify the primary employer of the professional's plans to see the client in private practice (d). If the employer is informed and raises no objections, then the employer cannot claim the professional caused a conflict of interest by seeing the client privately.

97. B: Berg et al (2007) surveyed 121 cochlear implant centers and their teams. They found that these groups informed families about issues of autonomy/identity and about deaf culture only (b) 45% of the time. They found that they did inform families of audiological information (a), medical and surgical risks (c) of implantation, and available options for education and communication (d) 100% of the time.

98. A: The implementation of newborn hearing screenings has made the average age of confirmation of hearing loss one tenth of what it was (a); specifically, the average age when hearing loss was confirmed used to be 24 to 30 months, but since the inception of newborn hearing screenings, it is now 2 to 3 months. Therefore, one fifth (b) and one half (c) of the former average age of confirmation are both incorrect answers. Since the change in the average age of hearing loss confirmation has changed dramatically, answer (d), that the average age is essentially unchanged, is also incorrect.

99. D: The CDC reports (2008) that of the newborns who fail hearing screenings and are referred for follow-up, almost half do not receive it, meaning that only a little more than half do receive follow-up (d). Thus 85% (a), 75% (b), and two thirds (c) are all overestimates of how many referred newborns actually receive follow-ups. The low statistic for follow-ups is attributed to ineffective means of assuring compliance in following up by families, and to the dearth of professionals available to deliver the needed services. Follow-up includes re-screening, complete audiological evaluation, medical referral when necessary, and remedial interventions such as medical and/or surgical treatment when indicated, aural rehabilitation, amplification, assistive technologies, communication methods, educational approaches, advocacy, and counseling services.

100. C: The only correct statement is (c): Instruments that are reliable obtain consistent results across repeated administrations. If the instrument cannot be used, or it does not obtain comparable results when it is, then it is not reliable. The term "test-retest reliability" reflects this principle. Validity means that an instrument measures what it is intended to measure. Validity and reliability are not both specific to each situation (a). Validity is situation-specific; an instrument can be valid for certain purposes but not others. If an instrument does measure something, but not what it purports to measure, then it is not valid for that purpose. Reliability is not situation-specific; a reliable instrument will have the same results each time it is used, no matter what it is purported to measure or actually does measure. It is not correct that where one of these exists, the other does, and vice versa (b). Validity and reliability do not mutually assure one another. Validity does predict reliability: the results of an instrument that measures what it is meant to measure can normally be replicated with consistency. However, reliability does not predict validity: an instrument can be used again with the same findings, but still not test what it is meant or claimed to test. It is incorrect that instruments need either one but not both (d): scientifically and statistically sound instruments must both be valid and reliable.

Secret Key #1 - Time is Your Greatest Enemy

Pace Yourself

Wear a watch. At the beginning of the test, check the time (or start a chronometer on your watch to count the minutes), and check the time after every few questions to make sure you are "on schedule."

If you are forced to speed up, do it efficiently. Usually one or more answer choices can be eliminated without too much difficulty. Above all, don't panic. Don't speed up and just begin guessing at random choices. By pacing yourself, and continually monitoring your progress against your watch, you will always know exactly how far ahead or behind you are with your available time. If you find that you are one minute behind on the test, don't skip one question without spending any time on it, just to catch back up. Take 15 fewer seconds on the next four questions, and after four questions you'll have caught back up. Once you catch back up, you can continue working each problem at your normal pace.

Furthermore, don't dwell on the problems that you were rushed on. If a problem was taking up too much time and you made a hurried guess, it must be difficult. The difficult questions are the ones you are most likely to miss anyway, so it isn't a big loss. It is better to end with more time than you need than to run out of time.

Lastly, sometimes it is beneficial to slow down if you are constantly getting ahead of time. You are always more likely to catch a careless mistake by working more slowly than quickly, and among very high-scoring test takers (those who are likely to have lots of time left over), careless errors affect the score more than mastery of material.

Secret Key #2 - Guessing is not Guesswork

You probably know that guessing is a good idea - unlike other standardized tests, there is no penalty for getting a wrong answer. Even if you have no idea about a question, you still have a 20-25% chance of getting it right.

Most test takers do not understand the impact that proper guessing can have on their score. Unless you score extremely high, guessing will significantly contribute to your final score.

Monkeys Take the Test

What most test takers don't realize is that to insure that 20-25% chance, you have to guess randomly. If you put 20 monkeys in a room to take this test, assuming they answered once per question and behaved themselves, on average they would get 20-25% of the questions correct. Put 20 test takers in the room, and the average will be much lower among guessed questions. Why?
    1. The test writers intentionally write deceptive answer choices that "look" right. A test

taker has no idea about a question, so picks the "best looking" answer, which is often wrong. The monkey has no idea what looks good and what doesn't, so will consistently be lucky about 20-25% of the time.

2. Test takers will eliminate answer choices from the guessing pool based on a hunch or intuition. Simple but correct answers often get excluded, leaving a 0% chance of being correct. The monkey has no clue, and often gets lucky with the best choice.

This is why the process of elimination endorsed by most test courses is flawed and detrimental to your performance- test takers don't guess, they make an ignorant stab in the dark that is usually worse than random.

$5 Challenge

Let me introduce one of the most valuable ideas of this course- the $5 challenge:

You only mark your "best guess" if you are willing to bet $5 on it.

You only eliminate choices from guessing if you are willing to bet $5 on it.

Why $5? Five dollars is an amount of money that is small yet not insignificant, and can really add up fast (20 questions could cost you $100). Likewise, each answer choice on one question of the test will have a small impact on your overall score, but it can really add up to a lot of points in the end.

The process of elimination IS valuable. The following shows your chance of guessing it right:

If you eliminate wrong answer choices until only this many remain:	Chance of getting it correct:
1	100%
2	50%
3	33%

However, if you accidentally eliminate the right answer or go on a hunch for an incorrect answer, your chances drop dramatically: to 0%. By guessing among all the answer choices, you are GUARANTEED to have a shot at the right answer.

That's why the $5 test is so valuable- if you give up the advantage and safety of a pure guess, it had better be worth the risk.

What we still haven't covered is how to be sure that whatever guess you make is truly random. Here's the easiest way:

Always pick the first answer choice among those remaining.

Such a technique means that you have decided, **before you see a single test question**, exactly how you are going to guess- and since the order of choices tells you nothing about which one is correct, this guessing technique is perfectly random.

This section is not meant to scare you away from making educated guesses or eliminating choices- you just need to define when a choice is worth eliminating. The $5 test, along with a pre-defined random guessing strategy, is the best way to make sure you reap all of the benefits of guessing.

Secret Key #3 - Practice Smarter, Not Harder

Many test takers delay the test preparation process because they dread the awful amounts of practice time they think necessary to succeed on the test. We have refined an effective method that will take you only a fraction of the time.
There are a number of "obstacles" in your way to succeed. Among these are answering questions, finishing in time, and mastering test-taking strategies. All must be executed on the day of the test at peak performance, or your score will suffer. The test is a mental marathon that has a large impact on your future.

Just like a marathon runner, it is important to work your way up to the full challenge. So first you just worry about questions, and then time, and finally strategy:

Success Strategy

1. Find a good source for practice tests.
2. If you are willing to make a larger time investment, consider using more than one study guide- often the different approaches of multiple authors will help you "get" difficult concepts.
3. Take a practice test with no time constraints, with all study helps "open book." Take your time with questions and focus on applying strategies.
4. Take a practice test with time constraints, with all guides "open book."
5. Take a final practice test with no open material and time limits

If you have time to take more practice tests, just repeat step 5. By gradually exposing yourself to the full rigors of the test environment, you will condition your mind to the stress of test day and maximize your success.

Secret Key #4 - Prepare, Don't Procrastinate

Let me state an obvious fact: if you take the test three times, you will get three different scores. This is due to the way you feel on test day, the level of preparedness you have, and, despite the test writers' claims to the contrary, some tests WILL be easier for you than others.
Since your future depends so much on your score, you should maximize your chances of success. In order to maximize the likelihood of success, you've got to prepare in advance.

This means taking practice tests and spending time learning the information and test taking strategies you will need to succeed.

Never take the test as a "practice" test, expecting that you can just take it again if you need to. Feel free to take sample tests on your own, but when you go to take the official test, be prepared, be focused, and do your best the first time!

Secret Key #5 - Test Yourself

Everyone knows that time is money. There is no need to spend too much of your time or too little of your time preparing for the test. You should only spend as much of your precious time preparing as is necessary for you to get the score you need.

Once you have taken a practice test under real conditions of time constraints, then you will know if you are ready for the test or not.

If you have scored extremely high the first time that you take the practice test, then there is not much point in spending countless hours studying. You are already there.

Benchmark your abilities by retaking practice tests and seeing how much you have improved. Once you score high enough to guarantee success, then you are ready.

If you have scored well below where you need, then knuckle down and begin studying in earnest. Check your improvement regularly through the use of practice tests under real conditions. Above all, don't worry, panic, or give up. The key is perseverance!

Then, when you go to take the test, remain confident and remember how well you did on the practice tests. If you can score high enough on a practice test, then you can do the same on the real thing.

General Strategies

The most important thing you can do is to ignore your fears and jump into the test immediately- do not be overwhelmed by any strange-sounding terms. You have to jump into the test like jumping into a pool- all at once is the easiest way.

Make Predictions

As you read and understand the question, try to guess what the answer will be. Remember that several of the answer choices are wrong, and once you begin reading them, your mind will immediately become cluttered with answer choices designed to throw you off. Your mind is typically the most focused immediately after you have read the question and digested its contents. If you can, try to predict what the correct answer will be. You may be surprised at what you can predict.

Quickly scan the choices and see if your prediction is in the listed answer choices. If it is, then you can be quite confident that you have the right answer. It still won't hurt to check the other answer choices, but most of the time, you've got it!

Answer the Question

It may seem obvious to only pick answer choices that answer the question, but the test writers can create some excellent answer choices that are wrong. Don't pick an answer just because it sounds right, or you believe it to be true. It MUST answer the question. Once you've made your selection, always go back and check it against the question and make sure that you didn't misread the question, and the answer choice does answer the question posed.

Benchmark

After you read the first answer choice, decide if you think it sounds correct or not. If it doesn't, move on to the next answer choice. If it does, mentally mark that answer choice. This doesn't mean that you've definitely selected it as your answer choice, it just means that it's the best you've seen thus far. Go ahead and read the next choice. If the next choice is worse than the one you've already selected, keep going to the next answer choice. If the next choice is better than the choice you've already selected, mentally mark the new answer choice as your best guess.

The first answer choice that you select becomes your standard. Every other answer choice must be benchmarked against that standard. That choice is correct until proven otherwise by another answer choice beating it out. Once you've decided that no other answer choice seems as good, do one final check to ensure that your answer choice answers the question posed.

Valid Information

Don't discount any of the information provided in the question. Every piece of information may be necessary to determine the correct answer. None of the information in the question is there to throw you off (while the answer choices will certainly have information to throw you off). If two seemingly unrelated topics are discussed, don't ignore either. You can be confident there is a relationship, or it wouldn't be included in the question, and you are probably going to have to determine what is that relationship to find the answer.

Avoid "Fact Traps"

Don't get distracted by a choice that is factually true. Your search is for the answer that answers the question. Stay focused and don't fall for an answer that is true but incorrect. Always go back to the question and make sure you're choosing an answer that actually answers the question and is not just a true statement. An answer can be factually correct, but it MUST answer the question asked. Additionally, two answers can both be seemingly correct, so be sure to read all of the answer choices, and make sure that you get the one that BEST answers the question.

Milk the Question

Some of the questions may throw you completely off. They might deal with a subject you have not been exposed to, or one that you haven't reviewed in years. While your lack of knowledge about the subject will be a hindrance, the question itself can give you many clues that will help you find the correct answer. Read the question carefully and look for clues. Watch particularly for adjectives and nouns describing difficult terms or words that you don't recognize. Regardless of if you completely understand a word or not, replacing it with a synonym either provided or one you more familiar with may help you to understand what the questions are asking. Rather than wracking your mind about specific detailed information concerning a difficult term or word, try to use mental substitutes that are easier to understand.

The Trap of Familiarity

Don't just choose a word because you recognize it. On difficult questions, you may not recognize a number of words in the answer choices. The test writers don't put "make-believe" words on the test; so don't think that just because you only recognize all the words in one answer choice means that answer choice must be correct. If you only recognize words in one answer choice, then focus on that one. Is it correct? Try your best to determine if it is correct. If it is, that is great, but if it doesn't, eliminate it. Each word and answer choice you eliminate increases your chances of getting the question correct, even if you then have to guess among the unfamiliar choices.

Eliminate Answers

Eliminate choices as soon as you realize they are wrong. But be careful! Make sure you consider all of the possible answer choices. Just because one appears right, doesn't mean that the next one won't be even better! The test writers will usually put more than one good answer choice for every question, so read all of them. Don't worry if you are stuck between two that seem right. By getting down to just two remaining possible choices, your odds are now 50/50. Rather than wasting too much time, play the odds. You are guessing, but guessing wisely, because you've been able to knock out some of the answer choices that you know are wrong. If you are eliminating choices and realize that the last answer choice you are left with is also obviously wrong, don't panic. Start over and consider each choice again. There may easily be something that you missed the first time and will realize on the second pass.

Tough Questions

If you are stumped on a problem or it appears too hard or too difficult, don't waste time. Move on! Remember though, if you can quickly check for obviously incorrect answer choices, your chances of guessing correctly are greatly improved. Before you completely give up, at least try to knock out a couple of possible answers. Eliminate what you can and then guess at the remaining answer choices before moving on.

Brainstorm

If you get stuck on a difficult question, spend a few seconds quickly brainstorming. Run through the complete list of possible answer choices. Look at each choice and ask yourself, "Could this answer the question satisfactorily?" Go through each answer choice and consider it independently of the other. By systematically going through all possibilities, you may find something that you would otherwise overlook. Remember that when you get stuck, it's important to try to keep moving.

Read Carefully

Understand the problem. Read the question and answer choices carefully. Don't miss the question because you misread the terms. You have plenty of time to read each question thoroughly and make sure you understand what is being asked. Yet a happy medium must be attained, so don't waste too much time. You must read carefully, but efficiently.

Face Value

When in doubt, use common sense. Always accept the situation in the problem at face value. Don't read too much into it. These problems will not require you to make huge leaps of logic. The test writers aren't trying to throw you off with a cheap trick. If you have to go beyond creativity and make a leap of logic in order to have an answer choice answer the question, then you should look at the other answer choices. Don't overcomplicate the problem by creating theoretical relationships or explanations that will warp time or space. These are normal problems rooted in reality. It's just that the applicable relationship or explanation may not be readily apparent and you have to figure things out. Use your common sense to interpret anything that isn't clear.

Prefixes

If you're having trouble with a word in the question or answer choices, try dissecting it. Take advantage of every clue that the word might include. Prefixes and suffixes can be a huge help. Usually they allow you to determine a basic meaning. Pre- means before, post- means after, pro - is positive, de- is negative. From these prefixes and suffixes, you can get an idea of the general meaning of the word and try to put it into context. Beware though of any traps. Just because con is the opposite of pro, doesn't necessarily mean congress is the opposite of progress!

Hedge Phrases

Watch out for critical "hedge" phrases, such as likely, may, can, will often, sometimes, often, almost, mostly, usually, generally, rarely, sometimes. Question writers insert these hedge phrases to cover every possibility. Often an answer choice will be wrong simply because it leaves no room for exception. Avoid answer choices that have definitive words like "exactly," and "always".

Switchback Words

Stay alert for "switchbacks". These are the words and phrases frequently used to alert you to shifts in thought. The most common switchback word is "but". Others include although, however, nevertheless, on the other hand, even though, while, in spite of, despite, regardless of.

New Information

Correct answer choices will rarely have completely new information included. Answer choices typically are straightforward reflections of the material asked about and will directly relate to the question. If a new piece of information is included in an answer choice that doesn't even seem to relate to the topic being asked about, then that answer choice is likely incorrect. All of the information needed to answer the question is usually provided for you, and so you should not have to make guesses that are unsupported or choose answer choices that require unknown information that cannot be reasoned on its own.

Time Management

On technical questions, don't get lost on the technical terms. Don't spend too much time on any one question. If you don't know what a term means, then since you don't have a dictionary, odds are you aren't going to get much further. You should immediately recognize terms as whether or not you know them. If you don't, work with the other clues that you have, the other answer choices and terms provided, but don't waste too much time trying to figure out a difficult term.

Contextual Clues

Look for contextual clues. An answer can be right but not correct. The contextual clues will help you find the answer that is most right and is correct. Understand the context in which a phrase or statement is made. This will help you make important distinctions.

Don't Panic

Panicking will not answer any questions for you. Therefore, it isn't helpful. When you first see the question, if your mind goes blank, take a deep breath. Force yourself to mechanically go through the steps of solving the problem and using the strategies you've learned.

Pace Yourself

Don't get clock fever. It's easy to be overwhelmed when you're looking at a page full of questions, your mind is full of random thoughts and feeling confused, and the clock is ticking down faster than you would like. Calm down and maintain the pace that you have set for yourself. As long as you are on track by monitoring your pace, you are guaranteed to have enough time for yourself. When you get to the last few minutes of the test, it may seem like you won't have enough time left, but if you only have as many questions as you should have left at that point, then you're right on track!

Answer Selection

The best way to pick an answer choice is to eliminate all of those that are wrong, until only one is left and confirm that is the correct answer. Sometimes though, an answer choice may immediately look right. Be careful! Take a second to make sure that the other choices are not equally obvious. Don't make a hasty mistake. There are only two times that you should stop before checking other answers. First is when you are positive that the answer choice you have selected is correct. Second is when time is almost out and you have to make a quick guess!

Check Your Work

Since you will probably not know every term listed and the answer to every question, it is important that you get credit for the ones that you do know. Don't miss any questions through careless mistakes. If at all possible, try to take a second to look back over your answer selection and make sure you've selected the correct answer choice and haven't made a costly careless mistake (such as marking an answer choice that you didn't mean to mark). This quick double check should more than pay for itself in caught mistakes for the time it costs.

Beware of Directly Quoted Answers

Sometimes an answer choice will repeat word for word a portion of the question or reference section. However, beware of such exact duplication – it may be a trap! More than likely, the correct choice will paraphrase or summarize a point, rather than being exactly the same wording.

Slang

Scientific sounding answers are better than slang ones. An answer choice that begins "To compare the outcomes..." is much more likely to be correct than one that begins "Because some people insisted..."

Extreme Statements

Avoid wild answers that throw out highly controversial ideas that are proclaimed as established fact. An answer choice that states the "process should be used in certain situations, if..." is much more likely to be correct than one that states the "process should be

- 167 -

discontinued completely." The first is a calm rational statement and doesn't even make a definitive, uncompromising stance, using a hedge word "if" to provide wiggle room, whereas the second choice is a radical idea and far more extreme.

Answer Choice Families

When you have two or more answer choices that are direct opposites or parallels, one of them is usually the correct answer. For instance, if one answer choice states "x increases" and another answer choice states "x decreases" or "y increases," then those two or three answer choices are very similar in construction and fall into the same family of answer choices. A family of answer choices is when two or three answer choices are very similar in construction, and yet often have a directly opposite meaning. Usually the correct answer choice will be in that family of answer choices. The "odd man out" or answer choice that doesn't seem to fit the parallel construction of the other answer choices is more likely to be incorrect.

Special Report: What Your Test Score Will Tell You About Your IQ

Did you know that most standardized tests correlate very strongly with IQ? In fact, your general intelligence is a better predictor of your success than any other factor, and most tests intentionally measure this trait to some degree to ensure that those selected by the test are truly qualified for the test's purposes.

Before we can delve into the relation between your test score and IQ, I will first have to explain what exactly is IQ. Here's the formula:

Your IQ = 100 + (Number of standard deviations below or above the average)*15

Now, let's define standard deviations by using an example. If we have 5 people with 5 different heights, then first we calculate the average. Let's say the average was 65 inches. The standard deviation is the "average distance" away from the average of each of the members. It is a direct measure of variability - if the 5 people included Jackie Chan and Shaquille O'Neal, obviously there's a lot more variability in that group than a group of 5 sisters who are all within 6 inches in height of each other. The standard deviation uses a number to characterize the average range of difference within a group.

A convenient feature of most groups is that they have a "normal" distribution- makes sense that most things would be normal, right? Without getting into a bunch of statistical mumbo-jumbo, you just need to know that if you know the average of the group and the standard deviation, you can successfully predict someone's percentile rank in the group.

Confused? Let me give you an example. If instead of 5 people's heights, we had 100 people, we could figure out their rank in height JUST by knowing the average, standard deviation, and their height. We wouldn't need to know each person's height and manually rank them, we could just predict their rank based on three numbers.

What this means is that you can take your PERCENTILE rank that is often given with your test and relate this to your RELATIVE IQ of people taking the test - that is, your IQ relative to the people taking the test. Obviously, there's no way to know your actual IQ because the people taking a standardized test are usually not very good samples of the general population- many of those with extremely low IQ's never achieve a level of success or competency necessary to complete a typical standardized test. In fact, professional psychologists who measure IQ actually have to use non-written tests that can fairly measure the IQ of those not able to complete a traditional test.

The bottom line is to not take your test score too seriously, but it is fun to compute your "relative IQ" among the people who took the test with you. I've done the calculations below. Just look up your percentile rank in the left and then you'll see your "relative IQ" for your test in the right hand column-

Percentile Rank	Your Relative IQ		Percentile Rank	Your Relative IQ
99	135		59	103
98	131		58	103
97	128		57	103
96	126		56	102
95	125		55	102
94	123		54	102
93	122		53	101
92	121		52	101
91	120		51	100
90	119		50	100
89	118		49	100
88	118		48	99
87	117		47	99
86	116		46	98
85	116		45	98
84	115		44	98
83	114		43	97
82	114		42	97
81	113		41	97
80	113		40	96
79	112		39	96
78	112		38	95
77	111		37	95
76	111		36	95
75	110		35	94
74	110		34	94
73	109		33	93
72	109		32	93
71	108		31	93
70	108		30	92
69	107		29	92
68	107		28	91
67	107		27	91
66	106		26	90
65	106		25	90
64	105		24	89
63	105		23	89
62	105		22	88
61	104		21	88
60	104		20	87

Special Report: What is Test Anxiety and How to Overcome It?

The very nature of tests caters to some level of anxiety, nervousness or tension, just as we feel for any important event that occurs in our lives. A little bit of anxiety or nervousness can be a good thing. It helps us with motivation, and makes achievement just that much sweeter. However, too much anxiety can be a problem; especially if it hinders our ability to function and perform.

"Test anxiety," is the term that refers to the emotional reactions that some test-takers experience when faced with a test or exam. Having a fear of testing and exams is based upon a rational fear, since the test-taker's performance can shape the course of an academic career. Nevertheless, experiencing excessive fear of examinations will only interfere with the test-takers ability to perform, and his/her chances to be successful.

There are a large variety of causes that can contribute to the development and sensation of test anxiety. These include, but are not limited to lack of performance and worrying about issues surrounding the test.

Lack of Preparation

Lack of preparation can be identified by the following behaviors or situations:

Not scheduling enough time to study, and therefore cramming the night before the test or exam
Managing time poorly, to create the sensation that there is not enough time to do everything
Failing to organize the text information in advance, so that the study material consists of the entire text and not simply the pertinent information
Poor overall studying habits

Worrying, on the other hand, can be related to both the test taker, or many other factors around him/her that will be affected by the results of the test. These include worrying about:

Previous performances on similar exams, or exams in general
How friends and other students are achieving
The negative consequences that will result from a poor grade or failure

There are three primary elements to test anxiety. Physical components, which involve the same typical bodily reactions as those to acute anxiety (to be discussed below). Emotional factors have to do with fear or panic. Mental or cognitive issues concerning attention spans and memory abilities.

Physical Signals

There are many different symptoms of test anxiety, and these are not limited to mental and emotional strain. Frequently there are a range of physical signals that will let a test taker know that he/she is suffering from test anxiety. These bodily changes can include the following:

Perspiring
Sweaty palms
Wet, trembling hands
Nausea
Dry mouth
A knot in the stomach
Headache
Faintness
Muscle tension
Aching shoulders, back and neck
Rapid heart beat
Feeling too hot/cold

To recognize the sensation of test anxiety, a test-taker should monitor him/herself for the following sensations:

The physical distress symptoms as listed above
Emotional sensitivity, expressing emotional feelings such as the need to cry or laugh too much, or a sensation of anger or helplessness
A decreased ability to think, causing the test-taker to blank out or have racing thoughts that are hard to organize or control.

Though most students will feel some level of anxiety when faced with a test or exam, the majority can cope with that anxiety and maintain it at a manageable level. However, those who cannot are faced with a very real and very serious condition, which can and should be controlled for the immeasurable benefit of this sufferer.

Naturally, these sensations lead to negative results for the testing experience. The most common effects of test anxiety have to do with nervousness and mental blocking.

Nervousness

Nervousness can appear in several different levels:

The test-taker's difficulty, or even inability to read and understand the questions on the test
The difficulty or inability to organize thoughts to a coherent form

The difficulty or inability to recall key words and concepts relating to the testing questions (especially essays)
The receipt of poor grades on a test, though the test material was well known by the test taker

Conversely, a person may also experience mental blocking, which involves:

Blanking out on test questions
Only remembering the correct answers to the questions when the test has already finished.

Fortunately for test anxiety sufferers, beating these feelings, to a large degree, has to do with proper preparation. When a test taker has a feeling of preparedness, then anxiety will be dramatically lessened.

The first step to resolving anxiety issues is to distinguish which of the two types of anxiety are being suffered. If the anxiety is a direct result of a lack of preparation, this should be considered a normal reaction, and the anxiety level (as opposed to the test results) shouldn't be anything to worry about. However, if, when adequately prepared, the test-taker still panics, blanks out, or seems to overreact, this is not a fully rational reaction. While this can be considered normal too, there are many ways to combat and overcome these effects.

Remember that anxiety cannot be entirely eliminated, however, there are ways to minimize it, to make the anxiety easier to manage. Preparation is one of the best ways to minimize test anxiety. Therefore the following techniques are wise in order to best fight off any anxiety that may want to build.

To begin with, try to avoid cramming before a test, whenever it is possible. By trying to memorize an entire term's worth of information in one day, you'll be shocking your system, and not giving yourself a very good chance to absorb the information. This is an easy path to anxiety, so for those who suffer from test anxiety, cramming should not even be considered an option.

Instead of cramming, work throughout the semester to combine all of the material which is presented throughout the semester, and work on it gradually as the course goes by, making sure to master the main concepts first, leaving minor details for a week or so before the test.

To study for the upcoming exam, be sure to pose questions that may be on the examination, to gauge the ability to answer them by integrating the ideas from your texts, notes and lectures, as well as any supplementary readings.

If it is truly impossible to cover all of the information that was covered in that particular term, concentrate on the most important portions, that can be covered very well. Learn these concepts as best as possible, so that when the test comes, a goal can be made to use these concepts as presentations of your knowledge.

In addition to study habits, changes in attitude are critical to beating a struggle with test anxiety. In fact, an improvement of the perspective over the entire test-taking

Copyright © Mometrix Media. You have been licensed one copy of this document for personal use only. Any other reproduction or redistribution is strictly prohibited. All rights reserved.

experience can actually help a test taker to enjoy studying and therefore improve the overall experience. Be certain not to overemphasize the significance of the grade - know that the result of the test is neither a reflection of self worth, nor is it a measure of intelligence; one grade will not predict a person's future success.

To improve an overall testing outlook, the following steps should be tried:

Keeping in mind that the most reasonable expectation for taking a test is to expect to try to demonstrate as much of what you know as you possibly can.
Reminding ourselves that a test is only one test; this is not the only one, and there will be others.
The thought of thinking of oneself in an irrational, all-or-nothing term should be avoided at all costs.
A reward should be designated for after the test, so there's something to look forward to. Whether it be going to a movie, going out to eat, or simply visiting friends, schedule it in advance, and do it no matter what result is expected on the exam.

Test-takers should also keep in mind that the basics are some of the most important things, even beyond anti-anxiety techniques and studying. Never neglect the basic social, emotional and biological needs, in order to try to absorb information. In order to best achieve, these three factors must be held as just as important as the studying itself.

Study Steps

Remember the following important steps for studying:

Maintain healthy nutrition and exercise habits. Continue both your recreational activities and social pass times. These both contribute to your physical and emotional well being.
Be certain to get a good amount of sleep, especially the night before the test, because when you're overtired you are not able to perform to the best of your best ability.
Keep the studying pace to a moderate level by taking breaks when they are needed, and varying the work whenever possible, to keep the mind fresh instead of getting bored.
When enough studying has been done that all the material that can be learned has been learned, and the test taker is prepared for the test, stop studying and do something relaxing such as listening to music, watching a movie, or taking a warm bubble bath.

There are also many other techniques to minimize the uneasiness or apprehension that is experienced along with test anxiety before, during, or even after the examination. In fact, there are a great deal of things that can be done to stop anxiety from interfering with lifestyle and performance. Again, remember that anxiety will not be eliminated entirely, and it shouldn't be. Otherwise that "up" feeling for exams would not exist, and most of us depend on that sensation to perform better than usual. However, this anxiety has to be at a level that is manageable.

Of course, as we have just discussed, being prepared for the exam is half the battle right away. Attending all classes, finding out what knowledge will be expected on the exam, and knowing the exam schedules are easy steps to lowering anxiety. Keeping up with work will remove the need to cram, and efficient study habits will eliminate wasted time. Studying should be done in an ideal location for concentration, so that it is simple to become interested in the material and give it complete attention. A method such as SQ3R (Survey, Question, Read, Recite, Review) is a wonderful key to follow to make sure that the study habits are as effective as possible, especially in the case of learning from a textbook. Flashcards are great techniques for memorization. Learning to take good notes will mean that notes will be full of useful information, so that less sifting will need to be done to seek out what is pertinent for studying. Reviewing notes after class and then again on occasion will keep the information fresh in the mind. From notes that have been taken summary sheets and outlines can be made for simpler reviewing.

A study group can also be a very motivational and helpful place to study, as there will be a sharing of ideas, all of the minds can work together, to make sure that everyone understands, and the studying will be made more interesting because it will be a social occasion.

Basically, though, as long as the test-taker remains organized and self confident, with efficient study habits, less time will need to be spent studying, and higher grades will be achieved.

To become self confident, there are many useful steps. The first of these is "self talk." It has been shown through extensive research, that self-talk for students who suffer from test anxiety, should be well monitored, in order to make sure that it contributes to self confidence as opposed to sinking the student. Frequently the self talk of test-anxious students is negative or self-defeating, thinking that everyone else is smarter and faster, that they always mess up, and that if they don't do well, they'll fail the entire course. It is important to decreasing anxiety that awareness is made of self talk. Try writing any negative self thoughts and then disputing them with a positive statement instead. Begin self-encouragement as though it was a friend speaking. Repeat positive statements to help reprogram the mind to believing in successes instead of failures.

Helpful Techniques

Other extremely helpful techniques include:

Self-visualization of doing well and reaching goals
While aiming for an "A" level of understanding, don't try to "overprotect" by setting your expectations lower. This will only convince the mind to stop studying in order to meet the lower expectations.
Don't make comparisons with the results or habits of other students. These are individual factors, and different things work for different people, causing different results.
Strive to become an expert in learning what works well, and what can be done in order to improve. Consider collecting this data in a journal.
Create rewards for after studying instead of doing things before studying that will only turn into avoidance behaviors.

Make a practice of relaxing - by using methods such as progressive relaxation, self-hypnosis, guided imagery, etc - in order to make relaxation an automatic sensation. Work on creating a state of relaxed concentration so that concentrating will take on the focus of the mind, so that none will be wasted on worrying.
Take good care of the physical self by eating well and getting enough sleep.
Plan in time for exercise and stick to this plan.

Beyond these techniques, there are other methods to be used before, during and after the test that will help the test-taker perform well in addition to overcoming anxiety.

Before the exam comes the academic preparation. This involves establishing a study schedule and beginning at least one week before the actual date of the test. By doing this, the anxiety of not having enough time to study for the test will be automatically eliminated. Moreover, this will make the studying a much more effective experience, ensuring that the learning will be an easier process. This relieves much undue pressure on the test-taker.

Summary sheets, note cards, and flash cards with the main concepts and examples of these main concepts should be prepared in advance of the actual studying time. A topic should never be eliminated from this process. By omitting a topic because it isn't expected to be on the test is only setting up the test-taker for anxiety should it actually appear on the exam. Utilize the course syllabus for laying out the topics that should be studied. Carefully go over the notes that were made in class, paying special attention to any of the issues that the professor took special care to emphasize while lecturing in class. In the textbooks, use the chapter review, or if possible, the chapter tests, to begin your review.

It may even be possible to ask the instructor what information will be covered on the exam, or what the format of the exam will be (for example, multiple choice, essay, free form, true-false). Additionally, see if it is possible to find out how many questions will be on the test. If a review sheet or sample test has been offered by the professor, make good use of it, above anything else, for the preparation for the test. Another great resource for getting to know the examination is reviewing tests from previous semesters. Use these tests to review, and aim to achieve a 100% score on each of the possible topics. With a few exceptions, the goal that you set for yourself is the highest one that you will reach.

Take all of the questions that were assigned as homework, and rework them to any other possible course material. The more problems reworked, the more skill and confidence will form as a result. When forming the solution to a problem, write out each of the steps. Don't simply do head work. By doing as many steps on paper as possible, much clarification and therefore confidence will be formed. Do this with as many homework problems as possible, before checking the answers. By checking the answer after each problem, a reinforcement will exist, that will not be on the exam. Study situations should be as exam-like as possible, to prime the test-taker's system for the experience. By waiting to check the answers at the end, a psychological advantage will be formed, to decrease the stress factor.

Another fantastic reason for not cramming is the avoidance of confusion in concepts, especially when it comes to mathematics. 8-10 hours of study will become one hundred percent more effective if it is spread out over a week or at least several days, instead of doing it all in one sitting. Recognize that the human brain requires time in order to assimilate new material, so frequent breaks and a span of study time over several days will be much more beneficial.

Additionally, don't study right up until the point of the exam. Studying should stop a minimum of one hour before the exam begins. This allows the brain to rest and put things in their proper order. This will also provide the time to become as relaxed as possible when going into the examination room. The test-taker will also have time to eat well and eat sensibly. Know that the brain needs food as much as the rest of the body. With enough food and enough sleep, as well as a relaxed attitude, the body and the mind are primed for success.

Avoid any anxious classmates who are talking about the exam. These students only spread anxiety, and are not worth sharing the anxious sentimentalities.

Before the test also involves creating a positive attitude, so mental preparation should also be a point of concentration. There are many keys to creating a positive attitude. Should fears become rushing in, make a visualization of taking the exam, doing well, and seeing an A written on the paper. Write out a list of affirmations that will bring a feeling of confidence, such as "I am doing well in my English class," "I studied well and know my material," "I enjoy this class." Even if the affirmations aren't believed at first, it sends a positive message to the subconscious which will result in an alteration of the overall belief system, which is the system that creates reality.

If a sensation of panic begins, work with the fear and imagine the very worst! Work through the entire scenario of not passing the test, failing the entire course, and dropping out of school, followed by not getting a job, and pushing a shopping cart through the dark alley where you'll live. This will place things into perspective! Then, practice deep breathing and create a visualization of the opposite situation - achieving an "A" on the exam, passing the entire course, receiving the degree at a graduation ceremony.

On the day of the test, there are many things to be done to ensure the best results, as well as the most calm outlook. The following stages are suggested in order to maximize test-taking potential:

Begin the examination day with a moderate breakfast, and avoid any coffee or beverages with caffeine if the test taker is prone to jitters. Even people who are used to managing caffeine can feel jittery or light-headed when it is taken on a test day.
Attempt to do something that is relaxing before the examination begins. As last minute cramming clouds the mastering of overall concepts, it is better to use this time to create a calming outlook.
Be certain to arrive at the test location well in advance, in order to provide time to select a location that is away from doors, windows and other distractions, as well as giving enough time to relax before the test begins.
Keep away from anxiety generating classmates who will upset the sensation of stability and relaxation that is being attempted before the exam.
Should the waiting period before the exam begins cause anxiety, create a self-distraction by reading a light magazine or something else that is relaxing and simple.

During the exam itself, read the entire exam from beginning to end, and find out how much time should be allotted to each individual problem. Once writing the exam, should more time be taken for a problem, it should be abandoned, in order to begin another problem. If there is time at the end, the unfinished problem can always be returned to and completed.

Read the instructions very carefully - twice - so that unpleasant surprises won't follow during or after the exam has ended.
When writing the exam, pretend that the situation is actually simply the completion of homework within a library, or at home. This will assist in forming a relaxed atmosphere, and will allow the brain extra focus for the complex thinking function.

Begin the exam with all of the questions with which the most confidence is felt. This will build the confidence level regarding the entire exam and will begin a quality momentum. This will also create encouragement for trying the problems where uncertainty resides.

Going with the "gut instinct" is always the way to go when solving a problem. Second guessing should be avoided at all costs. Have confidence in the ability to do well.

For essay questions, create an outline in advance that will keep the mind organized and make certain that all of the points are remembered. For multiple choice, read every answer, even if the correct one has been spotted - a better one may exist.

Continue at a pace that is reasonable and not rushed, in order to be able to work carefully. Provide enough time to go over the answers at the end, to check for small errors that can be corrected.

Should a feeling of panic begin, breathe deeply, and think of the feeling of the body releasing sand through its pores. Visualize a calm, peaceful place, and include all of the sights, sounds and sensations of this image. Continue the deep breathing, and take a few minutes to continue this with closed eyes. When all is well again, return to the test.

If a "blanking" occurs for a certain question, skip it and move on to the next question. There will be time to return to the other question later. Get everything done that can be done, first, to guarantee all the grades that can be compiled, and to build all of the confidence possible. Then return to the weaker questions to build the marks from there.

Remember, one's own reality can be created, so as long as the belief is there, success will follow. And remember: anxiety can happen later, right now, there's an exam to be written!

After the examination is complete, whether there is a feeling for a good grade or a bad grade, don't dwell on the exam, and be certain to follow through on the reward that was promised...and enjoy it! Don't dwell on any mistakes that have been made, as there is nothing that can be done at this point anyway.

Additionally, don't begin to study for the next test right away. Do something relaxing for a while, and let the mind relax and prepare itself to begin absorbing information again.

From the results of the exam - both the grade and the entire experience, be certain to learn from what has gone on. Perfect studying habits and work some more on confidence in order to make the next examination experience even better than the last one.

Learn to avoid places where openings occurred for laziness, procrastination and day dreaming.
Use the time between this exam and the next one to better learn to relax, even learning to relax on cue, so that any anxiety can be controlled during the next exam. Learn how to relax the body. Slouch in your chair if that helps. Tighten and then relax all of the different muscle groups, one group at a time, beginning with the feet and then working all the way up to the neck and face. This will ultimately relax the muscles more than they were to begin with. Learn how to breathe deeply and comfortably, and focus on this breathing going in and out as a relaxing thought. With every exhale, repeat the word "relax."

As common as test anxiety is, it is very possible to overcome it. Make yourself one of the test-takers who overcome this frustrating hindrance.

Special Report: Retaking the Test: What Are Your Chances at Improving Your Score?

After going through the experience of taking a major test, many test takers feel that once is enough. The test usually comes during a period of transition in the test taker's life, and taking the test is only one of a series of important events. With so many distractions and conflicting recommendations, it may be difficult for a test taker to rationally determine whether or not he should retake the test after viewing his scores.

The importance of the test usually only adds to the burden of the retake decision. However, don't be swayed by emotion. There a few simple questions that you can ask yourself to guide you as you try to determine whether a retake would improve your score:

1. What went wrong? Why wasn't your score what you expected?

Can you point to a single factor or problem that you feel caused the low score? Were you sick on test day? Was there an emotional upheaval in your life that caused a distraction? Were you late for the test or not able to use the full time allotment? If you can point to any of these specific, individual problems, then a retake should definitely be considered.

2. Is there enough time to improve?

Many problems that may show up in your score report may take a lot of time for improvement. A deficiency in a particular math skill may require weeks or months of tutoring and studying to improve. If you have enough time to improve an identified weakness, then a retake should definitely be considered.

3. How will additional scores be used? Will a score average, highest score, or most recent score be used?

Different test scores may be handled completely differently. If you've taken the test multiple times, sometimes your highest score is used, sometimes your average score is computed and used, and sometimes your most recent score is used. Make sure you understand what method will be used to evaluate your scores, and use that to help you determine whether a retake should be considered.

4. Are my practice test scores significantly higher than my actual test score?

If you have taken a lot of practice tests and are consistently scoring at a much higher level than your actual test score, then you should consider a retake. However, if you've taken five practice tests and only one of your scores was higher than your actual test score, or if your practice test scores were only slightly higher than your actual test score, then it is unlikely that you will significantly increase your score.

5. Do I need perfect scores or will I be able to live with this score? Will this score still allow me to follow my dreams?

What kind of score is acceptable to you? Is your current score "good enough?" Do you have to have a certain score in order to pursue the future of your dreams? If you won't be happy with your current score, and there's no way that you could live with it, then you should consider a retake. However, don't get your hopes up. If you are looking for significant improvement, that may or may not be possible. But if you won't be happy otherwise, it is at least worth the effort.
Remember that there are other considerations. To achieve your dream, it is likely that your grades may also be taken into account. A great test score is usually not the only thing necessary to succeed. Make sure that you aren't overemphasizing the importance of a high test score.

Furthermore, a retake does not always result in a higher score. Some test takers will score lower on a retake, rather than higher. One study shows that one-fourth of test takers will achieve a significant improvement in test score, while one-sixth of test takers will actually show a decrease. While this shows that most test takers will improve, the majority will only improve their scores a little and a retake may not be worth the test taker's effort.

Finally, if a test is taken only once and is considered in the added context of good grades on the part of a test taker, the person reviewing the grades and scores may be tempted to assume that the test taker just had a bad day while taking the test, and may discount the low test score in favor of the high grades. But if the test is retaken and the scores are approximately the same, then the validity of the low scores are only confirmed. Therefore, a retake could actually hurt a test taker by definitely bracketing a test taker's score ability to a limited range.

Special Report: Additional Bonus Material

Due to our efforts to try to keep this book to a manageable length, we've created a link that will give you access to all of your additional bonus material.

Please visit http://www.mometrix.com/bonus948/priiaudiology to access the information.